THE NAVARRE BIBLE

The Book of Revelation
and New Testament subject index

THE NAVARRE BIBLE
The Book of Revelation

in the Revised Standard Version and New Vulgate
with a commentary by members of the
Faculty of Theology of the University of Navarre

FOUR COURTS PRESS

Original title: *Sagrada Biblia: XII. Apocalipsis.*
Quotations from Vatican II documents
are based on the translation in *Vatican Council II:*
The Conciliar and Post Conciliar Documents,
ed. A. Flannery, OP (Dublin 1981).

Nihil obstat: Stephen J. Greene, *censor deputatus.*
Imprimi potest: Desmond, Archbishop of Dublin, 9 January 1992.

The typesetting of this book was produced by Gilbert Gough Typesetting.
The book, designed by Jarlath Hayes, is published by
Four Courts Press, Fumbally Lane, Dublin 8, Ireland.

First edition 1992
Reprinted 1994, 1998, 1999

A catalogue record for this book
is available from the British Library.

ISBN 1-85182-089-2

Printed in Ireland
by Colour Books Ltd, Dublin

Contents

Preface

In providing both undergraduate and postgraduate education, and in the research it carries out, a university is ultimately an institution at the service of society. It was with this service in mind that the theology faculty of the University of Navarre embarked on the project of preparing a translation and commentary of the Bible accessible to a wide readership—a project entrusted to it by the apostolic zeal of the University's founder and first chancellor, Monsignor Josemaría Escrivá de Balaguer.

Monsignor Escrivá did not live to see the publication of the first volume, the Gospel according to St Matthew; but he must, from heaven, continue to bless and promote our work, for the volumes, the first of which appeared in 1976, have been well received and widely read.

This edition of the Bible avoids many scholarly questions, discussion of which would over-extend the text and would be of no assistance to the immense majority of readers; these questions are avoided, but they have been taken into account.

The Spanish edition contains a new Spanish translation made from the original texts, always taking note of the Church's official Latin text, which is now that of the New Vulgate, a revision of the venerable Latin Vulgate of St Jerome: on 25 April 1979 Pope John Paul II, by the Apostolic Constitution *Scripturarum thesaurus*, promulgated the *editio typica prior* of the New Vulgate as the new official text; the *editio typica altera*, issued in 1986, is the Latin version used in this edition. For the English edition of this book we consider ourselves fortunate in having the Revised Standard Version as the translation of Scripture and wish to record our appreciation for permission to use that text, an integral part of which are the RSV notes, which are indicated by superior letters.

The introductions and notes have been prepared on the basis of the same criteria. In the notes (which are the most characteristic feature of this Bible, at least in its English version), along with scriptural and ascetical explanations we have sought to offer a general exposition of Christian doctrine—not of course a systematic exposition, for we follow the thread of the scriptural text. We have also tried to explain and connect certain biblical passages by reference to others, conscious that Sacred Scripture is ultimately one single entity; but, to avoid tiring the reader, most of the cross-references are given in the form of marginal notes (the marginal notes in this edition are, then, those of the Navarre Bible, not the RSV). The commentaries contained in the notes are the result of looking up thousands of sources (sometimes reflected in explicit references given in our text)—documents of the Magisterium, exegesis by Fathers and Doctors of the Church, works by important spiritual writers (usually saints, of every period) and writings of the founder of our University. It would have been impertinent of us to comment on the Holy Bible using our own expertise alone. Besides, a basic principle of exegesis is that Scripture should be interpreted in the context of Sacred Tradition and under the guidance of the Magisterium.

From the very beginning of our work our system has been to entrust each volume to a committee which then works as a team. However, the general editor of this edition takes ultimate responsibility for what it contains.

It is our pleasant duty to express our gratitude to the present chancellor of the University of Navarre, Bishop Alvaro del Portillo y Diez de Sollano, for his continued support and encouragement, and for reminding us of the good our work can do for the Church and for souls.

"Since Sacred Scripture must be read and interpreted with its divine authorship in mind,"[1] we pray to the Holy Spirit to help us in our work and to help our readers derive spiritual benefit from it. We also pray Mary, our Mother, Seat of Wisdom, and St Joseph, our Father and Lord, to intercede that this sowing of the Word of God may produce holiness of life in the souls of many Christians.

1   Vatican Council II, Dogm. Const. *Dei Verbum*, 12.

8

Abbreviations and Sources

1. BOOKS OF SACRED SCRIPTURE

Acts	Acts of the Apostles	2 Kings	2 Kings
Amos	Amos	Lam	Lamentations
Bar	Baruch	Lev	Leviticus
1 Chron	1 Chronicles	Lk	Luke
2 Chron	2 Chronicles	1 Mac	1 Maccabees
Col	Colossians	2 Mac	2 Maccabees
1 Cor	1 Corinthians	Mal	Malachi
2 Cor	2 Corinthians	Mic	Micah
Dan	Daniel	Mk	Mark
Deut	Deuteronomy	Mt	Matthew
Eccles	Ecclesiastes (Qohelet)	Nah	Nahum
Esther	Esther	Neh	Nehemiah
Eph	Ephesians	Num	Numbers
Ex	Exodus	Obad	Obadiah
Ezek	Ezekiel	1 Pet	1 Peter
Ezra	Ezra	2 Pet	2 Peter
Gal	Galatians	Phil	Philippians
Gen	Genesis	Philem	Philemon
Hab	Habakkuk	Ps	Psalms
Hag	Haggai	Prov	Proverbs
Heb	Hebrews	Rev	Revelation (Apocalypse)
Hos	Hosea	Rom	Romans
Is	Isaiah	Ruth	Ruth
Jas	James	1 Sam	1 Samuel
Jer	Jeremiah	2 Sam	2 Samuel
Jn	John	Sir	Sirach (Ecclesiasticus)
1 Jn	1 John	Song	Song of Solomon
2 Jn	2 John	1 Thess	1 Thessalonians
3 Jn	3 John	2 Thess	2 Thessalonians
Job	Job	1 Tim	1 Timothy
Joel	Joel	2 Tim	2 Timothy
Jon	Jonah	Tit	Titus
Josh	Joshua	Tob	Tobit
Jud	Judith	Wis	Wisdom
Jude	Jude	Zech	Zechariah
Judg	Judges	Zeph	Zephaniah
1 Kings	1 Kings		

Alphonsus Mary Liguori, St
The Love of Jesus Christ reduced to practice
Augustine, St
City of God, The
De Sermone Domini in monte
Sermo ad Casarriensis Ecclesiae plebem
Enarrationes in Psalmos
Sermons
Bede, St
Explanatio Apocalypsis
Bernard, St
De natura et dignitate divini amoris
Sermones de Beata Virgine
Bonaventure, St
Speculum Beatae Virgine
Cyprian, St
De bono patientiae
Liber de unitate Ecclesiae
Escrivá de Balaguer, J.
Christ is passing by (followed by section no.)
Friends of God (do.)
Furrow (do).
In Love with the Church (do.)
The Way (do.)
Eusebius of Caesarea
Ecclesiastical History
Francis of Sales, St
Treatise on the Love of God
Gregory the Great, St
Moralia in Job
Gregory of Nyssa
Oratio I in Christi resurrectionem
Hippolytus, St
De consummatione saeculi
Irenaeus, St
Against heresies
John of Avila, St
Audi, filia
John of the Cross, St
Ascent of Mount Carmel
John Cassian
Collationes
John Chrysostom, St
Homilies on St Matthew's Gospel
Paraeneses ad Theodorum lapsum
John Mary Vianney, St
Selected Sermons
John Paul II
Address (on date given)
Apos. Exhort. *Reconciliatio et paenitentia*, 2 December 1984

John Paul II
Apos. Exhort. *Salvifici doloris*, 11 February 1984
Enc. *Dives in misericordia*, 30 November 1980
Enc. *Redemptor hominis*, 4 March 1979
Homily (on date given)
Justin, St
Dialogue with Trypho
Lateran, Fourth Council of the
Decree *De fide catholica*
Lope de Vega
Rimas sacras
Minucius, Felix
Octavius
Nicene-Constantinopolitan Creed
Paul VI
Creed of the People of God: Solemn profession of faith, 30 June 1968
Pius V, St
Catechism of the Council of Trent
Pius X, St
Enc. *Ad Diem illum*
Pius XI
Enc. *Quas primas*, 11 December 1925
Enc. *Mens nostra*, 20 December 1929
Pius XII
Address, 14 November 1946
Enc. *Mystici corporis*, 29 June 1943
Pliny the Elder
Historia naturalis
Primasius
Commentariorum super Apocalypsium B. Ioannis libri quinque
Missal, Roman: Missale Romanum ex decreto sacrosancti oecumenici concilii Vatican II instauratum auctoritate Pauli PP. VI promulgatum, editio typica altera (Vatican City, 1975)
Sacred Congregation for the Doctrine of the Faith
Instruction, *Liberatis conscientia*, 22 March 1986
Instruction, *Libertatis nuntius*, 6 August 1984
Tacitus
Annals
Teresa of Avila, St
Way of Perfection
Tertullian
Apologeticum
Thomas Aquinas, St
Summa theologiae

Trent, Council of
De sacris imaginibus
Vatican, First Council of the
Dogm. Const. *Dei Filius*
Vatican, Second Council of the
Const. *Sacrosanctum concilium*
Decree *Nostra aetate*

Vatican, Second Council of the
Decree *Perfectae caritatis*
Dogm. Const. *Dei Verbum*
Dogm. Const. *Lumen gentium*
Past. Const. *Gaudium et spes*
Vincent of Lerins, St
Commonitorium

3. OTHER ABBREVIATIONS

ad loc.	*ad locum*, commentary on this passage	Enc.	Encyclical
Exhort.	Exhortation	f	and following (*pl.* ff)
Apost.	apostolic	*ibid.*	*ibidem*, in the same place
can.	canon	*in loc.*	*in locum*, commentary on this passage
chap.	chapter		
cf.	*confer*, compare	*loc.*	*locum*, place or passage
Const.	Constitution	n.	number (*pl.* nn.)
Decl.	Declaration	p.	page (*pl.* pp.)
Dz-Sch	Denzinger-Schönmetzer, *Enchiridion Symbolorum*	*pl.*	plural
		par.	and parallel passages
Dogm.	Dogmatic	Past.	Pastoral
EB	*Enchiridion Biblicum* (4th edition, Naples-Rome, 1961)	SCDF	Sacred Congregation for the Doctrine of the Faith
		sess.	session

Introduction to the Book of Revelation

The Apocalypse or Book of Revelation is the last book of Sacred Scripture and is the only prophetical book in the New Testament. The Church makes frequent use of it, particularly in the Liturgy, to sing the praises of the risen Christ and the splendour of the heavenly Jerusalem which symbolizes the Church in the glory of heaven.

A certain parallel can be seen between the Book of Revelation and Genesis, the first of the sacred books. Genesis describes the beginning of the world through the creative action of God. Using similar symbolism, the Apocalypse speaks at length of the new creation (cf. Rev 21:1, 5) initiated by the Redemption brought about by Christ which will reach its climax when he comes again at the end of the world. The last chapters of Revelation specifically mention the river which watered paradise (cf. Gen 2:6; Rev 22:1) and the tree of life (cf. Gen 2:8; Rev 22:14).

The Apocalypse is a book at once difficult and profound, and yet it focuses intense light on the figure of Christ in glory and builds up our hope of attaining eternal life.

AUTHORSHIP AND CANONICITY

The Apocalypse is one of the "deuterocanonical" books, that is, one of those which at one time were not accepted as sacred by all Christian communities. Its authenticity was suspect in parts of the Church, particularly in the East, probably because it was widely used by some early heretical sects in support of their teachings.

However, the earliest testimonies we have, which go back to the second century, are unanimous in recognizing the Apostle John as the author of the book. St Justin refers to "a man named John, one of the apostles of Christ", as having received the revelations contained in the Apocalypse.[1] This is a particularly valuable testimony in view of the fact that Justin was converted to Christianity in Ephesus in the year 135, only a few decades after John wrote the book to the seven churches of Asia, the foremost of which was Ephesus. Contemporary with Justin's text is the commentary on the Apocalypse written by St Melito, bishop of Sardis, another of the churches mentioned at the start

---

1. *Dialogue with Trypho*, 81, 3.

of the book. The bishop's commentary is not extant but it is referred to by Eusebius of Caesarea in his *Ecclesiastical History*.[2] Other second-century writers who support Johannine authorship of the Book of Revelation are Papias, bishop of Hierapolis,[3] and St Irenaeus, who frequently quotes from it.[4] The Muratorian Fragment, which dates from the end of the century, includes the Apocalypse in its list of sacred books.

An outstanding third-century testimony is that of Origen of Alexandria: he says that the author of it was the man who wrote the Fourth Gospel and had the good fortune to rest his head on Jesus' breast.[5] In the West, Tertullian also attributes the Book of Revelation to St John.[6] However, other views were being expressed around the same time as Tertullian: a Roman priest named Caius thought the Apocalypse was written by Cerinthus, a prominent Gnostic contemporary of John.[7] Other writers of the same period, called *alogoi* because they rejected the *Logos* of St John, refused to accept the authenticity of the Apocalypse.[8] Dionysius of Alexandria denied its canonicity because millenarianists were using it to support their arguments. To show that St John was not the author despite clear Church Tradition, Dionysius put forward arguments (not compelling ones) based on differences between the Apocalypse and the Fourth Gospel.[9]

In the fourth century, St Athanasius, bishop of Alexandria, recognized the Apocalypse as canonical and used it in his controversy with the Arians.[10] St Basil and St Gregory of Nyssa, for their part, accepted the tradition in favour of authenticity. However, the school of Antioch generally denied both the authenticity and the canonicity of the book; St Cyril of Jerusalem, St John Chrysostom, Theoderet and others do not use it.[11] This lack of conviction among some writers of the Eastern Church must be set against the unanimity of the Latin Church, which always accepted the Apocalypse as part of the canon of inspired books and as written by St John.

From the sixth to the sixteenth century the authenticity of the book was undisputed. Doubts which arose in Spain in the early seventh century were dispelled by the first Council of Toledo.[12] Once the danger from millenarianism was over, the Eastern Church came round again to accepting the Apocalypse as inspired.

In the sixteenth century Erasmus[13] expressed some doubts about its authenticity and canonicity, but his views were rejected and censored by the

2. *Ecclesiastical History*, IV, 26, 2.
3. Cf. Andrew of Caesarea, *Comment in Apoc.*, prologue.
4. Cf. *Against heresies*, 4, 20.
5. Cf. *In Ioann. comm.*, 1, 14.
6. Cf. *Against Marcion*, 3, 14; *De resurrectione carnis*, 25.
7. Cf. *Ecclesiastical History*, III, 28, 2.
8. Cf. St Epiphanius, *Haer.*, 51, 1-35.
9. Cf. Dionysius of Alexandria, *Ex libro de promission.*, 3-7.
10. Cf. *Oratio II contra Arianos*, 23.
11. Cf. *Ecclesiastical History*, III, 25, 2.
12. Cf. Mansi, 10, 624.
13. Cf. Erasmus, *In Apoc.*, 22, 21.

University of Paris. Luther[14] initially argued against authenticity but later changed his view. In the eighteenth century rationalists (who rejected prophecy out of hand) naturally had no place for the Book of Revelation: rationalist arguments were based on internal evidence (the same kind of arguments as put forward earlier by Dionysius of Alexandria). On the basis of a passage in Eusebius' *History*, rationalists attribute the Apocalypse to a personage called John the Presbyter; but these arguments are weak: what Eusebius says is far from clear, and his thinking was coloured by the danger posed by millenarianism.

At the present time there is a certain amount of disagreement among scholars. Some, Protestants for the most part, are of the opinion that the Apocalypse could not have been written by the author of the Fourth Gospel, given the differences in style and language. Others, mainly Catholics, accept that it is a Johannine text, given the antiquity of Tradition to this effect and the fact that the difference in subject matter between the two books can account for the differences in style.

The Magisterium has on different occasions pronounced on the authenticity and canonicity of the Apocalypse—for example, at the Council of Hippo (in 393), Carthage (397), and Toledo (633).[15] This teaching was confirmed later by the ecumenical Councils of Florence and Trent.[16] However, whereas the Church has dogmatically defined the book as canonical, it has not pronounced as strongly on who wrote it or how it was redacted.

PLACE AND DATE OF COMPOSITION

At the beginning of the book, we are told of how the hagiographer received this divine revelation: "I John, your brother, who share with you in Jesus the tribulation and the kingdom and the patient endurance, was on the island called Patmos on account of the word of God and the testimony of Jesus. I was in the Spirit on the Lord's day, and I heard behind me a voice like a trumpet . . ." (1:9-10). Patmos is a small island in the Aegean Sea, one of a group of islands known as the Dodecanese. It was a Sunday, the Lord's day, the day that ever since the beginning of the Church Christians had dedicated to divine worship in place of the Jewish sabbath; the *Didache* and St Ignatius of Antioch testify to this Christian practice. An ancient tradition, witnessed to by Tertullian, mentions that St John, the beloved disciple, was exiled on Patmos because of his preaching and apostolic ministry. The author of the Apocalypse seems to confirm this by saying at the outset that he shares the affliction, pain and patience experienced by those he is addressing.

St Irenaeus thinks that the book was written towards the end of the reign of Domitian, around the year 96.[17] Writing in the third century or towards the end of the second, Victorinus says that Domitian sent St John into exile, interning

14. Cf. Luther, *Praef. in Apoc.*
15. Cf. *EB* 17 and 34.
16. Cf. *EB* 47 and 59.
17. Cf. *Against heresies*, 5, 30.

him on the island of Patmos.[18] St Jerome[19] and Eusebius[20] say the same.

Information contained in the book itself confirm this date. We know in fact from the Acts of the Apostle (20:7) that the Christians met together on the "first day of the week", which Revelation 1:10 describes as "Dies Domini", "the Lord's Day" (our Sunday). Also, the life of the Christian communities of Asia Minor as reflected in the Book of Revelation clearly indicates they were at a more mature stage than the churches referred to in other New Testament texts. All this means that the year 95, given by tradition, is realistic and acceptable.

ADDRESSEES AND PURPOSE

The book is addressed to "the seven churches that are in Asia" (1:4)—Ephesus, Smyrna, Pergamum, Thyatira, Sardis, Philadelphia and Laodicea (cf. 1:11). Commentators are agreed that this number is symbolic and that the book is in fact addressed to the entire Church. The second-century Muratorian Canon puts it this way: "John in the Apocalpyse, although writing to seven churches, is however addressing all churches."[21] An early commentator called Primasius states that what the Lord says to his servant is addressed to the whole Church, "uni Ecclesiae septiforme", a single Church of which these seven are a symbol.[22]

Various things in the text confirm this world-wide reference—for example, when it says (without being specific), "Blessed is he who reads aloud the words of the prophecy, and blessed are those who hear, and who keep what is written therein (1:3)"; or its repeated warning, "he who has an ear, let him hear what the Spirit says to the churches" (2:7, 11, 17, 29; 3:6; etc.).

The book seeks to alert Christians to the grave dangers which threaten faith, while consoling and encouraging those who are suffering tribulation, particularly due to the fierce and long-drawn-out persecution mounted by Domitian. The very earliest heresies were already wreaking havoc among the Christian communities: the Nicolaitans were arguing in favour of some degree of compromise with idolatry and pagan lifestyles (cf. 2:7, 14) and there was evidence of a loss of early fervour (2:4) and a slackening of charity (3:2).

Persecution was coming from both Jews and pagans. Jewish persecutors are described as false Jews, "a synagogue of Satan" (2:9-10); pagan persecution had begun with the first great persecution (instigated by Nero), the memory of which was still fresh thirty years on (cf. 6:9-11; 17:6). The Empire would repeatedly persecute Christians up to the fourth century, when the advent of Constantine brought peace. Some emperors, Domitian for example, required idolatrous worship of their person, giving themselves the title of "our Lord and God". Christians refused, thereby incurring their wrath. However, as Tertullian put it, the blood of martyrs would prove to be the seed of Christians. St John

18. Cf. *In Apoc.*, 10, 11 and 17, 10.
19. Cf. *Of famous men*, 9.
20. Cf. *Ecclesiastical History*, III, 18, 4.
21. Cf. *EB* 4.
22. Cf. *Commentarium super Apoc.* 1, 1.

16

seeks to console Christians experiencing such cruel injustice and harassment, and strives to keep alive their hope in the ultimate victory of Christ and of all who stay true to him even to death if necessary (cf. 2:10).

LITERARY FORM

In line with the teaching of Pius XII,[23] the Second Vatican Council reminds us that to understand what sacred writers had in mind one needs to take into account, among other things, the literary forms they use, that is, the genre in which they are writing—historical narrative, prophecy, poetry, etc.—and the patterns of language prevailing in their time and culture.[24]

This principle needs to be particularly borne in mind in the case of the Book of Revelation, given its special characteristics and language, so remote from our own experience. In fact, during the two centuries before and after Christ there was quite a crop of Jewish and Christian writings entitled Apocalypse (Revelation), with a content and style of a type now called "apocalyptic writing"—for example, the Book of Enoch, the Apocalypse of Moses (which heretics attributed to St Paul) and others, including the Apocrypha of the Old and the New Testaments.

These books all had two basic features: (a) they dealt with the subject of the last age of the world, when good would triumph and evil be annihilated; (b) they made much use of symbolism taken from the animal kingdom, astrology, numbers and so forth, to depict past and present history and to prophesy the future. From the point of view of content and style these writings are a kind of late extension of prophetical literature, for the Prophets already spoke of the "day of Yahweh"[25] and used symbolism to convey their message.[26] Some Old Testament passages in fact have a markedly apocalyptic ring about them—for example, Isaiah 24-27, Zechariah 9-14 and, particularly, the Book of Daniel, which is clearly a precursor of apocalyptic literature. That literature, in turn, is influenced by wisdom literature: its visions are interwoven with moral exhortations, invitations to reflection and promises of future beatitude or retribution.

Compared with the Prophets, authors of apocalypses have distinct features of their own: a) they write under pseudonyms, using the names of celebrated figures who might have received divine revelations—men like Enoch who Genesis 5:24 tells us was taken to heaven at the end of his life; b) in general, they conceive this world as being in the power of Satan and incapable of regeneration, and therefore they place their hopes in a new world to be created by God: the most that man can contribute is prayer; c) they exhibit a marked tendency towards determinism: everything that has to be said is contained in these books, and very little room is left for freedom and personal conversion.

23. Cf. Pius XII, *Divino afflante Spiritu*, EB 558.
24. Cf. Vatican II, *Dei Verbum*, 12.
25. Cf. Amos 5:18-20; Is 2:6-21; Jer 30:5-7; Joel 2:1-17; etc.
26. Cf. Amos 7:1 - 8:3; Hos 13:7-8; Joel 2:10-11; Ezek 1-2; etc.

Although St John's work is entitled Apocalypse (Revelation), its key features are more akin to the books of the Prophets than to those of "apocalyptic writers". He in fact describes his book as "prophecy" (1:3; cf. 22:7, 10, 18, 19; 22:9), and although for the most part he uses language and symbolism akin to Jewish apocalyptic writing, his historical perspective is quite different, namely, that which human history acquires under the lordship of Christ, which is acknowledged and extolled in the Church, the new people of God, who like their Lord suffer in this present world at the hands of the forces of evil. However, the final outcome has already been revealed by the resurrection and ascension of Christ, and the ground is being laid for it all through the course of history by the holiness, good works and suffering of the just. Christ's definitive victory will come at the end and the Church will be raised on high in a new world where there will be no more mourning or pain (cf. 21:4) and where there will be room for all those who choose to repent (cf. 16:11).

The Revelation of John constitutes a strong call to conversion; it urges people to commit themselves to good and put their trust in God; in this it is like the oracles spoken by the prophets. Like other "apocalypses" it is a book of consolation written at a time of exceptional stress; but it also provides encouragement to holiness and fidelity in all ages. Those parts of the book which have epistolary features (at the beginning and end: 1:1 - 3:22; 22:21) and indeed to a lesser degree the whole text are in the tradition of didactical wisdom writing.

STYLE AND LANGUAGE

Symbolism is of the essence of apocalyptic literature: its lofty, supernatural message calls for the use of analogies and similes which will bring the reader not so much to understand its exact meaning as to grasp it intuitively.

The symbols used are in some cases physical objects, such as the seven-branched golden lampstand (cf. 1:12; Zech 4:2, 10), the book with the seven seals (cf. 5:1; Ezek 2:9), the two olive trees (cf. 11:4; Zech 4:2, 14). At other times the symbols are actions—the sealing of the foreheads of the elect (cf. 7:3; Ezek 9:4), the eating of the prophetical scroll (cf. 10:8-11; Ezek 2:8), the measurement of the temple (cf. 11:1; Ezek 40-41). Certain cities are also used as symbols—Zion, Jerusalem, Babylon and Armageddon.[27] Numbers also have a symbolic purpose: the number three refers to things supernatural and divine, four to created things; seven and twelve imply completion, fulness. Colours are used in a similar way: white stands for victory and purity, red for violence, black for death.

Another feature of apocalyptic writing is what we might call the "law of anticipation", that is, its tendency to refer briefly to some event which will be dealt with fully later on. And sometimes the narrative is interrupted to include a passage designed to provide consolation to the just.

27. Cf. Rev 14:1; 3:12; 21:2; 14:8; 18:2; 16:14, 16; etc.

Due to the wealth of symbolism in the book it has been interpreted in many different ways over the centuries. The four main interpretations are as follows:

a) The book is a history of the Church, proclaiming the main events and epochs of the Church, past and future. Seven periods are identified, the last being the reign of a thousand years which Christ and his followers will establish before the end of the world, if Revelation 20:1-7 is taken literally. This interpretation was widespread in the early centuries of the Church and in the middle ages; it is also popular in our own days among certain sects which have made a number of (mistaken) predictions of the date of the end of the world.

b) The Apocalypse has to do solely with events in St John's own time— persecutions and trials of the Church, for the most part the result of the actions of outsiders. This interpretation, first proposed in the sixteenth century, is still held by many scholars in the rationalist tradition. It sees the book as merely a symbolic description of first-century events.

c) The content of the Apocalypse is exclusively a proclamation and premonition of the last days: it refers to the eschatological era. This interpretation was very much in vogue in the eighteenth century and still has its followers today.

d) The Apocalypse is a theological vision of the entire panorama of history, a vision which underlines its transcendental and religious dimension. According to this interpretation (favoured by most Fathers of the Church) St John is describing the situation of the Church in his own time and he is also surveying the panorama of the last times; but for him these last times have already begun: they began with the entry into the world of Jesus Christ, the Son of God made man. This idea is very much in line with the Fourth Gospel, which also conceives the last era of the world, and eternal life, as having already in some way begun and as developing towards ultimate and total fulness. It provides a special perspective on events in history and is involved with expectation of final victory. The book does depict the cosmic struggle between good and evil, but it takes for granted Christ's ultimate triumph. This is, in our view, the most valid interpretation of the book and therefore it is the one we follow in the commentary provided.

THE HISTORICAL BACKGROUND

It is helpful to bear in mind the background against which the Apocalypse was written. The evangelization of Asia Minor began very early on and may well have been initiated by those Jews from Asia Minor who witnessed the events of Pentecost in Jerusalem (cf. Acts 2:9). When St Paul arrived in Ephesus he found followers of Christ there already (cf. Acts 19:1). However, until the period 53-56 and St Paul's missionary work, there were no Christian communities in these regions which could properly be called local churches. These now began to develop, and very soon there were signs of cockle growing up among the young wheat; persecution, too, was becoming part of the picture.

This period also saw the final break with the synagogue, and some Jews began to sow confusion (cf. 2:9; 3:9). There was, moreover, the threat of syncretism, as a result of the influence of oriental religions in the Roman empire. Phrygia, the centre of the cults of Cybele and Attis, was quite close to the churches mentioned in the Apocalypse; the sins denounced in the book reflect to some extent the mystery-rites of those pagan religions (cf. 13:11-13; 2:14; 2:20ff).

Another feature of the historical background is the persecution of Christianity by Rome. The more emperor-worship increased, the more difficult it was for Christians to stay loyal to their faith. With Domitian (81-96) the situation worsened, because those who refused him divine honours became liable to the death penalty.

From five of the seven cities to whose churches St John writes we have positive evidence of emperor-worship: Thyatira and Laodicea are the exceptions. Additionally, Ephesus had its famous temple dedicated to the goddess Artemis (cf. Acts 19:28). In Smyrna St Polycarp would later suffer martyrdom (*c.* 156) for refusing to acknowledge Caesar as *Kyrios*, Lord. Pergamum saw the martyrdom of Antipas, "my witness, my faithful one" (cf. 2:13). As time went on Christianity continued to spread, but opposition and violence towards Christians also increased. This grieves St John and, enlightened by the Holy Spirit, he tries to make the faithful see that Jesus Christ, the Lamb of God, will ultimately triumph over his enemies. In the meantime, however, the great struggle must go on, a struggle which involves Christians in every epoch of history. The enemy often gains the upper hand, but his victory is merely temporary and apparent. In fact things are quite the reverse of what they seem: martyrdom and suffering may appear to overwhelm Christians but really that experience guarantees their victory.

DIVISION AND CONTENTS

It is difficult to divide the book into parts which clarify its meaning; this is particularly so from chapter 4 onwards, when the author begins to describe his vision of the last times. For example, certain themes seem to be dealt with more than once—the scourges prior to the End (cf. 6:1-15; 8:6 - 9:21; 16:1-21), the victory of the elect (cf. 7:9-17; 14:1-5; 19:1-10), the fall of Babylon (cf. 14:6-11; 18:1-3), etc. Sometimes the rhythm of the narrative seems to break abruptly (cf. 8:2; 10:1; 12:1); it is broken, for example, by the episode of the two witnesses (cf. 11:1-13) and by that of the woman in heaven (cf. 12:1-17). This has led some scholars to suggest that the text of the Apocalypse in the form that has come down to us may be a fusion of two earlier works of St John on the same subject.

This is only a theory, however; besides, there is enough thematic development in the book to give it a strong basic unity. From chapter 4 onwards, everything is tending towards the final outcome of a dramatic battle between Christ and the powers of evil, a battle which reaches its climax in the last chapters (cf. 19:11 - 22:5). But it is true that we are already given the result of the last battle long before the detailed narrative of that event. As he describes each vision, the author seems to repeat his entire message: he feels under no restraint to deal with events or subjects in a tidy, systematic or chronological way: apocalyptic writing is different from other genres in this respect.

By using a series of literary devices he manages to keep the reader's interest alive right to the end. For example, he uses the number seven as a device of this kind: after the seven letters to the seven churches (cf. 1:4 - 3:22) the writer sees a scroll sealed with seven seals (cf. 5:1 - 8:1), hears the seven trumpets (cf. 8:2 - 11:15) and sees the seven plagues being poured out of the seven bowls (15:1 - 16:17). The seven letters seem to form a section of their own but all the other symbolic sevens appear to be connected with one another: the seventh seal introduces the vision of the seven angels with the seven trumpets (cf. 8:1-2), and once the seventh trumpet has been blown the author sees God's temple from which the seven angels with the seven plagues emerge (cf. 11:19; 15:5). After the seventh bowl has been poured, the author is shown, in detail, the various adversaries, the last battles, and the glorification of the Church (cf. chaps 17-22). To maintain the reader's interest and attention, the gap between the sixth and seventh events is sometimes extended by the introduction of a new vision (cf. 7:1-17; 10:1 - 11:14) or the appearance of the next set of seven (cf. 12:1 - 15:5) is delayed, so that when he thinks he is nearing the end the reader finds that preliminary episodes are still being introduced.

The number seven is so frequently used that some scholars have opted for dividing the book into seven acts, with seven scenes in each. But the text refuses to submit to this rigid scheme: the author writes with total freedom of style, though he clearly uses the "seven" device to help shape the book. However, after the seventh trumpet is sounded (11:15), this device becomes less prominent and the symbols of the woman, the beasts, the Lamb and the city occupy centre stage.

Given the way the various themes are developed and the literary aspects of the work, the following division is probably generally acceptable:

Prologue: The book and its author are introduced (1:1-3).

PART I: LETTERS TO THE SEVEN CHURCHES OF ASIA (1:4 - 3:22)

Formal address and greeting (1:4-8)

Introduction: Christ in glory commissions John to write the book (1:9-20)

Letters: to the churches of Ephesus (2:1-7), Smyrna (2:8-11), Pergamum (2:12-17), Thyatira (2:18-29), Sardis (3:1-6), Philadelphia (3:7-13) and Laodicea (3:14-22).

PART II: ESCHATOLOGICAL VISIONS (4:1 - 22:15)

1. Introductory vision. The author is taken up into heaven, where he sees God in majesty directing the destinies of the world and the Church. Only Christ can reveal what those destinies are, for only he can open the seven seals (chaps. 4-5).

2. First section. Events prior to the final outcome. A series of visions before the last trumpet is sounded (6:1 - 11:14):

Christ opens the first six seals. The great day of God's wrath has arrived (6:1-17).

The great multitude of the saved (7:1-17).

The opening of the seventh seal and the vision of the seven angels bearing seven trumpets (8:1-6).

The sounding of the first trumpets. They herald the coming of God and cause catastrophes which stir people to repent (8:7 - 9:21).

The author is given the little scroll to eat. What must still remain hidden and what is going to be prophetically revealed (10:1-11).

The death and resurrection of the two witnesses (11:1-14).

3. Second section. Christ's victory over the powers of evil, and the glorification of the Church (11:15 - 22:15).

The sounding of the seventh trumpet: the advent of the Kingdom of Christ (11:15-19).

The woman fleeing from the dragon: the Church (12:1-17).

The beasts given authority by the dragon (13:1-18).

The Lamb and his companions (14:1-5).

Proclamation and symbols of the Judgment; the harvest and the vintage (14:6-20).

The hymn of the saved: the song of Moses and the song of the Lamb (15:1-4).

The seven bowls of plagues: the last chance for conversion (15:5 - 16:21).

Description of the powers of evil: the harlot, Babylon and the beast (17:1-18).

The fall of Babylon proclaimed: joy and lamentation (18:1-24).

Songs of victory in heaven (19:1-10).

The first battle: the beast is destroyed (19:11-21).

The thousand-year reign of Christ and his people (20:1-6).

The second battle: Satan is overthrown (20:7-10).

The Last Judgment of the living and the dead (20:11-15).

A new world comes into being: the messianic Jerusalem is described (21:1 - 22:15).

CONCLUSION: A dialogue between Jesus and the Church. Warnings to the reader and words of farewell (22:16-2).

TEACHINGS CONTAINED IN THE BOOK OF REVELATION

The core of the teaching contained in the book concerns the second coming of our Lord—the Parousia—and the definitive establishment of his Kingdom at the end of time. Various elements go to make up this teaching.

1. *God the almighty* God is described as "the Alpha and the Omega, the beginning and the end" (1:8; 22:13), words which teach the sublimity and absolute authority of God. Alpha is the first letter of the Greek alphabet and Omega the last: the sacred author chooses this graphic method to explain that God is the source from which all created things derive their being: he wills that what did not exist should come to be (cf. 4:11); he is also the end or goal to which everything is directed and where it finds its fulfilment.

In another passage God is defined as he "who is and who was and who is to come" (1:4), a form of words also found in Jewish literature as an explanation of the name Yahweh, "I AM WHO I AM", revealed to Moses (Ex 3:14). This teaches that God is he who existed in the past (he is eternal); he who is (he is active in the world since its creation); and he who is to come (that is, his dynamic and saving presence will never cease).

Echoing the Book of Daniel, the Apocalypse teaches that God "lives for ever and ever" (4:9-10; cf. Dan 4:34). He is also called the "living God", an expression often met in the Old Testament, which underlines the essential difference between Yahweh (the living God) and idols, "the work of men's hands. They have mouths, but do not speak; eyes but do not see" (Ps 115:4-5). God is, then, eternal and immortal; he has no beginning or end. He is also the *Pantocrator*, the Almighty; his power is unique and all-embracing (cf. 1:8; 4:3). God is the Lord of history; nothing falls outside his providence; he is the just Father whose word is true, who will bestow himself on the victor as he promised: "I will be his God and he shall be my son" (21:7). Finally, God's creative power and unbounded love will lead him to restore all things and create a new world (cf. 21:5).

God is also presented as the universal Judge, against whose verdict there is no appeal; none can evade his judgment (cf. 20:12). However, at the end of time his infinite love will prevail and will cause all things to be made new (cf. 21:5), and night shall be no more, for the Lord will shine on them forever (cf. 22:5), nor shall there be any pain or tears, for the old world shall have passed away.

23

2. *Jesus Christ*   At the start of the book the figure of the suffering Christ is evoked by reference to "every one who pierced him" (1:7), and later on it speaks of the great city "where their Lord was crucified" (11:8). Elsewhere there is further reference to the saving blood of Christ (cf. 7:14; 12:11), particularly in connexion with the impressive yet humble figure of the Lamb, often depicted as "slain" (cf. 5:12; 22:14), the victim of the greatest of all sacrifices. However, our Lord is usually depicted in the glory of heaven under the tender symbol of the Lamb enthroned on Mount Zion, with the river of the water of life flowing from his throne (cf. 14:1; 5:6; 22:3; 22:1). He will shepherd and guide his people (7:17). His enemies will make war on him, but he will emerge victorious (cf. 17:14). He is worthy to receive power and glory and to be worshipped by all creation (cf. 5:12; 7:1; 13:8).

Jesus Christ is also given the title of "Son of man", destined to receive power and dominion over all nations and languages (cf. Dan 7:13-14; Rev 1:13-16). He is "Lord of lords and King of kings" (cf. 17:14; 19:12-16); he is above the angels, who are his emissaries, and unlike them he is rendered the worship due to God alone (cf. 1:1; 22:6; 19:10; 22:8-9). In other passages Christ is given divine titles and attributes (cf. 1:18; 3:7; 5:13; 22:1-3). He is also depicted as the Word of God: this is in line with the Fourth Gospel and clearly teaches that he is divine (cf. 19:13; Jn 1:1-14; 1 Jn 1:1).

3. *The Holy Spirit*   There are a number of passages which indirectly refer to the Holy Spirit—for example, when the book speaks of the seven spirits who are before the throne, or the seven torches of fire (1:4; 4:5). It also explicitly teaches that it is the Holy Spirit who is speaking to the churches (2:7, 11, 17; etc.). And, at the end, the voice of the Spirit joins with that of the Bride to make entreaty for the coming of Christ. This passage is reminiscent of St Paul's teaching about how the Holy Spirit prays by interceding for us with sighs too deep for words (cf. Rom 8:26). In the Book of Revelation, the Holy Spirit is presented in relation to the Church: he nourishes the Church with his word and moves it interiorly to pray earnestly for the coming of the Lord.

4. *The Church*   In a more or less explicit way the Church is present throughout the Book of Revelation. It teaches that the Church, which is one and universal, is the Bride of Christ, insistently making supplication for the Lord's coming (cf. 22:17, 20). But the Church is also depicted as Christian communities located in various cities of proconsular Asia (cf. chaps. 2-3). These communities do not constitute a Church distinct from the Church as such; rather, we can begin to perceive here the idea that all communities, taken together, make up the universal Church: the Church becomes present in these believing communities which are "parts" of the one Church of Christ.[28]

The apocalyptic vision of the woman in heaven (cf. chap. 12) has been interpreted in many different ways, particularly as referring to the Church. This interpretation sees her as the Church undergoing severe affliction. Her crown

28. Cf. Vatican II, *Christus Dominus*, 68.

of twelve stars is taken as symbolizing both the twelve tribes of Israel and the twelve Apostles, the pillars of the new Church. The passage is reminiscent of what the prophet Isaiah says when he compares the suffering of the people to those of a woman in labour.

The Apocalypse also uses a variety of symbols designed to convey the beauty and grandeur of the Church. Thus, it speaks of the holy city, the new Jerusalem, where God dwells; it is also the "beloved city" (cf. 3:12; 21:2, 10; 20:9). Its glory and splendour are described with a wealth of detail, ranging from the richness of its walls to the fruitfulness of its waters (cf. 21:16-27; 22:1-2). It is called the "temple of God", whose pillars are those who have won the victory; in it stands the Ark of the Covenant and there the countless multitudes of the elect render worship to God (cf. 3:12; 7:15; 11:19).

The text implies that in both its earthly stage and its heavenly stage, the Church is the chosen people of God. Thus, the voice from heaven warns the elect who live in Babylon, "Come out of her, my people, lest you take part in her sins, lest you share in her plagues" (18:4); and towards the end of the book we are reminded that God will dwell in the midst of his people (cf. 21:3): the Church is depicted as the new Israel, increasing in number, and at a future time preserved from all evil by the seal of God (cf. 7:4-8).

The image of the Kingdom also reveals the nature of the Church. John depicts it, now as sharing in tribulation and the Kingdom (cf. 1:9), now as singing the praises of Jesus Christ: he has "made us a kingdom", a royal line, "priests to his God and Father" (1:6).

One of the most important and revealing things the Bible tells us about the Church is God's love for his people as symbolized by the beloved Bride. The Apocalypse frequently speaks in these terms, focusing attention on the marriage of the Lamb, whose wife is decked out as a new bride (cf. 19:7; 21:9), eagerly calling for her beloved (cf. 22:17). One of the most significant moments described is the wedding of the Lamb, an occasion for great joy and exultation (cf. 19:7). The book also alludes to the Bride when it says, "Blessed are those who are invited to the marriage supper of the Lamb" (19:9).

5. *The angels* Throughout the book angels are very much in evidence. Etymologically, the word "angel" means "messenger"; this role of theirs in bringing God's messages to men is stressed continually. At the start of the book it is through an angel that John is given to know the things that are to come, and at the end it will also be an angel who shows him the final visions of the heavenly Jerusalem (cf. 1:1; 22:6, 16). At certain points an angel passes his message on to other angels (cf. 7:2; 8:2 - 11:15), or proclaims the Gospel to all mankind and makes known God's dire warnings and punishments (cf. 14:6-19; 16:17; 19:17).

The angels are also depicted as man's protectors. We see them standing at the four corners of the earth, holding back the winds to prevent their harming men (cf. 7:1), and standing as sentinels at the gates of the holy city (cf. 21:12). The angels of the churches (cf. 1:20; 2:1, 8, 12, 18; 3:1, 7, 14) are interpreted by some commentators as symbolizing the bishops of these churches, for the main mission of bishops is to watch over their flocks. However, these angels can also be seen as divine messengers who are given things by the Lord to communicate to the churches, whom they also have a mission to protect and govern.

On occasions the angels are deputed to carry out God's punishment (cf. 9:15; 14:18; etc.). With the archangel St Michael as their leader, they fight the great cosmic battle of Good and Evil (cf. 12:7ff) against the dragon, "that ancient serpent, who is called the Devil and Satan, the deceiver of the whole world" (12:9). But this is a war which goes on throughout history: thus, the demons, also called angels of Satan, are often shown as coming from the abyss, temporarily released to roam the earth, causing war and confusion (cf. 20:7-8); in the end, however, they will be cast down into hell where they will suffer everlasting torment (cf. 12:9; 20:10).

In addition to their important and varied mission on earth, the angels are also in heaven, in the presence of God, interceding on mankind's behalf, offering "upon the golden altar before the throne" the prayers of the saints, which reach God via the angels (cf. 8:4). Special emphasis is also put on the unceasing worship offered by the angels to God and to the Lamb (cf. 5:11; 7:11; etc.).

6. *The Virgin Mary*   The woman clothed with the sun, crowned with stars, and with the moon under her feet is undoubtedly a symbol of the Church. However, from very early on many Fathers also saw her as representing the Blessed Virgin. It is true that Mary suffered no birth-pangs when her Son was born, and had no children other than him to be "the rest of her offspring" (12:17). However, this vision does evoke the Genesis account, which speaks of enmity between the serpent and the woman. The Son who is caught up to God and to his throne is Jesus Christ (cf. 12:5). As in the case of the parables, not everything in the imagery necessarily happens in real life; and the same image can refer to one or more things—particularly when they are closely connected, as the Blessed Virgin and the Church are. So, the fact that this passage is interpreted as referring to the Church does not exclude its referring also to Mary. More than once, the Church's Magisterium has given it a Marian interpretation. For example, St Pius X says: "Everyone knows that this woman was the image of the Virgin Mary, who, in giving birth to our head, remained inviolate. 'And being with child,' the Apostle continues, 'she cried out in her travail and was there in the anguish of delivery' [. . .]. It was the birth of all of us who, while being exiles here below, are not yet brought forth into the perfect love of God and eternal happiness. The fact that the heavenly Virgin labours in childbirth shows her loving desire to watch over us and through unceasing prayer complete the number of the elect."[29]

John Paul II adopted this interpretation in a sermon at the shrine of Allötting: "Mary [. . .] carries the *features of that woman* whom the Apocalypse describes

29. Cf. *Ad Diem illum*, 15.

[. . .]. The woman, who stands *at the end* of the history of creation and salvation, corresponds evidently to the one about whom it is said *in the first pages* of the Bible that she 'is going to crush the head of the serpent'. Between this promising beginning and the apocalyptic end Mary *has brought to light a son* 'who is to rule all nations with an iron sceptre' (Rev 12:5) [. . .]. She it is with whom the *apocalyptic* dragon makes war, for being the mother of the redeemed, she is the image of the Church whom we likewise call mother."[30]

30. *Homily*, 18 November 1980.

THE EASTERN MEDITERRANEAN SEA IN THE FIRST CENTURY AD

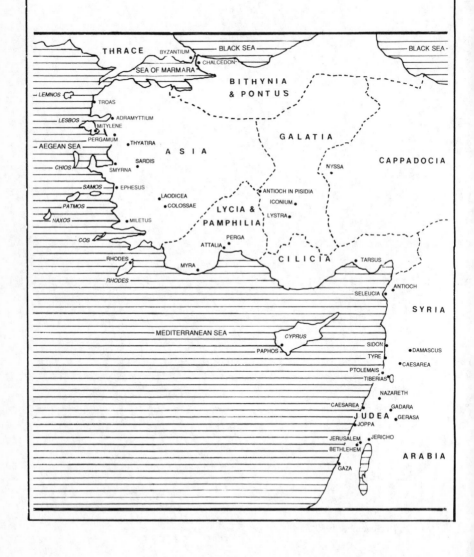

The Book of Revelation

ENGLISH AND LATIN VERSIONS, WITH NOTES

1

PROLOGUE

¹The revelation of Jesus Christ, which God gave him to show to his servants what must soon take place; and he made it known by sending his angel to his servant John, ²who bore witness to the word of God and to the testimony of Jesus Christ, even to all that he saw. ³Blessed is he who

Dan 2:28
Rev 22:6

Rev 6:9
1 Jn 1:1-3

Rev 22:7, 18

---

¹Apocalypsis Iesu Christi, quam dedit illi Deus palam facere servis suis, quae oportet fieri cito, et significavit mittens per angelum suum servo suo Ioanni,

---

1-20. After a brief prologue (vv. 1-3) and a letter-style greeting (vv. 4-8), St John describes a vision which acts as an introduction to the entire book; in it the risen Christ is depicted with features identifying his divinity and his position as Lord and Saviour of the churches.

In the course of the book Jesus Christ will also appear as God's envoy, sent to teach Christians of the time, and subsequent generations (chaps. 2-3), and to console them in the midst of persecution by proclaiming God's design for the future of the world and of the Church (chaps. 4-22).

1-3. Despite its brevity this prologue conveys the scope of the book, its authority and the effect it hopes to have on its readers.

The *content* of the letter is a revelation made by Jesus Christ about contemporary and future events (cf. 1:19; 4:1). Its author, John, gives it its *authority*: Christ's revelation has been communicated to him in a supernatural manner, and he bears faithful witness to everything revealed to him. The book's *purpose* is to have the reader prepare for his or her definitive encounter with Christ by obeying what is written in the book: blessed are those who read it and take it to heart and do what it says.

God made known his salvific purpose through everything Jesus did and said. However, after his resurrection Christ continues to speak to his Church by means of revelations such as that contained in this book and those made to St Paul (cf. Gal 1:15-16; etc.). These bring the Christian revelation to completion and apply the saving action of Jesus to concrete situations in the life of the Church. When revelations reach us through an inspired writer they have universal validity, that is, they are "public" revelation and are part and parcel of the message of salvation entrusted by Christ to his Apostles to proclaim to all nations (cf. Mt 28:18-20 and par.; Jn 17:18; 20:21). Public divine Revelation ceased with the death of the last Apostle (cf. Vatican II, *Dei Verbum*, 4).

1. "The revelation of Jesus Christ": The word in Greek is *apocalypsis*, hence the name often given to this book of Sacred Scripture. Revelation always

reads aloud the words of the prophecy, and blessed are those who hear, and who keep what is written therein; for the time is near.

---

²qui testificatus est verbum Dei et testimonium Iesu Christi, quaecumque vidit. ³Beatus, qui legit et qui audiunt verba prophetiae et servant ea, quae in ea scripta

---

implies the unveiling of something previously hidden—in this case, future events. The future is known to God the Father (the Greek text uses the definite article, "the God", which is how the New Testament usually refers to God the Father); and Jesus Christ, being the Son, shares in this knowledge which is being communicated to the author of the book. It speaks of "the revelation of Jesus Christ" not only because it has come to John from Christ but also because our Lord is the main subject, the beginning and end, of this revelation: he occupies the central position in all these great visions in which the veils concealing the future are torn to allow Light (Jesus Christ himself: cf. Rev 21:23; 22:5) to dispel the darkness.

"Soon": as regards how imminent or not all those events are, one needs to remember that the notion of time in Sacred Scripture, particularly in the Apocalypse, is not quite the same as ours: it is more qualitative than quantitative. Here indeed "with the Lord one day is as a thousand years, and a thousand years as one day" (2 Pet 3:8). So, when Scripture says that something is about to happen it is not necessarily referring to a date in the near future: it is simply saying that it will happen and even in some sense is happening already. Finally, one needs to bear in mind that if events are proclaimed as being imminent, this would have a desired effect of fortifying those who are experiencing persecution and would give them hope and consolation.

3. The Book of Revelation is a pressing call to commitment in fidelity to everything our Lord has chosen to reveal to us in the New Testament, in this instance from the pen of St John.

The book seems to be designed for liturgical assemblies, where someone reads it aloud and the others listen. This is the preferential place for Sacred Scripture, as Vatican II indicates: "The Church has always venerated the divine Scriptures as she venerated the Body of the Lord, in so far as she never ceases, particularly in the sacred liturgy, to partake of the bread of life and to offer it to the faithful from the one table of the Word of God and the Body of Christ" (*Dei Verbum*, 21).

"Sacred Scripture is of the greatest importance in the celebration of the liturgy. For it is from it that lessons are read and explained in the homily, and psalms are sung. It is from the scriptures that the prayers, collects, and hymns draw their inspiration and their force, and that actions and signs derive their meaning" (Vatican II, *Sacrosanctum Concilium*, 24).

The situation when St John was writing called for just the sort of exhortations and warnings this text contains. Its words call for a prompt, committed response which leaves no room for any kind of doubt or hesitation. They are also a dire

PART ONE
LETTERS TO THE SEVEN CHURCHES

Address and greeting

Ex 3:14
Is 11:2ff; 41:4

⁴John to the seven churches that are in Asia:
Grace to you and peace from him who is and who was

---

sunt; tempus enim prope est. ⁴Ioannes septem ecclesiis, quae sunt in Asia:

---

warning to those who try to hinder the progress of the Kingdom of God, a Kingdom which must inexorably come about and which in some way is already with us.

4-8. Following the prologue (vv. 1-3), a short reflection (vv. 4-8) introduces the series of seven letters which form the first part of the book (1:4 - 3:22). This introduction begins with a salutation to the seven churches of Asia Minor, located in the west of the region known at the time as 'proconsular Asia', the capital of which was Ephesus.

The salutation is in the usual New Testament style: it sends good wishes of grace and peace on behalf of God and Jesus Christ (vv. 4-5, cf. 1 Thess 1:1; 2 Thess 1:2; etc.); it depicts our Lord and his work of salvation (vv. 5-8) and projects that work onto the panorama of world history.

4. Even though there were other churches in Asia Minor, John addresses only seven, a number which stands for "totality", as an early ecclesiatical writer, Primasius, explains. "He writes to the seven churches, that is, to the one and only Church symbolized by these seven" (*Commentariorum super Apoc.*, 1, 1).

Grace and peace are the outstanding gifts of the messianic era (cf. Rom 1:7). This form of salutation embodies the normal forms of greeting used by Greeks (*jaire*, grace) and Jews (*shalom*, peace); but here the words mean the grace, forgiveness and peace extended to men by the redemptive action of Jesus Christ. Thus, St John is wishing these gifts on behalf of God, the seven spirits and Jesus Christ.

The description of God as he "who is and who was and who is to come" is an elaboration of the name of "Yahweh" ("I AM WHO I AM") which was revealed to Moses (cf. Ex 3:14), and underlines the fact that God is the Lord of history, of the past, the present and the future, and that he is at all times acting to effect salvation.

The "seven spirits" stand for God's power and omniscience and intervention in the events of history. In Zechariah 4:10 divine power is symbolized by the seven "eyes of the Lord, which range the whole earth". Further on in the Apocalypse (5:6), St John tells us that the seven spirits of God sent out into all the earth are the seven eyes of the Lamb, that is, Christ. This symbolism (also found in the Old Testament: cf. Is 11:2ff) is used to show that God the Father acts through his Spirit and that this Spirit has been communicated to Christ and

and who is to come, and from the seven spirits who are
before his throne, ⁵and from Jesus Christ the faithful
witness, the first-born of the dead, and the ruler of kings on
earth.

To him who loves us and has freed us from our sins by
his blood ⁶and made us a kingdom, priests to his God and

Ps 89:28, 38
Col 1:18
Rev 19:16

Ex 19:6
1 Pet 2:9
Rom 16:27
Is 61:6

Gratia vobis et pax ab eo, qui est et qui erat et qui venturus est, et a septem
spiritibus, qui in conspectu throni eius sunt, ⁵et ab Iesu Christo, qui est testis
fidelis, primogenitus mortuorum et princeps regum terrae. Ei, qui diligit nos et
solvit nos a peccatis nostris in sanguine suo ⁶et fecit nos regnum, sacerdotes

---

by him to mankind. So, when St John wishes grace and peace from the seven
spirits of God it is the same as saying "from the Holy Spirit", who is sent to the
Church after the death and resurrection of Christ. Patristic tradition has in fact
interpreted the seven spirits as meaning the septiform Spirit with his seven gifts
as described in Isaiah 11:1-2 in St Jerome's translation, the Vulgate.

5:6. Three messianic titles taken from Psalm 89:28-38 are given a new
meaning in the light of fulfilment of Christian faith and applied to Jesus Christ.
He is "the faithful witness" of the fulfilment of God's Old Testament promises
of a Saviour, a son of David (cf. 2 Sam 7:14; Rev 5:5;), for it is Christ who has
in fact brought about salvation. That is why, later on in the book, St John calls
Jesus Christ "the Amen" (Rev 3:4)—which is like saying that through what
Christ did God has ratified and kept his word; St John also calls him "Faithful
and True" (Rev 19;11), because God's fidelity and the truth of his promises
have been manifested in Jesus. This is to be seen in the Resurrection, which
made Jesus "the first-born from the dead", in the sense that the Resurrection
constituted a victory in which all who abide in him share (cf. Col 1:18). Christ
is also "the ruler of kings on earth" because he is Lord of the world: this will
be clearly seen when he comes a second time, but his dominion is already
making itself felt because he has begun to conquer the power of sin and death.

The second part of v. 5 and all v. 6 are a kind of paean in praise of Christ
recalling his great love for us as expressed in his words, "Greater love has no
man than this, that a man lay down his life for his friends" (Jn 15:13). Christ's
love for us knows no bounds: his generosity led him to sacrifice his life by the
shedding of his blood, which redeemed us from our sins. There was nothing
we could have done to redeem ourselves. "All were held captive by the devil",
St Augustine comments, "and were in the thrall of demons; but they have been
rescued from that captivity. The Redeemer came and paid the ransom: he shed
his blood and with it purchased the entire orb of the earth" (*Enarrationes in
Psalmos*, 95, 5).

Not content with setting us free from our sins, our Lord gave us a share in
his kingship and priesthood. "Christ the Lord, high priest taken from among
men (cf. Heb 5:1-5), made the new people 'a kingdom of priests to his God and

Father, to him be glory and dominion for ever and ever. Amen. ⁷Behold, he is coming with the clouds, and every eye will see him, every one who pierced him; and all tribes of the earth will wail on account of him. Even so. Amen.

Dan 7:13
Zech 12:10, 14
Jn 19:37
Mt 24:30

Deo et Patri suo, ipsi gloria et imperium in saecula saeculorum. Amen. ⁷*Ecce venit cum nubibus, et videbit* eum omnis oculus et qui eum *pupugerunt, et plangent se super eum omnes tribus terrae.* Etiam, amen. ⁸Ego sum Alpha et Omega, dicit Dominus Deus, qui est et qui erat et qui venturus est, Omnipotens. ⁹Ego Ioannes, frater vester et particeps in tribulatione et regno et patientia in Iesu, fui in insula, quae appellatur Patmos, propter verbum Dei et testimonium

---

Father' (Rev 1:6; cf. 5:9-10). The baptized, by regeneration and the anointing of the Holy Spirit, are consecrated to be a spiritual house and a holy priesthood, that through all the works of Christian men and women they may offer spiritual sacrifices and proclaim the perfection of him who has called them out of darkness into his marvellous light (cf. 1 Pet 2:4-10)" (Vatican II, *Lumen gentium*, 10).

7. Christ's work is not finished. He has assembled his holy people on earth to bring them enduring salvation, and he will be revealed in all his glory to the whole world at the end of time. Although the text speaks in the present tense—"he is coming with the clouds"—this should be understood as referring to the future: the prophet was seeing future events as if they were actually happening (cf. Dan 7:13). This will be the day of final victory, when those who crucified Jesus, "every one who pierced him" (cf. Zech 12:10; Jn 19:37), will be astonished by the grandeur and glory of the crucified One. "The Sacred Scriptures inform us that there are two comings of the Son of God—one when he assumed human flesh for our salvation in the womb of a virgin; the other when he shall come at the end of the world to judge all mankind [. . .]; and if, from the beginning of the world that day of the Lord, on which he was clothed with our flesh, was sighed for by all as the foundation of their hope of deliverance; so also, after the death and ascension of the Son of God, we should make that other day of the Lord the object of our most earnest desires, 'awaiting our blessed hope, the appearing of the glory of our great God' (Tit 2:13)" (*St Pius V Catechism*, I, 8, 2).

Commenting on this passage of the Apocalypse, St Bede says: "He who at his first coming came in a hidden way and in order to be judged (by men) will then come in a manifest way. (John) recalls these truths in order to help the Church bear its suffering: now it is being persecuted by its enemies, later it will reign at Christ's side" (*Explanatio Apocalypsis*, 1, 1).

The joy of those who put their hope in this glorious manifestation of Christ will contrast with the pains of those who reject God's love and mercy to the very end. "Then all the tribes of the earth will mourn, and they will see the Son of man coming in the clouds of heaven with power and great glory" (Mt 24:30).

Rev 1:4; 21:6   ⁸"I am the Alpha and the Omega," says the Lord God, who is and who was and who is to come, the Almighty.

Reason for writing

Rom 3:26   ⁹I John, your brother, who share with you in Jesus the tribulation and the kingdom and the patient endurance, was on the island called Patmos on account of the word of God

Rev 4:1   and the testimony of Jesus. ¹⁰I was in the Spirit on the Lord's day, and I heard behind me a loud voice like a trumpet ¹¹saying, "Write what you see in a book and send

---

Iesu. ¹⁰Fui in spiritu in dominica die et audivi post me vocem magnum tamquam tubae ¹¹dicentis: "Quod vides, scribe in libro et mitte septem ecclesiis: Ephesum

---

8. The coming of the Lord in glory, the climax of his dominion, is guaranteed by the power of God, the absolute master of the world and its destiny. Alpha and Omega are the first and last letters of the Greek alphabet; here they are used to proclaim that God is the beginning and end of all things, of the world and of history; he is present at all times—times past, present and future.

9-20. After greeting the churches (vv. 4-8) the author explains his reason for writing: he has been commanded to do so by his glorious Lord, in a vision of the risen Christ concerning his Church.

In Sacred Scripture God's messages are frequently communicated to prophets in the form of a vision (cf. Is 6; Ezek 1:4 - 3:15; etc.; Zech 1:7 - 2:9; etc.). Accounts of divine visions are particularly found in "books of revelation" or apocalypses, such as Daniel 8-12, and also in other Jewish and Christian writings of the time immediately before and after Christ's life on earth: although not included in the canon of the Bible, these writings were designed to keep up Christians' morale in times of persecution. In a genuinely prophetic vision God elevates the prophet's mind to enable him to understand what God desires to tell him (cf. *Summa theologiae*, II-II, q. 173, a. 3). In the Apocalypse, when St John reports his vision he is making known the message given him by the risen Christ: Christ is continuing to speak to his Church in a number of ways, including the exhortations and teachings contained in this book.

9-11. Like other prophets and apostles (cf. Ezek 3:12; Acts 10:10; 22:17; 2 Cor 12:2-3), John feels himself caught up by a divine force; in an ecstasy he hears the voice of our Lord; its power and strength he describes as a trumpet.

Some scholars think that the seven churches listed here were chosen because of their particular situation at the time. They stand for the entire Church universal, and therefore what is said in the seven letters is addressed to all Christians who, in one way or another, find themselves in situations similar to that of these churches of proconsular Asia.

it to the seven churches, to Ephesus and to Smyrna and
Pergamum and to Thyatira and to Sardis and to Philadelphia
and to Laodicea."

---

et Smyrnam et Pergamum et Thyatiram et Sardis et Philadelphiam et
Laodiciam." [12]Et conversus sum, ut viderem vocem, quae loquebatur mecum;
et conversus vidi septem candelabra aurea [13]et in medio candelabrorum *quasi
Filium hominis, vestitum podere et praecinctum* ad mamillas zonam *auream*;

The Apostles' vigilant care of the Church is discernible in many of the letters
they addressed to their communities. Like St Paul (cf. 2 Cor 11:28; 1 Thess
2:2), the other Apostles felt anxiety for all the churches. St Peter, for example,
wrote to elders telling them to be good shepherds of the flock God gave into
their care, tending it "not by constraint but willingly, as God would have you,
not for shameful gain but eagerly, not as domineering over those in your charge
but being examples to the flock" (1 Pet 5:2-3).

This pastoral solicitude leads St John to show solidarity with the joy and
affliction of Christians of his day. His consoling words come from someone
who well knows (because he has learned it from Jesus and later from his own
experience) that fidelity to the Gospel calls for self-denial and even martyrdom.
Communion and solidarity are wonderful features of the mystical body of
Christ: they stem from the fact that all Christians are united to each other and
to Jesus Christ, the head of that body which is the Church (cf. Col 1:18; Eph
4:16; etc.). The visionary of Patmos clearly has tremendous love for Christ and
for the Church. We should remember that "charity more than any other virtue,
unites us closely with Christ, and it is the heavenly ardour of this love which
has caused so many sons and daughters of the Church to rejoice in suffering
contumely for his sake, joyfully to meet and overcome the severest trials, and
even to shed their blood and die for him" (Pius XII, *Mystici corporis*, 33).

From the very start of his public ministry our Lord foretold how much his
followers would have to suffer for his sake. For example, in the Sermon on the
Mount, he said, "Blessed are you when men revile you and persecute you and
utter all kinds of evil against you falsely on my account. Rejoice and be glad,
for your reward is great in heaven, for so men persecuted the prophets who
were before you" (Mt 5:11-12).

"The Lord's day": the *dies Dominica*, Sunday, the day which the Church,
ever since the apostolic age, keeps as its weekly holy day in place of the Jewish
sabbath, because it is the day on which Jesus rose from the dead: "on this day
Christ's faithful are bound to come together into one place. They should listen
to the word of God and take part in the Eucharist, thus calling to mind the
passion, resurrection, and glory of the Lord Jesus, and giving thanks to God by
whom they have been begotten 'anew through the resurrection of Christ from
the dead, unto a living hope' (1 Pet 1:3)" (Vatican II, *Sacrosanctum Concilium*,
106). This day should be sanctified by attending Mass and also by giving time
to other devotions, rest, and activities which help build up friendship with
others, especially in the family circle.

Rev 1:4, 20
Dan 7:13; 10:5
Dan 7:9; 10:6
Rev 2:18;
19:12
Ezek 1:24; 43:2
Mt 17:2
Judg 5:31
Rev 2:12
Dan 8:18;
10:5-19
Is 41:4; 44:6
48:12

¹²Then I turned to see the voice that was speaking to me, and on turning I saw seven golden lampstands, ¹³and in the midst of the lampstands one like a son of man, clothed with a long robe and with a golden girdle round his breast; ¹⁴his head and his hair were white as white wool, white as snow; his eyes were like a flame of fire, ¹⁵his feet were like burnished bronze, refined as in a furnace, and his voice was like the sound of many waters; ¹⁶in his right hand he held seven stars, from his mouth issued a sharp two-edged sword, and his face was like the sun shining in full strength. ¹⁷When I saw him, I fell at his feet as though dead. But

¹⁴*caput* autem *eius et capilli erant candidi tamquam lana* alba, *tamquam nix, et oculi eius velut* flamma *ignis,* ¹⁵*et pedes eius similes orichalco* sicut in camino ardenti, *et vox illius tamquam vox aquarum multarum,* ¹⁶et habebat in dextera manu sua stellas septem, et de ore eius gladius anceps acutus exibat, et facies eius sicut sol lucet in virtute sua. ¹⁷Et cum vidissem eum, cecidi ad pedes eius

12-16. The lampstands in this first vision symbolize the churches at prayer; they remind us of the seven-branched candlestick (the *menorah*) which used to burn in the temple of Jerusalem and which is described in detail in Exodus 25:31-20. In the midst of the candlestick, as if guarding and governing the churches, a mysterious figure appears, in the form of a man. The expression "son of man" originates in Daniel 7:14 where, as here, it refers to someone depicted as Judge at the end of time. The various symbols used indicate his importance. His "long robe" shows his priesthood (cf. Ex 28:4; Zech 3:4); the golden girdle, his kingship (cf. 1 Mac 10:89); his white hair, his eternity (cf. Dan 7:9); his eyes "like a flame of fire" symbolize his divine wisdom (cf. Rev 2:23), and his bronze feet his strength and stability.

The seven stars stand for the angels of the seven churches (cf. v. 20), and our Lord's holding them in his hand is a sign of his power and providence. Finally, the splendour of his face recalls the Old Testament theophanies or apparitions, and the sword coming from his mouth shows the power of his word (cf. Heb 4:12).

It is interesting to note that our Lord used the title "son of man" to refer to himself (cf., e.g., Mt 9:6; Mk 10:45; Lk 6:22); it is always used in St John's Gospel to indicate Christ's divinity and transcendence (cf., e.g., Jn 1:51; 3:14; 9:35; 12:23).

"Burnished bronze": Latin versions transliterate the original as "orichalc", a shining alloy of bronze and gold.

17-19. When the glory of Christ, or the glory of God, is manifested, man becomes so conscious of his insignificance and unworthiness that he is unable to remain standing in his presence. This happened to the Israelites at Sinai (cf. Ex 19:16-24) and to the Apostles on Mount Tabor (cf. Mk 9:2-8 and par.). A

he laid his right hand upon me, saying, "Fear not, I am the first and the last, [18]and the living one; I died, and behold I am alive for evermore, and I have the keys of Death and Hades. [19]Now write what you see, what is and what is to take place hereafter. [20]As for the mystery of the seven stars

Heb 7:25
Mt 16:18

Rev 1:11,
12, 16

tamquam mortuus; et posuit dexteram suam super me dicens: "Noli timere! Ego sum primus et novissimus, [18]et vivens et fui mortuus et ecce sum vivens in saecula saeculorum et habeo claves mortis et inferni. [19]Scribe ergo, quae vidisti

person who experiences the divine presence in a vision reacts in the same way (cf. Ezek 1:29f; Dan 8:18; etc.), and in the case of the Apocalypse it happens when Christ is seen in glory surrounded by his Church. However, the risen Christ's first word to his followers was one of peace and assurance (cf., e.g., Mt 28:5, 10), and here he places his right hand on the seer's head in a gesture of protection.

The risen Christ is depicted as reassuring the Christian, who sees him as having absolute dominion over all things (he is the first and the last) though he shared man's mortal nature. By his death and resurrection Christ has overcome death; he has dominion over death and over the mysterious world beyond the grave—Hades, the place of the dead (cf. Num 16:33). "Christ is alive. This is the great truth which fills our faith with meaning. Jesus, who died on the cross, has risen. He has triumphed over death; he has overcome sorrow, anguish and the power of darkness" (J. Escrivá, *Christ is passing by*, 102).

The vision St John is given is meant for the benefit of the whole Church, as can be seen from the fact that he is told to write down what he sees; it is connected with contemporary events and with the future. The immediate context of the vision is the salvation of the churches mentioned and the glory of Christ who is caring for them (chaps. 2-3); the future has to do with the afflictions the Church must undergo and the full establishment of Christ's kingdom: his second coming will mean definitive victory over the powers of evil (cf. chaps. 4-22).

20. To understand the meaning of the revelation made to St John, which he is transmitting in this book, one needs to know the mysterious, hidden meaning behind the images which appear in the vision. When John says that Jesus Christ himself revealed this to him, he is saying that this is the true interpretation and he is inviting us to interpret the book's symbolism by using this key to its meaning; no parallel explanation is given of the other visions when he comes to describe them.

The angels of the seven churches may stand for the bishops in charge of them, or else the guardian angels who watch over them, or even the churches themselves insofar as they have a heavenly dimension and stand in God's presence as angels do. Whichever is the case, the best thing is to see the angels of the churches, to whom the letters are addressed, as meaning those who rule and protect each church in Christ's name. He is the only Lord, which is why

which you saw in my right hand, and the seven golden lampstands, the seven stars are the angels of the seven churches and the seven lampstands are the seven churches.

2

Letter to the church of Ephesus

Ps 36:5
Mic 2:1
Rev 1:13, 16, 20 [1]"To the angel of the church in Ephesus write: 'The words of him who holds the seven stars in his right hand, who walks among the seven golden lampstands.

---

et quae sunt et quae oportet fieri post haec. [20]Mysterium septem stellarum, quas vidisti ad dexteram meam, et septem candelabra aurea: septem stellae angeli sunt septem ecclesiarum, et candelabra septem septem ecclesiae sunt.
[1]Angelo ecclesiae, quae est Ephesi, scribe: Haec dicit, qui tenet septem stellas in dextera sua, qui ambulat in medio septem candelabrorum aureorum: [2]Scio

---

he is shown holding the stars (angels) in his right hand. In the Old Testament the "angel of Yahweh" is the one charged to guide the people of Israel (cf. Ex 14:19; 23:20; etc.); and in the Apocalypse itself angels are given the mission of ruling the material world (cf. Rev 7:1; 14:18; 16:5). So, Christ exercises his loving care and government of each Church through the mediation of "angels", but it is difficult to say whether this means angels as such, or bishops, or both.

Lampstands may be used as a symbol because the Church is being seen in liturgical terms: it is, from that point of new, like a lamp burning constantly and giving light in praise of Christ. The symbol is reminiscent of the seven-branched candlestick which used to burn continually in the presence of Yahweh (cf. Ex 27:20; Lev 24:2f) and which Zechariah saw in his visions (cf. Zech 4:1f). The lamps are a very good symbol, given that the churches are the light of the world (cf. Mt 5:14; Phil 2:15; etc.).

2:1 - 3:22. These chapters, which form the first part of the book, contain seven letters to the churches already mentioned (cf. 1:11), each represented by an angel to whom the letter is addressed. In these letters Christ (who is referred to in various ways) and the Holy Spirit speak: hence the warning at the end of each, "he who has an ear, let him hear what the Spirit says to the churches." The first part of that formula is reminiscent of things our Lord said in the Gospels (cf., e.g., Mt 11:15; 13:9, 43; Mk 9:23), while the second part underlines the influence of the Holy Spirit on the churches: one needs to belong to the Church, to "feel with" the Church, if one is to understand what the Spirit says and what is being committed to writing in this book. The book, therefore, must be taken as the true word of God. All Sacred Scripture needs to be approached in this way: "Since all that the inspired authors, or sacred writers, affirm should be regarded as affirmed by the Holy Spirit, we must acknowledge

2"'I know your works, your toil and your patient endurance, and how you cannot bear evil men but have tested those who call themselves apostles but are not, and found them to be false; ³I know you are enduring patiently

2 Cor 11:13
1 Jn 4:1

---

opera tua et laborem et patientiam tuam, et quia non potes sustinere malos et tentasti eos, qui se dicunt apostolos et non sunt, et invenisti eos mendaces; ³et

---

that the books of Scripture, firmly, faithfully and without error, teach that truth which God, for the sake of our salvation, wished to see confided to the sacred Scriptures. Thus 'all scripture is inspired by God, and profitable for teaching, for reproof, for correction and for training in righteousness, so that the man of God may be complete, equipped for every good work' (2 Tim 3:16-17)" (Vatican II, *Dei Verbum*, 11).

Although the letters are different from one another, they all have the same basic structure: there is reference to the past, which is contrasted with the present; various warnings are given and promises made; then there is an exhortation to repentance and conversion, a reminder that the end, and Christ's definitive victory, will soon come.

1. Ephesus, with its great harbour and commercial importance, was the leading city of Asia Minor at the time. It was also the centre of the cult of the goddess Artemis or Diana (cf. Acts 19:23ff).

St Paul spent three years preaching in Ephesus and had considerable success there: St Luke tells us that "the word of the Lord grew (there) and prevailed mightily" (Acts 19:20). In ancient times it was the most important Christian city in the whole region, especially after the fall of Jerusalem in the year 70. St John spent the last years of his life in Ephesus, where his burial place is still venerated.

In these letters in the Book of Revelation, Christ is depicted with attributes connected in some way with the circumstances of each church at the time. In the case of Ephesus the symbols described in the vision in 1:12, 16 appear again. The seven stars in his right hand signify his dominion over the whole Church, for he is the one who has power to instruct the angels who rule the various communities. His walking among the lampstands shows his loving care and vigilance for the churches (the lampstand symbolizing their prayer and liturgical life). Because the Church in Ephesus was the foremost of the seven, Christ is depicted to it as Lord of all the churches.

2-3. In these verses the church of Ephesus is praised for its endurance and for the resistance it has shown to false apostles. These two attributes— endurance or constancy, and holy intransigence—are basic virtues every Christian should have. Endurance means doggedly pursuing good and holding one's ground against evil influences; this virtue makes Christians "perfect and complete, lacking in nothing" (Jas 1:4). Indeed, St Paul asserts, "we rejoice in our sufferings, knowing that suffering produces endurance, and endurance

1 Tim 5:12
Rev 2:16,22;
3:3, 19

and bearing up for my name's sake, and you have not grown weary. ⁴But I have this against you, that you have abandoned the love you had at first. ⁵Remember then from what

patientiam habes et sustinuisti propter nomen meum et non defecisti. ⁴Sed habeo adversus te quod caritatem tuam primam reliquisti. ⁵Memor esto itaque unde excideris, et age paenitentiam et prima opera fac; sin autem, venio tibi et movebo candelabrum tuum de loco suo, nisi paenitentiam egeris. ⁶Sed hoc

produces character, and character produces hope" (Rom 5:3-4). In the Epistle to the Hebrews we read, "For you have need of endurance, so that you may do the will of God and receive what is promised" (10:36). Endurance, patience, is also the first mark of charity identified by St Paul (cf. 1 Cor 13:4) and one of the features of the true apostle (cf. 2 Cor 6:4; 12:12). Our Lord has told us that by endurance we will gain our lives, will save our souls (cf. Lk 21:19). As St Cyprian puts it, patience "is what gives our faith its firmest basis; it enables our hope to grow to the greatest heights; it guides our actions so as to enable us to stay on Christ's path and make progress with his help; it makes us persevere as children of God" (*De bono patientiae*, 20).

Another virtue of the church of Ephesus (mentioned again in v. 6) is firm rejection of false apostles. We know from other New Testament writings, especially those of St Paul (cf. 2 Cor 3:1; Gal 1:7; Col 2:8; etc.) and St John (cf. 1 Jn 2:19; etc.) that some people were falsifying the Christian message by distorting its meaning and yet seeming to be very devout and concerned about the poor. Reference is made here to the Nicolaitans, a heretical sect difficult to identify. However, the main thing to notice is the resolute way the Christians of Ephesus rejected that error. If one fails to act in this energetic way, one falls into a false kind of tolerance, "a sure sign of not possessing the truth. When a man gives way in matters of ideals, of honour or of faith, that man is a man without ideals, without honour and without faith" (J. Escrivá, *The Way*, 394).

4. "He does not say that he was without charity, but only that it was not such as in the beginning; that is, that it was not now prompt, fervent, growing in love, or fruitful: as we are wont to say of him who from being bright, cheerful and blithe, becomes sad, heavy and sullen, that he is not now the same man he was" (St Francis de Sales, *Treatise on the Love of God*, 4, 2). This is why our Lord complains that their early love has grown cold.

To avoid this danger, to which all of us are prone, we need to be watchful and correct ourselves every day and return again and again to God our Father. Love of God, charity, should never be allowed to die down; it should always be kept ardent; it should always be growing.

5. This is a call to repentance, to a change of heart which involves three stages. The first is recognizing that one is at fault—having the humility to admit one is a poor sinner: "To acknowledge one's sin, indeed—penetrating still more deeply into the consideration of one's own personhood—to recognize oneself

you have fallen, repent and do the works you did at first. If not, I will come to you and remove your lampstand from its place, unless you repent. [6]Yet this you have, you hate the works of the Nicolaitans, which I also hate. [7]He who has an ear, let him hear what the Spirit says to the churches. To him who conquers I will grant to eat of the tree of life, which is in the paradise of God.'

Rev 2:15
Ps 139:21

Gen 2:9
Rev 22:2

Letter to the church of Smyrna

[8]"And to the angel of the church in Smyrna write: 'The words of the first and the last, who died and came to life.

Is 44:6; 48:12
Rev 1:17
Jas 2:5

---

habes, quia odisti facta Nicolaitarum, quae et ego odi. [7]Qui habet aurem, audiat quid Spiritus dicat ecclesiis. Vincenti dabo ei edere de ligno vitae, quod est in paradiso Dei. [8]Et angelo ecclesiae, quae est Smyrnae, scribe: Haec dicit Primus

---

as being a sinner, capable of sin and inclined to commit sin, is the essential first step in returning to God" (John Paul II, *Reconciliatio et paenitentia*, 13). Then comes "love-sorrow" or contrition, which leads us to mend our ways. This is followed by acts of penance which enable us to draw closer to God and live in intimacy with him.

Evangelization is always calling us to repent. "To evoke conversion and penance in man's heart and to offer him the gift of reconciliation is the specific mission of the Church as she continues the redemptive work of her divine Founder" (*ibid.*, 23). The church of Ephesus is given a warning that if it does not change its course it will lose its leading position and possibly disappear altogether.

6. On the Nicolaitans, see the note on 2:14-16.

7. The image of the tree of life (cf. also Rev 22:2) is a reference to Genesis 2:9 and 3:22, where we find that tree in the middle of Paradise outside the reach of man; it is a symbol of immortality. The fruit of the tree is now to be found in Christ, and he promises to grant it to those who are victorious. This promise of a happiness that will last forever, rather than any threat of punishment, is what spurs us on to strive day in, day out, not knowing whether today's battle, no matter how small it is, may not be our last: "We cannot take it easy. Our Lord wants us to strive harder, on a broader front, more intensely each day. We have an obligation to outdo ourselves, for in this competition the only goal is to reach the glory of heaven. If we do not get there, the whole thing will have been useless" (J. Escrivá, *Christ is passing by*, 77).

8. Smyrna was a port some 60 kilometres (35 miles) north of Ephesus; one of the main cities of the region, it was renowned for its loyalty to Rome and its ritual worship of the emperor. Christ is depicted to this church as truly God, "the first and the last" (cf. 1:8), that is, he who has had no beginning and will have no end. Despite the vigorous emperor worship which was a feature of

9"'I know your tribulation and your poverty (but you are rich) and the slander of those who say that they are Jews

---

et Novissimus, qui fuit mortuus et vixit: ⁹Scio tribulationem tuam et pauper-

Smyrna, its Christians were very assiduous in the practice of their faith in Christ as the only true God and Lord, as verified especially by his glorious resurrection. That is why we are reminded that Christ died and then rose again: the words used emphasize that Christ's death was something quite transitory, whereas his return to life is something permanent and irreversible (cf. 1:18).

9. The Christians of Smyrna had to endure persecution and deprivation, due no doubt to the fact that they refused to take part in ceremonies connected with emperor worship. Their poverty can become something of great value, for God has high regard for the poor and despised (cf. 1 Cor 1:27-28; Jas 2:5). As an ancient Christian writer puts it, "They say that most of us are poor. That is nothing to be ashamed of; rather, we glory in it, because man's soul is demeaned by easy living and strengthened by frugality. Besides, can a person be poor who is in need of nothing, who does not covet the goods of others, who is rich in the eyes of God? That person is truly poor who has much and yet desires to have more [. . .]. Just as the wayfarer is happier the less he has to carry, so in this journey of life the poor person who is unencumbered is happier than the well-to-do person burdened with riches" (Minucius Felix, *Octavius*, 36, 3-6).

In addition to poverty, the Christians of Smyrna had to bear with the lies spread by certain Jews, who were accusing them of being agitators against the civil authorities and against pagans in general. Jews were quite influential in the Empire: for example, the *Martyrdom of St Polycarp* tells of how, fifty years after the Apocalypse was written, the saintly bishop Polycarp of Smyrna was martyred because the Jews of that city incited the people to clamour for his death.

Because they were collaborating in this way with idolatry instead of defending worshippers of the true God, these people did not deserve the honourable title of "Jews": "ministers of Satan", God's adversary, was a better label for them. In opposing Christians, they were adopting the same attitude as those who opposed Jesus Christ, an attitude which earned them the title of children of the devil (cf. Jn 8:44). Although they bore the name of Jews, they were not really members of the people of God, because, as St Paul teaches, "Not all who are descended from Israel belong to Israel, and not all are children of Abraham because they are his descendants [. . .]. This means that it is not the children of the flesh who are the children of God, but the children of the promise are reckoned as descendants" (Rom 9:6-8). The new Israel, the true Israel, is the Church of Jesus Christ who "acknowledges that in God's plan of salvation the beginning of her faith and election is to be found in the patriarchs, Moses and the prophets. She professes that all Christ's faithful, who as men of faith are sons of Abraham (cf. Gal 3:7), are included in the same patriarch's call" (Vatican II, *Nostra aetate*, 4).

and are not, but are a synagogue of Satan. ¹⁰Do not fear what you are about to suffer. Behold, the devil is about to throw some of you into prison, that you may be tested, and for ten days you will have tribulation. Be faithful unto death, and I will give you the crown of life. ¹¹He who has an ear, let him hear what the Spirit says to the churches. He who conquers shall not be hurt by the second death.'

Dan 1:12, 14
Mt 10:28
1 Cor 9:25

Rev 20:14; 21:8

---

tatem tuam—sed dives es—et blasphemiam ab his, qui se dicunt Iudaeos esse et non sunt, sed sunt synagoga Satanae. ¹⁰Nihil horum timeas, quae passurus

---

The harsh accusation made in this passage of the book refers to those Jews who at that time were denouncing Christians in Smyrna: it should not be applied to Jews in general; similarly, "even though the Jewish authorities and those who followed their lead pressed for the death of Christ (cf. Jn 19:6), neither all Jews indiscriminately at that time, nor Jews today, can be charged with the crimes committed during his passion. It is true that the Church is the new people of God, yet the Jews should not be spoken of as rejected or accursed as if this followed from Holy Scripture" (*ibid.*, 4).

10. The church of Smyrna receives no words of reproach from our Lord, only encouragement: God has foreseen the situation it finds itself in, and things will get even worse for a while—"ten days" (cf. Dan 1:12). He therefore exhorts them to stay true to the very end, even to death, so as to win the crown of victory (cf. 1 Cor 9:25; Phil 3:14; 1 Pet 5:4). The simile of the crown comes from athletic contests of the time, in which victors received a crown of laurels or a floral wreath—a symbol of enduring glory, but in fact something very perishable.

This passage, in fact, provides us with an entire programme for living—faithfulness to commitments, enduring loyalty to the love of Christ. If we want to be saved we need to persevere to the very end; as St Teresa of Avila puts it, "by making an earnest and most determined resolve not to halt until the goal [eternal life] is reached, whatever may come, whatever may happen, however much effort one needs to make, whoever may complain about one, whether one dies on the road or has no heart to face the trials one meets, even if the ground gives away under one's feet" (*Way of Perfection*, 21, 2). "It is easy", John Paul II has reminded us, "to stay true to the faith for a day or for a few days. The difficult thing, the important thing, is to do so right through life. It is easy to keep the faith when things are going well, and difficult to do so when obstacles are met. Consistent behaviour which lasts one's whole life is the only kind which deserves to be called 'fidelity'" (*Homily*, 27 January 1979).

11. "Second death": a reference to irreversible, enduring, condemnation. Further on, the book is more specific about what this involves, and who will suffer it (cf. 20:6, 14; 21:8).

Letter to the church of Pergamum

Rev 1:16; 19:15
Is 49:2
Heb 4:12
¹²"And to the angel of the church in Pergamum write: 'The words of him who has the sharp two-edged sword.

Rev 3:8; 14:12
¹³"'I know where you dwell, where Satan's throne is; you hold fast my name and you did not deny my faith even in the days of Antipas my witness, my faithful one, who

---

es. Ecce missurus est Diabolus ex vobis in carcerem, ut tentemini, et habebitis tribulationem diebus decem. Esto fidelis usque ad mortem, et dabo tibi coronam

---

12-13. Pergamum, some 70 kilometres (40 miles) to the north of Smyrna, was renowned for its temples, among other things. It was the first city in Asia Minor to erect a temple to the "divine Augustus" and "divine Rome" (in the year 29 B.C.). The temple had a huge altar, of the whitest marble, dedicated to Zeus. The city was also a place of pilgrimage where sick people flooded to the temple of Aesculapius, the god of health and miracles. For all these reasons it is described as the place where Satan has his throne. Pergamum was also noted for its great library and for its manufacture of parchment.

Christ is portrayed to this church as a judge, that is, one whose word distinguishes good from evil, and who distributes rewards and punishments (cf. Rev 1:16; 19:15, 21; Heb 4:12)—the reason being that the church at Pergamum is a mix of truth and error, with some people holding on to sound teaching and others supporting the Nicolaitans (cf. v. 15).

The letter begins by praising the fidelity of this church despite the persecution which has led to the death of Antipas. We do not know for sure who Antipas was; some traditions refer to his undergoing ordeal by fire in the reign of Domitian. The emperors of the time insisted on being acknowledged as *Kyrios* (Lord), which amounted to divine honours: this implied a form of idolatry, to which no Christian could subscribe. Tertullian says that there was nothing against acknowledging the emperor as *Kyrios*, if the title referred to his temporal power, but he could not be given it if it had a different, religious, meaning—"ut dominum dei vice dicam", as if it meant treating him as a god (cf. *Apologeticum*, 34).

The title given to this Christian who died for the faith—"my witness, my faithful one"—was and is an outstanding title of honour for a believer, applied as it is to one who has kept faith with Christ even at the cost of life itself. In the early times of the Church (a time of unique persecution), many Christians followed the example of the first martyr, St Stephen (cf. Acts 7:55-60) and bore heroic witness to the faith by shedding their blood. Their deaths, marked as they were by serenity and hope, played an important part in the spread of Christianity, so much so that, as Tertullian put it, the blood of the martyrs was the seed from which Christians grew (cf. *Apologeticum*, 197). St Justin also notes that the more martyrs there were, the more Christians increased in number; the same is true of the vine when it is pruned: the branches which are pruned put out many more shoots (cf. *Dialogue with Trypho*, 110, 4).

was killed among you, where Satan dwells. [14]But I have a few things against you: you have some there who hold the teaching of Balaam, who taught Balak to put a stumbling block before the sons of Israel, that they might eat food sacrificed to idols and practise immorality. [15]So you also have some who hold the teaching of the Nicolaitans. [16]Repent then. If not, I will come to you soon and war

Num 25:1, 2;
31:16
2 Pet 2:15
Jude 11

Rev 2:6

Rev 1:16; 2:5

vitae. [11]Qui habet aurem, audiat quid Spiritus dicat ecclesiis. Qui vicerit non laedetur a morte secunda. [12]Et angelo ecclesiae, quae est Pergami, scribe: Haec dicit, qui habet romphaeam ancipitem acutam: [13]Scio, ubi habitas, ubi thronus est Satanae, et tenes nomen meum et non negasti fidem meam et in diebus Antipas, testis meus fidelis, qui occisus est apud vos, ubi Satanas habitat. [14]Sed habeo adversus te pauca, quia habes illic tenentes doctrinam Balaam, qui docebat Balac mittere scandalum coram filiis Israel, edere idolothyta et fornicari; [15]ita habes et tu tenentes doctrinam Nicolaitarum similiter. [16]Ergo paenitentiam age; si quo minus, venio tibi cito et pugnabo cum illis in gladio oris mei. [17]Qui habet aurem, audiat quid Spiritus dicat ecclesiis. Vincenti dabo ei de manna abscondito et dabo illi calculum candidum, et in calculo nomen novum scriptum, quod nemo scit, nisi qui accipit. [18]Et angelo ecclesiae, quae

14-16. After being praised for their fidelity, the Christians of Pergamum are told where they are going wrong; some of them are compromising their faith by taking part in pagan ritual banquets and "sacred fornication" rites. A comparison is drawn with Balaam, who encouraged the Moabite women to marry Israelites and draw them to worship the god of Moab (cf. Num 31:16). As regards the Nicolaitans, some early authors suggest that this was a heresy started by Nicholas, one of the first seven deacons (cf. Acts 6:5); but their view is not well founded. It is easy to understand how this aberration could have arisen in a society where Christians were living cheek by jowl with pagans who went in for sacred banquets in honour of idols, and rites of an erotic character. It was a situation which arose more than once (cf., e.g., Rom 14:2, 15; 1 Cor 8:10; 2 Cor 2:16).

As in v. 5, there is a new call to conversion, and the same pattern is found in the subsequent letters. John Paul II states that "in all periods of history this invitation constitutes the very basis of the Church's mission" (*Address*, 28 February 1982). Elsewhere, he points out where conversion begins: "Authentic knowledge of the God of mercy, the God of tender love, is a constant and inexhaustible source of conversion, not only as a momentary interior act but also as a permanent attitude, as a state of mind. Those who come to know God in this way, who 'see' him in this way, can live only in a state of being continually converted to him. They live, therefore, *in statu conversionis*; and it is this state of conversion which marks out the most profound element of the pilgrimage of every man and woman on earth *in statu viatoris*" (*Dives in misericordia*, 13).

Is 62:2; 65:15
Rev 3:12; 19:12
Ps 78:24 against them with the sword of my mouth. [17]He who has an ear, let him hear what the Spirit says to the churches. To him who conquers I will give some of the hidden manna, and I will give him a white stone, with a new name written on the stone which no one knows except him who receives it.'

Letter to the church of Thyatira

Rev 1:14, 15
Dan 10:6 [18]"And to the angel of the church in Thyatira write: 'The

est Thyatirae, scribe: Haec dicit Filius Dei, qui habet oculos ut flammam ignis,

17. The promise of the hidden manna to the victors can be seen as a counter to the sin of indulging in idolatrous meals. St Paul also contrasts sacrifices to idols with the eucharistic sacrifice; and tells the Corinthians that they cannot "drink the cup of the Lord and the cup of demons [. . .], cannot partake of the table of the Lord and the table of demons" (1 Cor 10:21). Elsewhere, St John tells us of our Lord's referring to manna when speaking about the Eucharist (cf. Jn 6:31-33). The nourishment which Yahweh gave his people in the desert was described as "bread from heaven" (cf. Ex 16:4) and "the bread of the angels" (Ps 78:25), kept in the Ark of the Covenant to be revered by the people (cf. Heb 9:4). Here it is described as "hidden" manna, a reference to the supernatural, divine, character of the reward of heavenly beatitude; we share in this in Holy Communion, to a degree; in eternal life it is partaken of fully.

The "white stone" is a reference to the custom of showing a little stone, with some appropriate mark on it, to gain entrance to a feast or banquet. The name inscribed on the stone referred to here shows that the Christian has a right to partake of the good things which the Lord reserves for those who win the victory.

The fact that only the recipient knows what is written on the stone points to the personal, intimate relationship between God (who issues the invitation) and the invited guest. "Go over, calmly, that divine admonition which fills the soul with disquiet and which at the same time tastes as sweet as honey from the comb: *redemi te, et vocavi te, nomine tuo: meus es tu* (Is 43:1); I have redeemed you, I have called you by your name, you are mine" (J. Escrivá, *Friends of God*, 312).

18. Thyatira, located some 75 kilometres (48 miles) to the south-east of Pergamum, was the least important of the seven churches mentioned; the city was noted for smelting, weaving and dyeing. Acts 16:13-15 gives an account of the conversion of a native of Thyatira, a dealer in purple called Lydia. The city had many craft guilds which organized festivities in honour of the gods. This involved danger for Christians, because they felt obliged to take part.

Jesus Christ is depicted explicitly as "the Son of God". This is the only time he is given this title in the Apocalypse, but it is implicit in the many references

words of the Son of God, who has eyes like a flame of fire, and whose feet are like burnished bronze.

[19]"'I know your works, your love and faith and service and patient endurance, and that your latter works exceed the first. [20]But I have this against you, that you tolerate the woman Jezebel, who calls herself a prophetess and is teaching and beguiling my servants to practise immorality and to eat food sacrificed to idols. [21]I gave her time to

Rev 2:14
2 Kings 9:22

---

et pedes eius similes orichalco: [19]Novi opera tua et caritatem et fidem et ministerium et patientiam tuam et opera tua novissima plura prioribus. [20]Sed habeo adversus te, quia permittis mulierem Iezabel, quae se dicit prophetissam,

---

to God as his Father (cf. 1:6; 3:5, 21; 14:1). As Son of God, Christ appears clothed in the attributes proper to the Godhead—divine knowledge, which enables him to search man's soul (cf. v. 23) and divine power (cf. note on 1:14-15). These attributes are revealed particularly by the way he deals with the church of Thyatira.

19. The letter begins with praise of the good works of this Church, the most outstanding of which is its service (*diakonia*) to the poor (cf. Acts 11:28; Rom 15:25, 31; 1 Cor 16:15; 1 Pet 4:10; etc.). Unlike Ephesus, its "latter works" are more perfect than its earlier works; in other words, it is making progress in virtue.

20-23. Our Lord again inveighs against those Christians who are compromising themselves by taking part in pagan worship, involving, as it does, idolatry and moral aberration. The letter seems to refer to the same (Nicolaitan) heresy, here symbolized by Jezebel, the wife of King Ahab, who led many of the people of Israel into the sin of idolatry (cf. 1 Kings 16:31; 2 Kings 9:22). This may be a reference to a real person (described here symbolically by this biblical name) who projected herself as a prophetess and led many people astray by getting them to take part in idolatrous rites and banquets. When wrong is being done and one fails to point it out, one's silence is really a form of complicity.

The passage reveals how patient God is: he has waited for this people to mend their ways and only at a later stage condemned them for not doing so. This is a warning which those who persist in evil must bear in mind, for "the more we postpone getting out of sin and turning to God", the Curé of Ars warns us, "the greater the danger we run of dying with our sins on us, for the simple reason that bad habits become more and more difficult to shed. Every time we despise a grace, our Lord is going further away from us, and we are growing weaker, and the devil gets more control of us. So, my conclusion is that the longer we remain in sin, the greater the risk we run of never being converted" (*Selected Sermons*, fourth Sunday in Lent).

repent, but she refuses to repent of her immorality. [22]Behold, I will throw her on a sickbed, and those who commit adultery with her I will throw into great tribulation, unless they repent of her doings; [23]and I will strike her children dead. And all the churches shall know that I am he who searches mind and heart, and I will give to each of you as your works deserve. [24]But to the rest of you in Thyatira, who do not hold this teaching, who have not learned what some call the deep things of Satan, to you I say, I do not lay upon you any other burden; [25]only hold fast what you have, until I come. [26]He who conquers and who keeps my works until the end, I will give him power over the nations, [27]and he shall rule them with a rod of iron, as when earthen pots are broken in pieces, even as I myself have received power from my Father; [28]and I will give him the morning star. [29]He who has an ear, let him hear what the Spirit says to the churches.'

Ps 7:10; 62:13
Jer 11:20; 17:10

Rev 3:11

Ps 2:8
Rev 12:5; 19:15

2 Pet 1:19
Is 14:12

---

et docet et seducit servos meos fornicari et manducare idolothyta. [21]Et dedi illi tempus, ut paenitentiam ageret, et non vult paeniteri a fornicatione sua. [22]Ecce mitto eam in lectum et, qui moechantur cum ea, in tribulationem magnam, nisi paenitentiam egerint ab operibus eius. [23]Et filios eius interficiam in morte, et scient omnes ecclesiae quia ego sum scrutans renes et corda, et dabo unicuique vestrum secundum opera vestra. [24]Vobis autem dico ceteris, qui Thyatirae estis, quicumque non habent doctrinam hanc, qui non cognoverunt altitudines

---

The punishment meted out to Jezebel is quite frightening: she will be afflicted with a grievous illness (cf. Ex 21:18; Jud 8:3; 1 Mac 1:5). The same will happen to her followers they are warned, in the hope that this will cause them to repent. In other words, our Lord still has hopes of their conversion, and even uses the threat of punishment to move sinners to think again and repent.

24-28. Knowledge of the "deep things of Satan" was another aspect of the Nicolaitan heresy, which claimed to possess secrets leading to salvation. Some scholars link this kind of arcane knowledge with Gnosticism, which was making headway in the East at the time.

The promise made to the victors (taken from Psalm 2:9) involves sharing in Christ's sovereignty and power because one is in full communion with him.

The "morning star" is an expression also applied to Christ in Revelation 22:16. It may refer to the perfect communion with the Lord enjoyed by those who persevere to the end: the symbolism of the power given to the victors (vv. 26-27) is followed in v. 28 by reference to sharing in the resurrection and glory of Christ, expressed by the image of the "morning star", which heralds the day, that is, rebirth, resurrection.

3

1"And to the angel of the church in Sardis write: 'The words   Rev 1:16
of him who has the seven spirits of God and the seven stars.
"'I know your works; you have the name of being alive,

Satanae, quemadmodum dicunt, non mittam super vos aliud pondus; [25]tamen id quod habetis, tenete, donec veniam. [26]Et, qui vicerit et qui custodierit usque in finem opera mea, *dabo illi* potestatem super *gentes*, [27]et *reget illas in virga ferrea, tamquam vasa fictilia confringentur*, [28]sicut et ego accepi a Patre meo, et dabo illi stellam matutinam. [29]Qui habet aurem, audiat quid Spiritus dicat ecclesiis.

[1]Et angelo ecclesiae, quae est Sardis, scribe: Haec dicit, qui habet septem spiritus Dei et septem stellas: Scio opera tua, quia nomen habes quod vivas, et mortuus es. [2]Esto vigilans et confirma cetera, quae moritura erant, non enim

---

1. Sardis, about 50 kilometres (30 miles) south-east of Thyatira, was an important hub in the highway system; it was also famous for its acropolis, which was located in an unassailable position. Herodotus describes its inhabitants as immoral, licentious people (cf. *History*, 1, 55). The Christians of the city were probably somewhat infected by the general atmosphere.

Christ is now depicted as possessing the fulness of the Spirit, with the power to effect radical change by sanctifying the churches from within (cf. note on 1:4). He is also portrayed as the sovereign Lord of the universal Church (cf. note on 2:1), ever ready to imbue it with new life.

The church of Sardis is accused of seeming to be alive but in fact being dead: in other words, although its external practice of religion makes it look Christian, most of its members (not all: cf. v. 4) are estranged from Christ, devoid of interior life, in a sinful condition. Anyone who lives like that is dead. Our Lord himself described the situation of the prodigal son as being a kind of death: "my son was dead, and is alive again", the father exclaims in the parable (Lk 15:24); and St Paul invites Christians to offer themselves to God "as men who have been brought from death to life" (Rom 6:13). Now, in this passage of Revelation, we are told that the cause of this spiritual, but real, death is the fact that the works of this church are imperfect in the sight of God (v. 2); they were works which led to spiritual death, that is, what we would term mortal sins. "With the whole tradition of the Church", John Paul II says, "we call *mortal sin* the act by which man freely and consciously rejects God, his law, the covenant of love that God offers, preferring to turn in on himself or to some created and finite reality, something contrary to the divine will (*conversio ad creaturam*) [. . .]. Man perceives that this disobedience to God destroys the bond that unites him with his life-principle: it is a *mortal sin*, that is, an act which gravely offends God and ends in turning against man himself with a dark and powerful force of destruction" (*Reconciliatio et Paenitentia*, 17).

Ezek 34:4

1 Thess 5:2
Mt 24:43

Jude 23

and you are dead. ²Awake, and strengthen what remains and is on the point of death, for I have not found your works perfect in the sight of my God. ³Remember then what you received and heard; keep that, and repent. If you will not awake, I will come like a thief, and you will not know at what hour I will come upon you. ⁴Yet you have still a few names in Sardis, people who have not soiled their garments; and they shall walk with me in white, for they are worthy.

---

invenio opera tua plena coram Deo meo; ³in mente ergo habe qualiter acceperis

2-3. Vigilance is always necessary, particularly in certain situations like that of Sardis where there was a number of people who had not fallen victim to sin. In this kind of peril, Christians need to be alerted and confirmed in the faith. They need to remember what they learned at the beginning, when they were instructed in the faith, and try to bring their lives into line with that teaching. And so they are not simply exhorted to conversion but told how to go about it—by comparing their lives with the Word of God and making the necessary changes: "no one is safe if he ceases to strive against himself. Nobody can save himself by his own efforts. Everyone in the Church needs specific means to strengthen himself—humility, which disposes us to accept help and advice; mortifications, which temper the heart and allow Christ to reign in it; the study of abiding, sound doctrine, which leads us to conserve and spread our faith" (J. Escrivá, *Christ is passing by*, 81).

"I will come like a thief": an image also found elsewhere in the New Testament (cf. Mt 24:42-51, Mk 13:36; Lk 12:39ff; 1 Thess 5:2; 2 Pet 3:10). This does not mean that our Lord is lying in wait, ready to pounce on man when he is unawares, like a hunter waiting for his prey. It is simply a warning to us to live in the grace of God and be ready to render our account to him. If we do that we will not run the risk of being found empty-handed at the moment of death. "That day will come for us. It will be our last day, but we are not afraid of it. Trusting firmly in God's grace, we are ready from this very moment to be generous and courageous, and take loving care of little things: we are ready to go and meet our Lord, with our lamps burning brightly. For the feast of feasts awaits us in heaven" (J. Escrivá, *Friends of God*, 40).

4-5. Despite the corrupt environment in which they were living, there were some Christians who had not been contaminated by the immoral cults and lifestyles of the pagans: their loyalty is symbolized by white garments. In the course of narrating his visions St John mentions white garments a number of times (cf. 7:9, 13; 15:6; 19:14); this colour symbolizes purity and also the joy of victory.

The symbol of the "book of life", which occurs often in the Apocalypse (cf. 13:8; 17:8; 20:12, 15; 21:27; etc.), is taken from the Old Testament, where those who belong to the people of Israel are described as enrolled in the "book of the

⁵He who conquers shall be clad thus in white garments, and I will not blot his name out of the book of life; I will confess his name before my Father and before his angels. ⁶He who has an ear, let him hear what the Spirit says to the churches.'

Rev 4:4; 20:12
Mt 10:32
Ex 32:32
Ps 69:29

Letter to the church of Philadelphia

⁷"And to the angel of the church in Philadelphia write:

Rev 1:18
Is 6:3; 22:22

---

et audieris, et serva et paenitentiam age. Si ergo non vigilaveris, veniam

---

living", which is also referred to as the book of the Lord (cf. Ps 69:28; Ex 32:32ff). Those whose names are in the book will share in the promises of salvation (cf. Is 4:3), whereas those who are unfaithful to the Law will be excluded from the people of God and their names blotted out of the "book of the living". Other New Testament texts use the same image (cf., e.g., Lk 10:20; Phil 4:3).

The names of the victors will stay in the "book of life" which lists those who have proved loyal to Christ, as well as those who belonged to the people of Israel.

Finally, on Judgment Day, those Christians who have kept the faith, will be spoken for by Christ (cf. Mt 10:32; Lk 12:8).

7. Philadelphia, in the province of Lydia, was about 45 kilometres (25 miles) south-east of Sardis. Its geographical location made it a gateway to all of Phrygia—hence the sacred writer's reference to its having an open door (the same turn of phrase is used by St Paul to refer to scope for apostolate: cf. 1 Cor 16:9; 2 Cor 2:12; Col 4:3).

Philadephia had suffered an earthquake around the year A.D. 17: there is a possible allusion to this in the promise to make it a supportive pillar in God's temple (v. 12). When the city was rebuilt, it was given the new name of Neocaesarea, but that name soon fell into disuse. Here, however, it is promised another new name (v. 12), the name of God and the name New Jerusalem, and this name will endure forever. There was quite a sizeable and influential Jewish community in Philadelphia (cf. v. 9), many of whom will later become converts and recognize the Church, the beloved Bride of Jesus Christ.

The titles given to Jesus in this letter clearly indicate his divinity: "the holy one" is proper to Yahweh, as can be seen frequently in the Old Testament (cf. Lev 11:44; Josh 24:19; Is 6:3; 12:6; Job 6:10; etc.). The title of "the true one" (also used by St John in his Gospel: cf., e.g., Jn 1:9; 4:23; 7:28; 15:1; 17:3) conveys the idea of the complete reliability and faithfulness of the Lord with regard to keeping his promises (cf. Ps 86:15; 116; 135). And the words "who has the key of David" and the power to open and shut signify the absolute sovereignty of Christ in the messianic Kingdom. Our Lord used this metaphor when he confirmed St Peter in the primacy (cf. Mt 16:19) and when he passed on his own powers to the College of Apostles (cf. Mt 18:18).

'The words of the holy one, the true one, who has the key of David, who opens and no one shall shut, who shuts and no one opens.

⁸"'I know your works. Behold, I have set before you an open door, which no one is able to shut; I know that you have but little power, and yet you have kept my word and have not denied my name. ⁹Behold, I will make those of the synagogue of Satan who say that they are Jews and are not, but lie—behold, I will make them come and bow down before your feet, and learn that I have loved you. ¹⁰Because you have kept my word of patient endurance, I will keep you from the hour of trial which is coming on the whole world, to try those who dwell upon the earth. ¹¹I am coming soon; hold fast what you have, so that no one may seize your crown. ¹²He who conquers, I will make him a pillar in

Acts 14:27
1 Cor 16:9

Rev 2:9
Is 43:4; 45:14;
49:23; 60:14

2 Pet 2:9
2 Thess 2:12

Rev 2:25
1 Cor 9:25

---

tamquam fur, et nescies qua hora veniam ad te. ⁴Sed habes pauca nomina in Sardis, qui non inquinaverunt vestimenta sua et ambulabunt mecum in albis, quia digni sunt. ⁵Qui vicerit, sic vestietur vestimentis albis, et non delebo nomen

---

8-12. The fidelity of these Christians is praised despite their limitations. As a reward they are given an open door which no enemy can shut—an assurance of evangelical success, despite opposition and perhaps also a promise of unimpeded access to the Kingdom.

On the "synagogue of Satan, see the note on Revelation 7:9. The promise that their enemies will admit defeat and do obeisance to the victor is reminiscent of Isaiah 49:23 and 60:14, which contain a prediction that the nations will do homage to the chosen people. Before that happens, however, the entire world will experience tribulation, as described later on in the book (cf. Rev 8-9 and 16); but those who stay faithful will be protected. As to the imminence of these predicted events, see what is said in the note on Revelation 1:1 about the whole matter of timing (cf. also 22:12, 20). When all is over, the strife and the victory, the conquering church will be a pillar of the temple, that is, it will have a place of honour (cf. Gal 2:9).

When it says that despite their weakness they have not denied Christ's name (v. 8), this implies that the strength which enables them to win victory is something given them by God, who often acts and triumphs amidst man's weakness and shortcomings. St Paul says as much to the faithful of Corinth: "Consider your call, brethren; not many of you were wise according to worldly standards, not many were powerful, not many were of noble birth; but God chose what is foolish in the world to shame the wise, God chose what is weak in the world to shame the strong. God chose what is low and despised in the world, even things that are not, to bring to nothing things that are, so that no human being might boast in the presence of God" (1 Cor 1:26-29).

the temple of my God: never shall he go out of it, and I will write on him the name of my God, and the name of the city of my God, the new Jerusalem which comes down from my God out of heaven, and my own new name. [13]He who has an ear, let him hear what the Spirit says to the churches.'

Rev 21:2
Gal 2:9
Ezek 48:35
Is 62:2; 65:15

Letter to the church of Laodicea

[14]"And to the angel of the church in Laodicea write: 'The words of the Amen, the faithful and true witness, the beginning of God's creation.

Ps 89:38
2 Cor 1:20

---

eius de libro vitae et confitebor nomen eius coram Patre meo et coram angelis eius. [6]Qui habet aurem, audiat quid Spiritus dicat ecclesiis. [7]Et angelo ecclesiae, quae est Philadelphiae, scribe: Haec dicit Sanctus, Verus, qui habet *clavem David, qui aperit, et nemo claudet; et claudit, et nemo aperit*; [8]Scio opera tua—ecce dedi coram te ostium apertum, quod nemo potest claudere—quia modicam habes virtutem, et servasti verbum meum et non negasti nomen meum. [9]Ecce dabo de synagoga Satanae, qui dicunt se Iudaeos esse et non sunt, sed mentiuntur; ecce faciam illos, ut veniant et adorent ante pedes tuos et scient quia ego dilexi te. [10]Quoniam servasti verbum patientiae meae, et ego te servabo ab hora tentationis, quae ventura est super orbem universum tentare habitantes in terra. [11]Venio cito; tene quod habes, ut nemo accipiat coronam tuam. [12]Qui vicerit, faciam illum columnam in templo Dei mei, et foras non egredietur amplius, et scribam super eum nomen Dei mei et nomen civitatis Dei mei, novae Ierusalem, quae descendit de caelo a Deo meo, et nomen meum novum. [13]Qui habet aurem, audiat quid Spiritus dicat ecclesiis. [14]Et angelo ecclesiae, quae est Laodiciae, scribe: Haec dicit Amen, testis fidelis et verus, principium creaturae Dei: [15]Scio opera tua, quia neque frigidus es neque calidus. Utinam frigidus

---

14. Laodicea was a city on the border of Phrygia, about 75 kilometres (45 miles) south-west of Philadelphia. It is also mentioned by St Paul when he suggests to the Colossians that they exchange his letter to them for the one he sent the Laodiceans (cf. Col 4:16).

Jesus Christ is given the title of "the Amen"; a similar description is applied to Christ in 2 Corinthians 1:20. Both texts are instances of a divine name being applied to Christ, thereby asserting his divinity. "Amen", so be it, is an assertion of truth and veracity and connects with the title of "the true one" in the previous letter. It highlights the fact that our Lord is strong, dependable and unchangeable; the words that follow, "faithful and true witness", spell out the full meaning of the "Amen" title (cf. 1:5).

The most satisfactory interpretation of the phrase "the beginning of God's creation" is in terms of Jesus Christ's role in creation: for "all things were made through him" (Jn 1:3) and therefore he, along with the Father and the Holy Spirit, is the Creator of heaven and earth.

Col 1:15
Jn 1:3
Hos 12:9
1 Cor 4:8
1 Pet 1:7
Rev 4:4; 16:15

15"'I know your works: you are neither cold nor hot. Would that you were cold or hot! 16So, because you are lukewarm, and neither cold nor hot, I will spew you out of my mouth. 17For you say, I am rich, I have prospered, and I need nothing; not knowing that you are wretched, pitiable, poor, blind, and naked. 18Therefore I counsel you to buy from me gold refined by fire, that you,may be rich, and

---

esses aut calidus! 16Sic quia tepidus es et nec calidus nec frigidus, incipiam te evomere ex ore meo. 17Quia dicis: 'Dives sum et locupletatus et nullius egeo', et nescis quia tu es miser et miserabilis et pauper et caecus et nudus, 18suadeo

15-16. The prosperity Laodicea enjoyed may have contributed to the laxity and lukewarmness the church is accused of here (Israel tended to take the same direction when living was easy: the people would become forgetful of Yahweh and adopt an easy-going lifestyle: cf., e.g., Deut 31:20; 32:15; Hos 13:6; Jer 5:7).

The presence of hot springs close to the city explains the language used in this passage, which amounts to a severe indictment of lukewarmness. It shows God's repugnance for mediocrity and bourgeois living. As observed by Cassian, one of the founders of Western monasticism, lukewarmness is something that needs to be nipped in the bud: "No one should attribute his going astray to any sudden collapse, but rather [. . .] to his having moved away from virtue little by little, through prolonged mental laziness. That is the way bad habits gain ground without one's even noticing it, and eventually lead to a sudden collapse. 'Pride goes before destruction, and a haughty spirit before a fall' (Prov 16:18). The same thing happens with a house: it collapses one fine day due to some ancient defect in its foundation or long neglect by the occupiers" (*Collationes*, VI, 17).

Spiritual lukewarmness and mediocrity are very closely related: neither is the route Christian life should take. As Monsignor Escrivá puts it, "'In medio virtus'. . . . Virtue is to be found in the middle, so the saying goes, warning us against extremism. But do not make the mistake of turning that advice into a euphemism to disguise your own comfort, calculation, lukewarmness, easy-goingness, lack of idealism and mediocrity.

"Meditate on these words of Sacred Scripture: 'Would that you were cold or hot. So, because you are lukewarm, and neither cold nor hot, I will spew you out of my mouth'" (*Furrow*, 541).

17-19. The Christians of Laodicea did not realize how precarious their spiritual situation was. The city's flourishing trade and industry, and the fact that the church was not being persecuted in any way, made them feel prosperous and content: they were proud as well as lukewarm. They had fallen victim to that self-conceit the wealthy are always inclined to feel and which moved our Lord to say that rich people enter heaven only with difficulty (cf. Mt 19:23);

white garments to clothe you and to keep the shame of your
nakedness from being seen, and salve to anoint your eyes, Prov 3:12
that you may see. ¹⁹Those whom I love, I reprove and 1 Cor 11:32
chasten; so be zealous and repent. ²⁰Behold, I stand at the Heb 12:6
door and knock; if any one hears my voice and opens the Jn 14:23
door, I will come in to him and eat with him, and he with
me. ²¹He who conquers, I will grant him to sit with me on Mt 19:28 Rev 20:4

---

tibi emere a me aurum igne probatum, ut locuples fias et vestimentis albis
induaris, et non appareat confusio nuditatis tuae, et collyrium ad inunguendum
oculos tuos ut videas. ¹⁹Ego, quos amo, arguo et castigo. Aemulare ergo et
paenitentiam age. ²⁰Ecce sto ad ostium et pulso. Si quis audierit vocem meam

---

he often pointed to the dangers of becoming attached to material things (cf. Lk
1:53; 6:24; 12:21; 16:19-31; 18:23-25). The Laodiceans had become proud in
their prosperity and did not see the need for divine grace (which is worth more
than all the wealth in the world). As St Paul says in one of his letters: "Whatever
gain I had, I counted as loss for the sake of Christ. Indeed I count everything
as loss because of the surpassing worth of knowing Christ Jesus my Lord. For
his sake I have suffered the loss of all things, and count them as refuse, in order
that I may gain Christ" (Phil 3:7-8).

There was an important textile industry in Laodicea which specialized in the
manufacture of black woollen cloth. Instead of wearing that material, the
Laodiceans must dress in garments which only our Lord can provide and which
are the mark of the elect (cf., e.g., Mt 17:2 and par; Rev 3:4-5; 7:9). The city
was also famous for its oculists, like Zeuxis and Philetos, who had developed
a very effective ointment for the eyes. Jesus offers an even better ointment—one
which will show them the dangerous state they are in. This dire warning comes
from God's love, not his anger: it is his affection that leads him to reprove and
correct his people: "the Lord reproves whom he loves, as a father the son in
whom he delights" (Prov 3:12). After quoting these same words the Epistle to
the Hebrews adds: "It is for discipline that you have to endure. God is treating
you as sons; for what son is there whom his father does not discipline? If you
are left without discipline, in which all have participated, then you are ille-
gitimate children and not sons" (12:7-8).

"Be zealous": stop being lukewarm and enter the fervour of charity, have an
ardent zeal for the glory of God.

20-21. Christ knocking on the door is one of the most touching images in
the Bible. It is reminiscent of the Song of Songs, where the bridegroom says,
"Open to me, my sister, my dove, my perfect one; for my head is wet with dew,
my locks with the drops of the might" (Song 5:2). It is a way of describing
God's love for us, inviting us to greater intimacy with him, as happens in a
thousand ways in the course of our life. We should be listening for his knock,
ready to open the door to Christ. A writer from the Golden Age of Spanish

my throne, as I myself conquered and sat down with my Father on his throne. [22]He who has an ear, let him hear what the Spirit says to the churches.' "

et aperuerit ianuam, introibo ad illum et cenabo cum illo, et ipse mecum. [21]Qui vicerit, dabo ei sedere mecum in throno meo, sicut et ego vici et sedi cum Patre meo in throno eius. [22]Qui habet aurem, audiat quid Spiritus dicat ecclesiis."

literature evokes this scene in poetry: "How many times the angel spoke to me:/'Look out of your window now,/you'll see how lovingly he calls and calls.'/ Yet, sovereign beauty, how often/I replied, 'We'll open for you tomorrow',/to reply the same when the morrow came" (Lope de Vega, *Rimas sacras*, Sonnet 18).

Our Lord awaits our response to his call, and when we make the effort to revive our interior life we experience the indescribable joy of intimacy with him. "At first it will be a bit difficult. You must make an effort to seek out the Lord, to thank him for his fatherly and practical concern for us. Although it is not really a matter of feeling, little by little the love of God makes itself felt like a rustle in the soul. It is Christ who pursues us lovingly: 'Behold, I stand at the door and knock' (Rev 3:20). How is your life of prayer going? At times during the day don't you feel the impulse to have a longer talk with him? Don't you then whisper to him that you will tell him about it later, in a heart-to-heart conversation [. . .]. Prayer then becomes continuous, like the beating of our heart, like our pulse. Without this presence of God, there is no contemplative life; and without contemplative life, our working for Christ is worth very little, for vain is the builder's toil if the house is not of the Lord's building (cf. Ps 126:1)" (J. Escrivá, *Christ is passing by*, 8).

Jesus promises that those who conquer will sit beside him on his throne. He gave a similar promise to St Peter about how the Apostles would sit on twelve thrones to judge the twelve tribes of Israel (cf. Mt 19:28; 20:20ff). The "throne" is a reference to the sovereign authority Christ has received from the Father. Therefore, the promise of a seat beside him is a way of saying that those who stay faithful will share in Christ's victory and kingship (cf. 1 Cor 6:2-3).

PART TWO
ESCHATOLOGICAL VISIONS

4

INTRODUCTORY VISION

God in majesty

¹After this I looked, and lo, in heaven an open door! And the first voice, which I had heard speaking to me like a trumpet, said, "Come up hither, and I will show you what must take place after this." ²At once I was in the Spirit, and lo, a throne stood in heaven, with one seated on the throne! ³And he who sat there appeared like jasper and carnelian,

Ex 19:16, 24
Dan 2:29
Rev 1:10, 19
Rev 1:10
Ezek 1:26
Is 6:1
Ps 47:9
Ezek 1:26; 10:1f
Is 6:1

---

¹Post haec vidi: et ecce ostium apertum in caelo, et vox prima, quam audivi, tamquam tubae loquentis mecum dicens: "Ascende huc, et ostendam tibi, quae oportet fieri post haec." ²Statim fui in spiritu: et ecce thronus positus erat in

1. The second part of the Apocalypse begins at this point and extends to the start of the Epilogue. The author describes visions concerning the future of mankind, particularly the ultimate outcome of history when our Lord Jesus Christ will obtain the final victory at his second coming. It begins with a formal introduction (chaps. 4-5); this is followed by a first section as it were (6:11 - 11:14) covering the visions of the seven seals and the first six trumpets, which describes the event prior to the final battle. The war begins with the sound of the seventh trumpet and it goes on (this is the second section 11:15 - 22:5) until the beast is completely routed and the Kingdom of God is definitively established in the heavenly Jerusalem.

This introductory vision (chaps. 4-5) begins with God in heaven in all his glory being worshipped and celebrated by all creation (chap. 4). He alone controls the destiny of the world and the Church.

Only Jesus knows God's salvific plans, and he, through his death and resurrection, reveals them to us. All this is expressed in chapter 4 by the image of the Lamb who is able to open the scroll and its seven seals.

1-3. The risen and glorified Christ, who spoke to St John previously (cf. 1:10-13), now invites him, in a new vision, to go up into heaven to be told God's plan for the world. "I looked," "I was in the Spirit," "I went up to heaven" all describe the same phenomenon—God revealing something to the writer. Because the things he is being told are things man could not possibly discover for himself, the writer speaks about going up to heaven: this enables him to contemplate heavenly things, that is, God. Going up to heaven is the same as being in ecstasy, "being in the Spirit", being taken over by the Holy Spirit so as to be able to understand what God wants to reveal to him (cf. note on 1:10).

and round the throne was a rainbow that looked like an emerald. [4]Round the throne were twenty-four thrones, and seated on the thrones were twenty-four elders, clad in white

---

caelo; et supra thronum sedens; [3]et, qui sedebat, similis erat aspectu lapidi iaspidi et sardino; et iris erat in circuitu throni, aspectu similis smaragdo. [4]Et

He is going to be shown "what must take place after this"; it is something which has already begun to happen in the writer's own time but it will not reach its climax until the end of the world. The revelation he is given shows him the ultimate meaning of contemporary events, the outcome of which is guaranteed by the authority of the revealer, Jesus Christ.

The description given here of heaven stresses the majesty and power of God. Heaven is depicted with a throne at its centre, an image taken from Isaiah (cf. Is 6:1) and Ezekiel (cf. Ezek 1:26-28; 10:1). God's appearance is described in terms of the vivid colouring of precious stones; this avoids the danger of defining God in human terms (an inversion of values). The rainbow round the throne further emphasizes the sublimity of God and is also a reminder (cf. Gen 9:12-17) of God's merciful promise never to destroy mankind.

4. God's sovereignty over the world—as symbolized by the throne—is shared in by others whom the vision also portrays as seated on thrones. They are symbolically described as twenty-four elders who act as a kind of heavenly council or senate. These elders appear frequently in the course of the book, always positioned beside God, rendering him tribute of glory and worship (cf. 4:10; 5:9; 19:4), offering him the prayers of the faithful (cf. 5:8) or explaining events to the seer (cf. 5:5; 7:13). It is not clear whether they stand for angels or saints; the Fathers and recent commentators offer both interpretations.

The symbolic number (twenty-four) and the way they are described suggest that they stand for saints in the glory of heaven. They are twenty-four—twelve plus twelve, that is, the number of the tribes of Israel plus that of the Apostles. Our Lord in fact promised the latter that they would sit on thrones (cf. Mt 19:28). The twenty-four elders, then, would represent the heavenly Church, which includes the old and the new Israel and which, in heaven, renders God the tribute of perfect praise and intercedes for the Church on earth. The number twenty-four has also been seen as reflecting the twenty-four priestly classes of Judaism, thereby emphasizing the liturgical dimension of heaven (cf. 1 Chron 24:7-18; 25:1, 9-13). Whichever is the case, the white garments indicate that they have achieved everlasting salvation (cf. 3:5); and the golden crowns stand for the reward they have earned (cf. 2:10), or their prominence among Christians, who have been promised that, if they come out victorious, they will sit on Christ's throne (cf. 3:21).

Through these visions laden with symbolism the Apocalypse shows the solidarity that exists between the Church triumphant and the Church militant—specifically, the connexion between the praise that is rendered God in heaven and that which we offer him on earth, in the liturgy. The Second Vatican Council refers to this: "In the earthly liturgy we take part in the foretaste of that

garments, with golden crowns upon their heads. ⁵From the throne issue flashes of lightning, and voices and peals of thunder, and before the throne burn seven torches of fire, which are the seven spirits of God; ⁶and before the throne there is as it were a sea of glass, like crystal.

And round the throne, on each side of the throne, are four living creatures, full of eyes in front and behind: ⁷the first

Ex 19:16
Ezek 1:13
Rev 8:5; 11:9;
16:18
Zech 4:2

Ezek 1:5-26;
10:1f

Ezek 1:10; 10:14

---

in circuitu throni, viginti quattuor thronos et super thronos viginti quattuor seniores sedentes circumamictos vestimentis albis et super capita eorum coronas aureas. ⁵Et de throno procedunt fulgura et voces et tonitrua; et septem lampades ignis ardentes ante thronum, quae sunt septem spiritus Dei, ⁶et in

---

heavenly liturgy which is celebrated in the Holy City of Jerusalem toward which we journey as pilgrims, where Christ is sitting at the right hand of God [. . .]. With all the warriors of the heavenly army we sing a hymn of glory to the Lord; venerating the memory of the saints, we hope for some part and fellowship with them; we eagerly await the Saviour, our Lord Jesus Christ, until he our life shall appear and we too will appear with him in glory" (*Sancrosanctum Concilium*, 8).

5. This vision is similar to the Old Testament theophanies, especially that of Sinai. There too the Lord's presence was revealed with thunder and lightning (cf. Ex 19:16). Storms are frequently used to symbolize the salvific power and majesty of God at the moment of revelation (cf. Ps 18:14; 50:3; etc.). Further on, the author will again describe, in more detail, the signs accompanying God's self-revealing; this gives the book a sense of on-going revelation with an increasing tempo (cf. Rev 8:5; 11:19; 16:18; etc.). It is generally accepted Church tradition to interpret fire as a manifestation of the Spirit of God. On the seven spirits, see the note on 1:4.

6-7. To describe the majesty of God, St John uses symbols which are sometimes quite difficult to interpret. This is the case with the sea as transparent as glass, and the four living creatures round the throne and on each side of it. The scene may be a kind of heavenly replica of the arrangements in Solomon's temple where there stood in front of the Holy of Holies a huge water container called the "molten sea" supported by figures of oxen, twelve in number (cf. 1 Kings 7:23-26; 2 Chron 4:2-5). This similarity between heaven and the temple would be a a way of expressing the connexion between liturgy on earth and worship of God in heaven.

The crystal sea may also be an allusion to God's absolute dominion over all forms of authority on earth. In biblical tradition the sea is often used as a symbol for the powers of darkness (cf. Rev 13:1; 21:1). To God, however, the sea is crystal-clear, that is, he is its master; cf. the way the spirit of God moved over the surface of the waters in Genesis 1:2.

Is 6:2, 3
Ezek 1:18; 10:12
Ex 3:14

living creature like a lion, the second living creature like an ox, the third living creature with the face of a man, and the fourth living creature like a flying eagle. [8]And the four living creatures, each of them with six wings, are full of eyes all round and within, and day and night they never cease to sing,

"Holy, holy, holy, is the Lord God Almighty,
who was and is and is to come!"

---

conspectu throni tamquam mare vitreum simile crystallo. Et in medio throni et in circuitu throni quattuor animalia, plena oculis ante et retro: [7]et animal *primum* simile *leoni et secundum* animal simile *vitulo et tertium* animal habens *faciem* quasi *hominis et quartum* animal simile *aquilae* volanti. [8]Et quattuor animalia

---

Elsewhere in the Apocalypse (15:2) it speaks of the sea of glass supporting the blessed while they praise God: just as the Israelites passed through the Red Sea, so those who have conquered the beast will cross this solid sea to make their way to God.

The author of the Book of Revelation avails of images used by the prophets to describe the glory of Yahweh. The four living creatures are very like those in the prophet Ezekiel's vision of the chariot of the Lord drawn by four angels representing intelligence, nobility, strength and agility (cf. Ezek 1:10; 10:12; Is 6:2).

Christian tradition going back as far as St Irenaeus has interpreted these four creatures as standing for the four evangelists because they "carry" Jesus Christ to men. The one with the face of a man is St Matthew, who starts his book with the human genealogy of Christ; the lion stands for St Mark: his Gospel begins with the voice crying in the wilderness (which is where the lion's roar can be heard); the ox is a reference to the sacrifices in the temple of Jerusalem, which is where St Luke begins his account of Christ's life, and the eagle represents St John, who soars to the heights to contemplate the divinity of the Word.

8-11. The chant of the four living creatures is virtually the same as that which the prophet Isaiah heard the six-winged seraphim sing in his vision of God in the temple of Jerusalem (cf. Is 6:1-3). St John changes the ending by bringing in the new name of God which is an elaboration of the name "Yahweh" (cf. note on Rev 1:4). The four creatures (who, because there are four of them, stand for government of the entire universe) take the lead in worshipping and praising God; but they are joined by all the people of God, as represented by the twenty-four elders, that is, the Church victorious in heaven. They throw down their crowns to show that they realize their victory is due to God, and that all power belongs to him. Essentially what they are praising here is God as creator. By reporting this vision the author of the Apocalypse is inviting the pilgrim Church on earth to associate with the worship and praise offered God the creator in heaven.

⁹And whenever the living creatures give glory and honour and thanks to him who is seated on the throne, who lives for ever and ever, ¹⁰the twenty-four elders fall down before him who is seated on the throne and worship him who lives for ever and ever; they cast their crowns before the throne, singing,

¹¹"Worthy art thou, our Lord and God,
to receive glory and honour and power,
for thou didst create all things,
and by thy will they existed and were created."

---

singula eorum habebant *alas senas*, in circuitu et intus plenae sunt oculis; et requiem non habent die et nocte dicentia: *"Sanctus, sanctus, sanctus Dominus, Deus omnipotens,* qui erat et qui est et qui venturus est!" ⁹Et cum darent illa animalia gloriam et honorem et gratiarum actionem sedenti super thronum, viventi in saecula saeculorum, ¹⁰procidebant viginti quattuor seniores ante sedentem in throno et adorabant viventem in saecula saeculorum et mittebant coronas suas ante thronum dicentes: ¹¹"Dignus es, Domine et Deus noster, accipere gloriam et honorem et virtutem, quia tu creasti omnia, et propter voluntatem tuam erant et creata sunt."

The Church uses these words of praise in its eucharistic liturgy: at the end of the Preface, it chants the angelic *Sanctus* in preparation for the Canon. This angelic chant, performed as it is in heaven and on earth, reminds us of the sublimity of the Mass, where the worship of God crosses the frontiers of time and space and has a positive influence on the entire world, for, "through the communion of the saints, all Christians receive grace from every Mass that is celebrated, regardless of whether there is an attendance of thousands or whether it is only a boy with his mind on other things who is there to serve. In either case, heaven and earth join with the angels of the Lord to sing: *Sanctus, Sanctus, Sanctus . . .*" (J. Escrivá, *Christ is passing by*, 88). The saintly Curé of Ars refers to this intercommunion of praise and thanksgiving, of grace and forgiveness: "The Holy Mass is a source of joy to all the heavenly court; it alleviates the poor souls in purgatory; it draws down to earth all kinds of blessings; and it gives more glory to God than all the sufferings of all the martyrs taken together, than all the penances of all the hermits, than all the tears shed for them [the holy souls] since time began and all that will be shed from now till the end of time" (*Selected Sermons*, second Sunday after Pentecost).

5

The sealed scroll and the Lamb

Is 29:11
Ezek 2:9, 10
Dan 12:4, 9
Rev 4:2

¹And I saw in the right hand of him who was seated on the throne a scroll written within and on the back, sealed with seven seals; ²and I saw a strong angel proclaiming with a loud voice, "Who is worthy to open the scroll and break its seals?" ³And no one in heaven or on earth or under the earth was able to open the scroll or to look into it, ⁴and I wept much that no one was found worthy to open the scroll or to look into it. ⁵Then one of the elders said to me, "Weep not; lo, the Lion of the tribe of Judah, the Root of David, has conquered, so that he can open the scroll and its seven seals."

Gen 49:9f
Is 11:1, 10
Rom 15:12

---

¹Et vidi in dextera sedentis super thronum librum scriptum intus et foris, signatum sigillis septem. ²Et vidi angelum fortem praedicantem voce magna: "Quis est dignus aperire librum et solvere signacula eius?" ³Et nemo poterat in caelo neque in terra neque subtus terram aperire librum neque respicere illum. ⁴Et ego flebam multum, quoniam nemo dignus inventus est aperire librum nec respicere eum. ⁵Et unus de senioribus dicit mihi: "Ne fleveris; ecce vicit leo de

---

1-5. The sealed scroll contains God's mysterious plans for the salvation of mankind; no one on earth can disclose them (v. 3). Only the risen Christ can take the scroll and make its contents known (vv. 6-7). On this account he is praised by the four living creatures, by the elders (vv. 8-10), by a whole host of angels (vv. 11-12) and by all creation (vv. 13-14).

The image of a scroll (or book) containing God's hidden plans for mankind was used before, particularly by the prophet Daniel (cf. Dan 12:4 - 9; also Is 29:11), who refers to a prophecy remaining sealed until the end of time. St John uses this image to make the point that the End Time, the Last Days, have already begun with Christ, so now he can reveal God's plans. The fact that there are *seven* seals stresses the hidden nature of the scroll's contents; and its being written on both sides shows its richness.

The author of the Book of Revelation, and everyone in fact, really does need to know what is written on the scroll; for, if he knows God's plans he will be able to discover the meaning of life and cease to be anxious about events past, present and future. Yet no one is able to open the scroll: that is why the author weeps so bitterly.

The scroll is sealed: the Revelation of the salvation of mankind and the consolation of the Church is being delayed. Soon, however, the seer ceases to weep, for he learns that Christ (here called "the Lion of the tribe of Judah" and "the Root" or descendant of David: cf. Gen 49:9; Is 11:1, 10) has conquered and therefore is able to break the seven seals.

⁶And between the throne and the four living creatures and among the elders, I saw a Lamb standing, as though it had been slain, with seven horns and with seven eyes, which are the seven spirits of God sent out into all the earth; ⁷and he went and took the scroll from the right hand of him who

Is 53:7; 11:2
Jn 1:29
Rev 4:5
Zech 3:9; 4:6

---

tribu Iudae, radix David, aperire librum et septem signacula eius." ⁶Et vidi in medio throni et quattuor animalium et in medio seniorum Agnum stantem tamquam occisum, habentem cornua septem et oculos septem, qui sunt septem spiritus Dei missi in omnem terram. ⁷Et venit et accepit de dextera sedentis in

---

The Church contemplates Christ's victory when it "believes that Christ, who died and was raised for the sake of all, can show man the way and strengthen him through the Spirit in order to be worthy of his destiny [. . .]. The Church likewise believes that the key, the centre and the purpose of the whole of man's history is to be found in its Lord and Master" (Vatican II, *Gaudium et spes*, 10). "In fact," the Council adds, "it is only in the mystery of the Word made flesh that the mystery of man truly becomes clear. For Adam, the first man, was a type of him who was to come (cf. Rom 5:14). Christ the Lord, Christ the new Adam, in the very revelation of the mystery of the Father and of his love, fully reveals man to himself and brings to light his most high calling" (*ibid.*, 22).

6-7. Christ is able to open the scroll on account of his death and resurrection —an event symbolized by the Lamb standing upright and victorious and at the same time looking as though it had been immolated. In the Fourth Gospel, John the Baptist calls Christ "the Lamb of God" (Jn 1:29, 36); in the Apocalypse this expression is the one most often used to refer to him: he is the Lamb raised to the very height of God's throne and has dominion over the entire cosmos (cf. 5:8, 12-13; 6:1, 16; 7:9-10; 13:8; 15:3; etc.). This Christological title, which is a feature of St John's writings, has great theological depth; the Church venerates it greatly, often using it in the liturgy—particularly in the Mass, after the kiss of peace when the Lamb of God is invoked three times; also, just before Holy Communion is distributed the host is shown to the faithful as him who takes away the sin of the world and those who are called to his marriage supper are described as "happy" (cf. Rev 19:9).

The image of the Lamb reminds us of the passover lamb, whose blood was smeared on the door frames of houses as a sign to the avenging angel not to inflict on Israelites the divine punishment being dealt out to the Egyptians (cf. Ex 12:7, 13). St Paul refers to the Lamb in one of his letters: "Christ, our paschal lamb, has been sacrificed" (1 Cor 5:7). At a high point in Old Testament prophecy Isaiah portrays the Messiah as the suffering Servant of Yahweh, "a lamb that is led to the slaughter" (Is 53:7). St Peter, on the basis of that text, states that our Lord "bore our sins in his body on the tree, that we might die to sin and live to righteousness" (1 Pet 2:24).

The Lamb is a sacrifice for sin, but the Apocalypse also focuses attention

65

Rev 14:2
Ps 141:2

was seated on the throne. [8]And when he had taken the scroll, the four living creatures and the twenty-four elders fell down before the Lamb, each holding a harp, and with golden bowls full of incense, which are the prayers of the

Rev 14:3, 4
Rom 3:24

saints; [9]and they sang a new song, saying,

"Worthy are thou to take the scroll and to open its seals, for thou wast slain and by thy blood didst ransom men for God

Ex 19:6
Is 61:6
Rev 1:6; 20:6;
22:5

from every tribe and tongue and people and nation, [10]and hast made them a kingdom and priests to our God, and they shall reign on earth."

---

throno. [8]Et cum accepisset librum, quattuor animalia et viginti quattuor seniores ceciderunt coram Agno, habentes singuli citharas et phialas aureas plenas incensorum, quae sunt orationes sanctorum. [9]Et cantant novum canticum dicentes: "Dignus es accipere librum et aperire signacula eius, quoniam occisus

---

on the victorious power of the risen Lamb by showing him standing on the throne, in the centre of the vision; the horns symbolize his power and the eyes his knowledge, both of which he has to the fullest degree as indicated by the number seven. The seven spirits of Christ also indicate the fulness of the Spirit with which Christ is endowed and which he passes on to his Church (cf. notes on Rev 1:4 and 4:5). This completes the description of the risen Christ, who through his victory reveals the mystery of God.

8-10. The greatness of Christ the Lamb is duly acknowledged and proclaimed through the worship rendered him, firstly, from the four living creatures and the twenty-four elders, then from all the angels and finally from the whole of creation (vv. 11-13). St John selects these three points to highlight the praise rendered by the heavenly Church, with which the pilgrim Church on earth joins through its own prayer (symbolized by the image of the golden bowls). Later on (15:7ff), seven bowls appear again, this time filled with God's wrath, which is caused by the complaint of the righteous who are being cruelly tormented by the agents of evil.

All this shows the value of the prayers of those who stay loyal to God: "the prayer of a righteous man has great power in its effects" (Jas 5:16), for "the prayer of the humble pierces the clouds, and he will not be consoled until it reaches the Lord" (Sir 35:17).

The "new song" proclaims that Christ alone decides the destinies of the world and of mankind; this is a consequence of himself being offered in sacrifice as the atoning victim *par excellence*. By shedding his blood Christ has won for himself an immense people, from every nation under heaven; in them, a holy people, his chosen ones, that people which was originally assembled in the Sinai desert (cf. Ex 19:6; 1 Pet 2:9f) has come to full maturity. When it says

¹¹Then I looked, and I heard around the throne and the living creatures and the elders the voice of many angels, numbering myriads of myriads and thousands of thousands, ¹²saying with a loud voice, "Worthy is the Lamb who was slain, to receive power and wealth and wisdom and might and honour and glory and blessing!" ¹³And I heard every

Dan 7:10

Is 53:7
1 Chron 29:11
Phil 2:9

Phil 2:10
1 Tim 1:17

---

es et redemisti Deo in sanguine tuo ex omni tribu et lingua et populo et natione ¹⁰et fecisti eos Deo nostro regnum et sacerdotes, et regnabunt super terram." ¹¹Et vidi et audivi vocem angelorum multorum in circuitu throni et animalium et seniorum, et erat numerus eorum myriades myriadum et milia milium ¹²dicentium voce magna: "Dignus est Agnus, qui occisus est, accipere virtutem et divitias et sapientiam et fortitudinem et honorem et gloriam et benedictionem." ¹³Et omnem creaturam, quae in caelo est et super terram et sub terra

---

that they have been ransomed from every tribe and nation, it is pointing out that God's salvific plans extend to the whole human race: he "desires all men to be saved and to come to the knowledge of the truth" (1 Tim 2:4). This does not exempt us from making an effort to merit salvation, for, as St Augustine teaches, "God who created you without your cooperation will not save you without your cooperation" (*Sermon* 169, 11). Here is how another early writer puts it: "we know that God will give to each individual the opportunity to be saved—to some in one way, to others in another. But whether we respond eagerly or listlessly depends on ourselves" (Cassian, *Collationes*, 3, 12).

"Didst ransom men for God": in many important Greek manuscripts this reads, "you ransomed us for God", and some even change the reading of the following verse: "you made us a kingdom . . . and we will reign". The earlier Latin translation, the Vulgate, chose that reading, which emphasizes that those who are intoning the chant are men, that is, members of the Church triumphant in heaven. The new official Latin version, the New Vulgate, follows what it considers to be the most reliable Greek text. But the meaning does not really change.

11-14. The host of angels around the throne act as a kind of guard of honour proclaiming the sublime perfection of Christ the Lamb (v. 12); they list seven attributes which all point to the fact that he has everything that belongs to the Godhead.

After the song of the spiritual, invisible, creation, there follows the hymn of the material, visible, world. This hymn (v. 14) differs from the previous one in that it is also addressed to him who sits upon the throne. It thereby puts on the same level God and the Lamb, whose Godhead is being proclaimed. This marks the climax of the universal, cosmic praise that is rendered the Lamb. The emphatic "Amen!" of the four living creatures, and the worship offered by the elders bring this introductory vision to a close.

creature in heaven and on earth and under the earth and in the sea, and all therein, saying, "To him who sits upon the throne and to the Lamb be blessing and honour and glory and might for ever and ever!" [14]And the four living creatures said, "Amen!" and the elders fell down and worshipped.

---

et super mare et quae in eis omnia, audivi dicentes: "Sedenti super thronum et Agno benedictio et honor et gloria et potestas in saecula saeculorum." [14]Et quattuor animalia dicebant: "Amen"; et seniores ceciderunt et adoraverunt.

As in other passages of the book, mention is made of the role of the angels in heaven, particularly the worship and praise they offer God before his throne (cf. Rev 7:11), their role in putting God's plans into operation (cf. 11:15; 16:17; 22:6, etc.) and their intercession with God on behalf of mankind (cf. 8:4).

The Church has always encouraged special devotion to the angels (cf. *Lumen gentium*, 50). Sacred Scripture and the teaching of the Church clearly tells us about the existence of angels and about their mission to guide and protect us; cf. Exodus 23:20: "Behold, I send an angel before you, to guard you on the way and to bring you to the place which I have prepared. Give heed to him and harken to his voice." Echoing these words the Catechism of St Pius V states that "by God's providence angels have been entrusted with the office of guarding the human race and of accompanying every human being [. . .]. (God) not only deputes angels on particular and private occasions, but also appoints them to take care of us from our very births. He furthermore appoints them to watch over the salvation of every member of the human race" (IV, 9). Devotion to one's guardian angel, a part of ordinary Christian practice, is something we learn as children and should keep up during our adult lives: "Have confidence in your guardian Angel. Treat him as a lifelong friend—that is what he is—and he will render you a thousand services in the ordinary affairs of each day" (J. Escrivá, The Way, 562).

6

EVENTS PRIOR TO THE FINAL OUTCOME

Christ opens the first six seals. Vision of the four horsemen

[1]Now I saw when the Lamb opened one of the seven seals, and I heard one of the four living creatures say, as with a voice of thunder, "Come!" [2]And I saw, and behold, a white horse, and its rider had a bow; and a crown was given to him, and he went out conquering and to conquer.

Rev 5:1, 2; 4:6;
5:6, 8

Zech 1:8-10;
6:1-3

---

[1]Et vidi, cum aperuisset Agnus unum de septem sigillis, et audivi unum de quattuor animalibus dicens tamquam vox tonitrui: "Veni." [2]Et vidi: et ecce equus albus; et, qui sedebat super illum, habebat arcum, et data est ei corona, et exivit vincens et ut vinceret. [3]Et cum aperuisset sigillum secundum, audivi

---

6.1 - 11:14. After describing his vision of heaven, especially the risen Christ empowered to reveal God's hidden plans (chaps. 4-5), the author now begins to disclose that revelation little by little as each of the seven seals is opened (chaps. 6-7). When he comes to the seventh seal, the main one, a new series of visions or revelations begins. These are symbolized by the blowing of the seven trumpets in turn; when the seventh is sounded (cf. 11:15) the description begins of the last battles fought by Christ and his followers against the powers of evil, the beast and its followers. The sound of the seventh trumpet marks the fulfilment of "the mystery of God" (cf. 10:7).

In its description of the opening of the first six seals, this section covers, firstly, the arrival of the day of the wrath of God (cf. 6:17), which is heralded by natural calamities and social upheaval (a foretaste of God's judgment on mankind). This gives the author the opportunity to jump ahead and describe a vision of the saved in heaven (chap. 7)—putting human history into its proper perspective: all its tragedies and untoward events are a kind of forewarning of the punishment that lies in wait for the evildoer.

The vision then describes another series of catastrophes akin to the plagues of Egypt; preceded by the blowing of the trumpets, they herald the coming of God. Like the earlier disasters they are designed to provoke men to a change of heart; because they fail to have any effect, these people will incur God's wrath and will each be judged by him in due course (cf. 9:20-21; 11:18).

At the end of this section, as a kind of transition to the next, the author stresses the prophetic character of his words: evil seems to have come out winning (as symbolized by the death of the two witnesses: cf. 11:1-13), but this is only apparently so, for Christ, who has already won the victory by his death and resurrection, will be seen to triumph at his second coming. The Lamb will confront the beast and overwhelm it. Until that moment, there is still time for conversion, for opting for or against God. There is no middle course.

³When he opened the second seal, I heard the second
Ezek 21:14-16   living creature say, "Come!" ⁴And out came another horse,

---

secundum animal dicens: "Veni." ⁴Et exivit alius equus rufus; et, qui sedebat

1-8. The first four seals have various things in common: as they are opened horsemen appear, each of a different colour; and it is always one of the four living creatures that calls up the horsemen.

The last three horsemen are easy to identify: the second carries a sword, which stands for war; the third a balance, here a symbol of famine, to do with the measuring out of rations; and the fourth represents plague, as indicated by the colour of his horse. All three are forms of divine punishment already predicted in the Old Testament: "I will send famine and wild beasts against you, and they will rob you of your children; pestilence and blood shall pass through you; and I will bring the sword upon you. I, the Lord, have spoken" (Ezek 5:17). Jesus used similar language in his eschatological discourse: "And when you hear of wars and tumults, do not be terrified [. . .]; there will be great earthquakes, and in various places famines and pestilence" (Lk 21:9, 11).

The first rider is, however, difficult to interpret: his features suggest that he is some type of power in the service of God. The colour white is symbolic of belonging to the heavenly sphere and of having won victory with God's help (cf., e.g., Rev 3:4, 5, 18; 14:14; 20:11). The crown he is given and the words "he went out conquering and to conquer" would refer to the victory of good over evil (cf. 2:7, 11, 17, 28; 3:5, 12; etc.); and the bow indicates the connexion between this horse and the other three: these latter will be as it were arrows loosed from a distance to implement God's plans.

This first rider, who goes forth "conquering and to conquer", refers to Christ's victory in his passion and resurrection, as St John has already mentioned (cf. 5:5), and also announces the final victory of the Word of God which first will come about later (cf. 19:11). The horseman is a kind of key which provides a specifically Christian meaning for all the terrifying scenes described in the book. A propos of this figure, Pius XII wrote: "He is Jesus Christ. The inspired evangelist not only saw the devastation brought about by sin, war, hunger and death; he also saw, in the first place, the victory of Christ. It is certainly true that the course the Church takes down through the centuries is a *via crucis*, a way of the cross, but it is also a victory march. It is the Church of Christ, men and women of Christian faith and love, who are always bringing light, redemption and peace to a mankind without hope. 'Jesus Christ, the same yesterday and today and for ever' (Heb 13:8)" (*Address*, 15 November 1946).

4. The sword carried by the rider on the red horse stands for war (cf. Mt 10:34), referring to the wars being waged at the time in the Roman empire, but also to war in general, the scourge of mankind, which at the time of the End will be a signal of the imminent destruction of the world (cf. Mt 24:6 and par.).

The Church has had much to say about war in recent times. Thus, the Second Vatican Council says that "insofar as men are sinners, the threat of war hangs

bright red; its rider was permitted to take peace from the earth, so that men should slay one another; and he was given a great sword. ⁵When he opened the third seal, I heard the third living creature say, "Come!" And I saw, and behold, a black horse, and its rider had a balance in his hand; ⁶and I heard what seemed to be a voice in the midst of the four living creatures saying, "A quart of wheat for a denarius,ᵃ and three quarts of barley for a denarius;ᵃ but do not harm oil and wine!" ⁷When he opened the fourth seal, I heard the voice of the fourth living creature say, "Come!" ⁸And I saw, and behold,

Ezek 4:16f
1 Kings 6:25f

super illum, datum est ei, ut sumeret pacem de terra, et ut invicem se interficiant, et datus est illi gladius magnus. ⁵Et cum aperuisset sigillum tertium, audivi tertium animal dicens: "Veni." Et vidi: et ecce equus niger; et, qui sedebat super eum, habebat stateram in manu sua. ⁶Et audivi tamquam vocem in medio quattuor animalium dicentem: "Bilibris tritici denario, et tres bilibres hordei denario; et oleum et vinum ne laeseris." ⁷Et cum aperuisset sigillum quartum,

over them and will so continue until the coming of Christ; but insofar as they can vanquish sin by coming together in charity, violence itself will be vanquished and they will make these words come true: 'They shall beat their swords into ploughshares, and their spears into pruning hooks; nation shall not lift up sword against nation, neither shall they learn war any more' (Is 2:4)" (*Gaudium et spes*, 78).

5-6. A sudden (perhaps tenfold) rise in the price of wheat and barley, part of the staple diet at the time, signals a period of famine. If we bear in mind that a "quart" (Greek: *choinix*) was about one kilo or 30 ounces and a denarius a day's wage for a labourer (cf. Mt 20:13), these are clearly very high prices.

Famine and hunger are ultimately a consequence of sin and therefore can be interpreted as a "punishment". The Church reminds us all that we have a strict duty to help alleviate the needs of others, for this is a way of combatting evil. "The Council asks individuals and governments to remember the saying of the Fathers: 'Feed the man dying of hunger, because if you do not feed him you are killing him' (Gratian, *Decretum*, 21, 86) and it urges them according to their ability to share and dispose of their goods to help others, above all by giving them aid which will enable them to help and develop themselves" (*Gaudium et spes*, 69).

8. "Pale horse": the fourth horse has a strange colour, which some translate as greenish or ashen; it probably means a death-like colour. Death is personified by the horse's sinister rider; this symbol is reinforced by his companion *Hades* or *Sheol*, the dark abode of the dead (cf. Rev 1:18).

ᵃThe denarius was a day's wage for a labourer

71

Hos 13:14
Ezek 5:12;
14:21
Jer 14:12

a pale horse, and its rider's name was Death, and Hades followed him and they were given power over a fourth of the earth, to kill with sword and with famine and with pestilence and by wild beasts of the earth.

Rev 20:4

⁹When he opened the fifth seal, I saw under the altar the souls of those who had been slain for the word of God and for the witness they had borne; ¹⁰they cried out with a loud voice, "O Sovereign Lord, holy and true, how long before thou wilt judge and avenge our blood on those who dwell

Rev 3:7
Zech 1:12
Ps 79:5
Deut 32:43
Gen 4:10
Lk 18:7

---

audivi vocem quarti animalis dicentis: "Veni." ⁸Et vidi: et ecce equus pallidus; et, qui sedebat desuper, nomen illi Mors, et Infernus sequebatur eum, et data est illis potestas super quartam partem terrae, interficere gladio et fame et morte et a bestiis terrae. ⁹Et cum aperuisset quintum sigillum, vidi subtus altare animas interfectorum propter verbum Dei et propter testimonium, quod habebant. ¹⁰Et clamaverunt voce magna dicentes: "Usquequo, Domine, sanctus et verus, non iudicas et vindicas sanguinem nostrum de his, qui habitant in terra?" ¹¹Et datae sunt illis singulae stolae albae, et dictum est illis, ut requiescant tempus adhuc

---

All this is meant to show that in the midst of all the terrible chastisement God has pity on mankind: most (three quarters, that is) will manage to survive the test.

9-11. Here St John sees all who gave their lives for God. The vision takes in the Old Testament martyrs from Abel down to Zechariah (cf. Mt 23:35-37; Heb 11:35-40), and Christian martyrs of all eras; St John sees them under the altar of holocausts where victims were sacrificed in honour of God and their blood collected beneath. Here we see a heavenly copy of that altar, meaning that the martyrs are very close to God and that their death has been a most acceptable offering to him (cf. Phil 2:17; 2 Tim 4:6).

The presence of the martyrs in heaven shows that when man dies his soul receives its reward or punishment immediately. God's judgment of each soul begins to take effect the moment he dies, although it is not until the resurrection of all the dead that it will have its full effect, on body as well as soul.

The martyrs' song is a clamour for justice: our Lord refers to it in the Gospel (cf. Lk 18:7) and it echoes the aboriginal lament raised at Abel's death (cf. Gen 4:10). What the martyrs say seems to be at odds with Christ's prayer on the cross (cf. Lk 23:24) and Stephen's on the eve of his martyrdom (cf. Acts 7:60), but there is really no contradiction. "This prayer of the martyrs", St Thomas says, "is nothing other than their desire to obtain resurrection of the body and to share in the inheritance of those who will be saved, and their recognition of God's justice in punishing evildoers" (*Summa theologiae*, III, q. 72, a. 3, ad. 1).

It is, thus, a prayer for the establishment of the Kingdom of God and his justice, which causes his divine holiness and fidelity to shine forth.

upon the earth?" [11]Then they were each given a white robe and told to rest a little longer, until the number of their fellow servants and their brethren should be complete, who were to be killed as they themselves had been.

[12]When he opened the sixth seal, I looked, and behold, there was a great earthquake; and the sun became black as sackcloth, the full moon became like blood, [13]and the stars of the sky fell to the earth as the fig tree sheds its winter fruit when shaken by a gale; [14]the sky vanished like a scroll that is rolled up, and every mountain and island was removed from its place. [15]Then the kings of the earth and the great men and the generals and the rich and the strong, and every one, slave and free, hid in the caves and among the rocks of the mountains, [16]calling to the mountains and rocks, "Fall on us and hide us from the face of him who is seated on the throne, and from the wrath of the Lamb; [17]for the great day of their wrath has come, and who can stand before it?"

Is 13:10
Ezek 32:7, 8
Joel 3:3, 4
Mt 24:29

Is 34:4

Rev 16:20; 20:11

Ps 2:2
Is 2:10; 24:21
Jer 4:29

Hos 10:8
Lk 23:30
Ps 47:9

Joel 2:11; 3:4
Rom 2:5
Mal 3:2
Zeph 1:14

---

modicum, donec impleantur et conservi eorum et fratres eorum, qui interficiendi sunt sicut et illi. [12]Et vidi, cum aperuisset sigillum sextum, et terraemotus factus est magnus, et sol factus est niger tamquam saccus cilicinus, et luna tota facta est sicut sanguis, [13]et stellae caeli ceciderunt in terram, sicut ficus mittit grossos suos, cum vento magno movetur, [14]et caelum recessit sicut liber involutus, et omnis mons et insula de locis suis motae sunt. [15]Et reges terrae et magnates et tribuni et divites et fortes et omnis servus et liber absconderunt se in speluncis et in petris montium; [16]*et dicunt montibus et petris: "Cadite super nos et abscondite nos* a facie sedentis super thronum et ab ira Agni, [17]quoniam venit dies magnus irae ipsorum, et quis poterit stare?"

12-17. This passage predicts the events which will occur just before the second coming of our Lord Jesus Christ. It does not refer to the very End, but to the fact that it is imminent. The terrifying symbols used to indicate these events derive from literary style and language used in the Old Testament (cf., e.g., Amos 8:9; Is 13:98f; 34:4; 50:3; Job 3:4). This was the prophets' way of warning the people—and of consoling them by telling them that Christ's definitive victory would soon come. Jesus speaks in the same way to the grieving women of Jerusalem whom he meets on his way to Calvary (cf. Lk 23:30).

In v. 15 there is a reference to seven social groups embracing all mankind, ranging from the highest to the lowest. Nothing escapes God's judgment and there is no appeal against it. The *Dies Irae* has come, the day of the Lamb's wrath. The Lamb symbolizes the innocence and immolation of the Messiah; but it also stands for messianic royalty, symbolized here by his fury.

73

The great multitude of the saved

Jer 49:36
Ezek 7:2; 37:9
Dan 7:2
Zech 6:5
Mt 24:31

[1]After this I saw four angels standing at the four corners of the earth, holding back the four winds of the earth, that no wind might blow on earth or sea or against any tree. [2]Then I saw another angel ascend from the rising of the sun, with the seal of the living God, and he called with a loud voice

Ezek 9:4, 6
Rev 9:6

to the four angels who had been given power to harm earth and sea, [3]saying, "Do not harm the earth or the sea or the

---

[1]Post haec vidi quattuor angelos stantes super quattuor angulos terrae tenentes quattuor ventos terrae, ne flaret ventus super terram neque super mare neque in ullam arborem. [2]Et vidi alterum angelum ascendentem ab ortu solis, habentem sigillum Dei vivi, et clamavit voce magna quattuor angelis, quibus datum est nocere terrae et mari, [3]dicens: "Nolite nocere terrae neque mari

---

1-17. This chapter consists of two visions designed to illustrate God's protection of Christians and the happy circumstances of the martyrs. The victory of the Church is depicted—of the entire Church, made up of people from the four points of the compass (vv. 9-12). What is not so clear, however, is who the one hundred and forty four thousand are, drawn from the twelve tribes of Israel, whom an angel has marked with the seal of the living God (vv. 1-8). Some commentators interpret them as all being Christians of Jewish background (Judaeo-Christians). Others say that they are those who make up the new Israel which St Paul speaks about in Galatians 6:17; that is, all the baptized viewed first as still engaged in their battle (vv. 1-8) and then after they have won victory (vv. 9-17). The most plausible interpretation is that the one hundred and forty four thousand stand for the Jews converted to Christianity (as distinct from those not converted)—the 'remnant of Israel' (cf. Is 4:2-4; Ezek 9; etc.). St Paul says that they prove the irrevocable nature of God's election (cf. Rom 11:1-5) and are the first-fruits of the restoration which will come about at the End (cf. Rom 11:25-32).

The hundred and forty-four thousand are included in the second vision; they would be part of the great multitude "from all tribes and people and tongues". Thus, the vision in vv. 9-17 takes in the entire Church without any distinctions, whereas the vision in vv. 1-8 can refer only to a part of the Church—those Jews who, by becoming Christians, made up the original nucleus of the Church. The Church admits these on the same basis as all those who become Christians later without having had to pass through any stage of Jewish observance.

1-8. In Jewish tradition angels were divided into two groups—angels of the Presence and sanctification, and those charged with controlling the forces of nature. Both kinds appear in this passage.

trees, till we have sealed the servants of our God upon their foreheads." [4]And I heard the number of the sealed, a hundred and forty-four thousand sealed, out of every tribe of the sons of Israel, [5]twelve thousand sealed out of the tribe of Judah, twelve thousand of the tribe of Reuben, twelve thousand of the tribe of Gad, [6]twelve thousand of the tribe of Asher, twelve thousand of the tribe of Naphtali, twelve thousand of the tribe of Manasseh, [7]twelve thousand of the tribe of Simeon, twelve thousand of the tribe of Levi, twelve thousand of the tribe of Issachar, [8]twelve thousand of the tribe of Zebulun, twelve thousand of the tribe of Joseph, twelve thousand sealed out of the tribe of Benjamin.

Rev 14:1, 3

Num 1:21-43

neque arboribus, quoadusque signemus servos Dei nostri in frontibus eorum." [4]Et audivi numerum signatorum, centum quadraginta quattuor milia signati ex omni tribu filiorum Israel: [5]ex tribu Iudae duodecim milia signati, ex tribu Ruben duodecim milia, ex tribu Gad duodecim milia, [6]ex tribu Aser duodecim milia, ex tribu Nephthali duodecim milia, ex tribu Manasse duodecim milia, [7]ex tribue Simeon duodecim milia, ex tribu Levi duodecim milia, ex tribu Issachar duodecim milia, [8]ex tribu Zabulon duodecim milia, ex tribu Ioseph

According to the custom of the time, when something bore the mark of a seal or brand that meant that it belonged to the seal's owner. This passage is saying that the one hundred and forty four thousand belong to God and therefore will be protected by him as his property. This fulfils what Ezekiel prophesied about the inhabitants of Jerusalem (cf. Ezek 9:1-7): some would be sealed on the forehead with a *tau* (the last letter of the Hebrew alphabet) and would therefore escape the punishment to be inflicted on all the rest: this shows the special way God makes provision for those who are his not only because he created them but also by a new title.

The Fathers of the Church saw this mark as symbolizing the character Baptism impresses on the souls of the faithful to show that they are destined for eternal life. Thus, the persons preserved from harm are the Jews who were converts to Christianity: their Baptism marked them out from those Jews who rejected Christ and were not baptized.

The list of tribes is somewhat different from the usual list which keeps the order of Genesis 29. The name of Judah is put first because the Messiah came from that tribe, as St John recently mentioned (cf. 5:5); and there is no mention of the tribe of Dan, presumably because it fell into idolatry (cf. Judg 17-18) and eventually disappeared. To make up the tally of twelve the tribe of Joseph is mentioned twice—as that of Joseph and as that of Manasseh, his first-born.

The number of those sealed (12 x 12 x 1000) symbolizes completeness, totality—in this instance, a huge multitude, depicted as the new Israel. Included in this number are the descendants of Jacob who receive Baptism, irrespective of when they do. Obviously this number is not meant to be taken literally, as if

Rev 15:2-5
Gen 15:5

Rev 19:1
Ps 47:9

Rev 5:11; 11:16

⁹After this I looked, and behold, a great multitude which no man could number, from every nation, from all tribes and peoples and tongues, standing before the throne and before the Lamb, clothed in white robes, with palm branches in their hands,¹⁰ and crying out with a loud voice, "Salvation belongs to our God who sits upon the throne, and to the Lamb!" ¹¹And all the angels stood round the throne and round the elders and the four living creatures, and they fell on their faces before the throne and worshipped God, ¹²saying, "Amen! Blessing and glory and wisdom and thanksgiving and honour and power and might be to our God for ever and ever! Amen."

duodecim milia, ex tribu Beniamin duodecim milia signati. ⁹Post haec vidi: et ecce turba magna, quam dinumerare nemo poterat, ex omnibus gentibus et tribubus et populis et linguis stantes ante thronum et in conspectu Agni, amicti stolis albis, et palmae in manibus eorum; ¹⁰et clamant voce magna dicentes: "Salus Deo nostro, qui sedet super thronum, et Agno." ¹¹Et omnes angeli stabant in circuitu throni et seniorum et quattuor animalium, et ceciderunt in conspectu throni in facies suas et adoraverunt Deum ¹²dicentes: "Amen! Benedictio et

only one hundred and forty-four thousand people will attain salvation. In this scene all those of Gentile background who become Christians over the course of history are explicitly not included. They will appear in the vision which follows.

9-17. Pope John Paul II has commented on this passage as follows: "The people dressed in white robes whom John sees with his prophetic eye are the redeemed, and they form a 'great multitude', which no one could count and which is made up of people of the most varied backgrounds. The blood of the Lamb, who has been offered in sacrifice for all, has exercised its universal and most effective redemptive power in every corner of the earth, extending grace and salvation to that 'great multitude'. After undergoing the trials and being purified in the blood of Christ, they—the redeemed—are now safe in the Kingdom of God, whom they praise and bless for ever and ever" (*Homily*, 1 November 1981). This great crowd includes all the saved and not just the martyrs, for it says that they washed their robes in the blood of the Lamb, not in their own blood.

Everyone has to become associated with Christ's passion through suffering, as St Augustine explains, not without a certain humour: "Many are martyrs in their beds. The Christian is lying on his couch, tormented by pain. He prays and his prayers are not heard, or perhaps they are heard but he is being put to the test . . . so that he may be received as a son. He becomes a martyr through illness and is crowned by him who hung upon the Cross" (*Sermon* 286, 8).

It is consoling and encouraging to know that those who attain heaven

¹³Then one of the elders addressed me, saying, "Who are these, clothed in white robes, and whence have they come?" ¹⁴I said to him, "Sir, you know." And he said to me, "These are they who have come out of the great tribulation; they have washed their robes and made them white in the blood of the Lamb.

¹⁵Therefore are they before the throne of God,
and serve him day and night within his temple;
and he who sits upon the throne will shelter them with
his presence.
¹⁶They shall hunger no more, neither thirst any more;
the sun shall not strike them, nor any scorching heat.
¹⁷For the Lamb in the midst of the throne will be their
shepherd,
and he will guide them to springs of living water;
and God will wipe away every tear from their eyes."

Rev 22:14
Dan 12:1
Mt 24:21
Gen 49:11

Is 6:1
Rev 15:5

Is 49:10
Ps 121:6

Ps 23:2
Is 25:8; 49:10
Rev 21:4

gloria et sapientia et gratiarum actio et honor et virtus et fortitudo Deo nostro in saecula saeculorum. Amen." ¹³Et respondit unus de senioribus dicens mihi: "Hi qui amicti sunt stolis albis, qui sunt et unde venerunt?" ¹⁴Et dixi illi: "Domine mi, tu scis." Et dixit mihi: "Hi sunt qui veniunt de tribulatione magna et laverunt stolas suas et dealbaverunt eas in sanguine Agni. ¹⁵Ideo sunt ante thronum Dei et serviunt ei die ac nocte in templo eius; et, qui sedet in throno, habitabit super illos. ¹⁶Non *esurient* amplius *neque sitient* amplius, *neque cadet super illos sol neque* ullus *aestus,* ¹⁷quoniam Agnus, qui in medio throni est,

constitute a huge multitude. The passages of Matthew 7:14 and Luke 13:24 which seem to imply that very few will be saved should be interpreted in the light of this vision, which shows that the infinite value of Christ's blood makes God's will be done: "(God) desires all men to be saved and to come to the knowledge of the truth" (1 Tim 2:4).

In vv. 14-17 we see the blessed in two different situations—first, before the resurrection of the body (v. 14) and, then, after it, when body and soul have been reunited (vv. 15-17). In this second situation the nature of risen bodies is highlighted: they cannot suffer pain or inconvenience of any kind: they are out of harm's reach; they have the gift of "impassibility" (cf. *St Pius V Catechism*, I, 12, 13).

This consoling scene is included in the vision to encourage believers to imitate those Christians who were like us and now find themselves in heaven because they have come through victorious. The Church invites us to pray along similar lines: "Father, you sanctified the Church of Rome with the blood of its first martyrs. May we find strength from their courage and rejoice in their triumph" (*Roman Missal*, Feast of the First Martyrs of the Church of Rome, opening prayer).

The opening of the seventh seal

Zech 2:17
Hab 2:20
Mt 24:31
Tob 12:15

Rev 5:8
Ps 141:2

Lev 16:12
Ezek 10:2
Rev 4:5
Ex 19:16

¹When the Lamb opened the seventh seal, there was silence in heaven for about half an hour. ²Then I saw the seven angels who stand before God, and seven trumpets were given to them. ³And another angel came and stood at the altar with a golden censer; and he was given much incense to mingle with the prayers of all the saints upon the golden altar before the throne; ⁴and the smoke of the incense rose with the prayers of the saints from the hand of the angel before God. ⁵Then the angel took the censer and filled it

---

pascet illos et deducet eos ad vitae fontes aquarum, et absterget Deus omnem lacrimam ex oculis eorum."

¹Et cum aperuisset sigillum septimum, factum est silentium in caelo quasi media hora. ²Et vidi septem angelos, qui stant in conspectu Dei, et datae sunt illis septem tubae. ³Et alius angelus venit et stetit ante altare habens turibulum aureum, et data sunt illi incensa multa, ut daret orationibus sanctorum omnium

---

1-2. The silence is a signal that the End has come: it expresses the Lord's patient waiting—as if he were putting off the day of judgment, to the chagrin of the faithful. However, "the Lord is not slow about his promise as some count slowness, but is forebearing toward you, not wishing that any should perish, but that all should reach repentance" (2 Pet 3:9).

The opening of the seventh seal leads to another "seven", the seven trumpets; and the last of these leads to the seven bowls (cf. Rev 11:15). But first we are told what happens when the first six trumpets are blown (chap. 8-9) and God's judgments are visited on the earth. There is a certain parallel here with the plagues of Egypt (cf. Ex 7:14 - 12:34). Before the seventh trumpet is sounded, there is a sort of interlude (cf. 10:1 - 11:14).

Trumpets were used by the Israelites not only in battle (cf. Josh 6:5) but also in the temple liturgy, where they proclaimed the presence of Yahweh (cf. Ps 47:6). In accounts of our Lord's second coming we find references to trumpets being sounded to signal that divine intervention is imminent (cf., e.g., Mt 24:31; 1 Cor 15:52; 1 Thess 4:15).

3-5. The prayers of the saints, previously identified by bowls of incense (cf. 5:8), are now mingled with the aromatic incense rising from the golden censer. All this is a reference to the fact that the saints in heaven intercede with God on our behalf. The Second Vatican Council reminds us that "the Church has always believed that the apostles and Christ's martyrs, who gave the supreme witness of faith and charity by the shedding of their blood, are closely united with us in Christ; she has always venerated them, together with the Blessed

with fire from the altar and threw it on the earth; and there were peals of thunder, loud noises, flashes of lightning, and an earthquake.

⁶Now the seven angels who had the seven trumpets made ready to blow them.

Joel 2:1

The first six trumpet calls. The three woes

⁷The first angel blew his trumpet, and there followed hail and fire, mixed with blood, which fell on the earth; and a third of the earth was burnt up, and a third of the trees were burnt up, and all green grass was burnt up.

Joel 3:3
Ex 9:23-26
Ezek 38:22
Rev 16:2

---

super altare aureum, quod est ante thronum. ⁴Et ascendit fumus incensorum de orationibus sanctorum de manu angeli coram Deo. ⁵Et accepit angelus turibulum et implevit illud de igne altaris et misit in terram; et facta sunt tonitrua et voces et fulgura et terraemotus. ⁶Et septem angeli, qui habebant septem tubas,

---

Virgin Mary and the holy angels, with a special love, and has asked piously for the help of their intercession" (*Lumen gentium*, 50). The Council of Trent recommends that the faithful be taught how profitable it is to have recourse to the intercession of the saints: "it is a good and useful thing to invoke the saints humbly and to have recourse to their prayers" (*De sacris imaginibus*).

The usefulness of intercessory prayer is something we learn about first in the Old Testament. For example, we are told how Moses, with his hands raised to heaven, pleaded successfully for Israelite victory over the Amalekites (cf. Ex 17:8f). Also, the references here to the altar of incense recall elements of Jewish worship (cf. Ex 29:13; Lev 21:6; Ps 141:2; etc.), which was a prefiguration of the worship "in spirit and truth" (Jn 4:23) announced by Jesus.

In response to the prayers of the saints, the Lord once again manifests his presence in the way he did at Sinai (cf. note on 4:5). The angel's action is reminiscent of Ezekiel 10:2, where the angel fills his hands with burning coals and scatters them over Jerusalem. This rain of fire now signals the start of God's fury on the world and on mankind, which is described here in stages marked by trumpet blasts.

6-12. The blowing of the first four trumpets is separated from that of the following ones by a vision (v. 13); the same pattern applied to the seven seals. The punishments the trumpet calls herald are reminiscent of the plagues of Egypt. No necessary historical sequence of events is being described here; the order is more logical than historical. Each successive divine intervention is simply a further manifestation of God's power and justice. The devastation which the trumpets introduce is greater than that produced by the opening of the first four seals: a third of the earth is affected, not just a quarter (cf. 6:8). Divine mercy, however, still controls the range of the punishment and prevents total annihilation.

79

Jer 51:25
Ex 7:20f

⁸The second angel blew his trumpet, and something like a great mountain, burning with fire, was thrown into the sea; ⁹and a third of the sea became blood, a third of the living creatures in the sea died, and a third of the ships were destroyed.

Rev 16:4
Dan 8:10
Is 14:12

Jer 9:14

¹⁰The third angel blew his trumpet, and a great star fell from heaven, blazing like a torch, and it fell on a third of the rivers and on the fountains of water. ¹¹The name of the star is Wormwood. A third of the waters became wormwood, and many men died of the water, because it was made bitter.

Ex 10:21
Rev 6:12; 16:8

¹²The fourth angel blew his trumpet, and a third of the sun was struck, and a third of the moon, and a third of the stars, so that a third of their light was darkened; a third of the day was kept from shining, and likewise a third of the night.

---

paraverunt se, ut tuba canerent. ⁷Et primus tuba cecinit. Et facta est grando et ignis mixta in sanguine, et missum est in terram: et tertia pars terrae combusta est, et tertia pars arborum combusta est, et omne fenum viride combustum est. ⁸Et secundus angelus tuba cecinit. Et tamquam mons magnus igne ardens missus est in mare: et facta est tertia pars maris sanguis, ⁹et mortua est tertia pars creaturarum, quae in mari sunt, quae habent animas, et tertia pars navium interiit. ¹⁰Et tertius angelus tuba cecinit. Et cecidit de caelo stella magna ardens tamquam facula et cecidit super tertiam partem fluminum et super fontes aquarum. ¹¹Et nomen stellae dicitur Absinthius. Et facta est tertia pars aquarum in absinthium, et multi hominum mortui sunt de aquis, quia amarae factae sunt. ¹²Et quartus angelus tuba cecinit. Et percussa est tertia pars solis et tertia pars lunae et tertia pars stellarum, ut obscuraretur tertia pars eorum, et diei non luceret pars tertia, et nox similiter. ¹³Et vidi et audivi unam aquilam volantem per medium caelum dicentem voce magna: "Vae, vae, vae habitantibus in terra de ceteris vocibus tubae trium angelorum, qui tuba canituri sunt!"

Following the logical order which classifies the cosmos into land, sea and sky, the blowing of the first trumpet affects the vegetation (v. 7); the description is parallel to the account of the seventh plague in Exodus 9:13-35.

The blowing of the two next trumpets affects seas and rivers (vv. 10-11). Many perish as a result of the pollution of the waters. Both these calamities are connected with the first plague of Egypt (cf. Ex 7:19-21).

After this contamination of land and sea, the heavens are affected by the fourth trumpet. The sun and the heavenly bodies are darkened, so that their power is reduced by a third: these effects are reminiscent to some degree of Exodus 10:21-29

¹³Then I looked, and I heard an eagle crying with a loud voice, as it flew in midheaven, "Woe, woe, woe to those who dwell on the earth, at the blasts of the other trumpets which the three angels are about to blow!"

Rev 14:6; 9:12; 11:14

9

¹And the fifth angel blew his trumpet, and I saw a star fallen from heaven to earth, and he was given the key of the shaft of the bottomless pit; ²he opened the shaft of the bottomless

Rev 8:10; 20:1
Is 14:12
Gen 19:28
Ex 19:18
Joel 2:10

¹Et quintus angelus tuba cecinit. Et vidi stellam de caelo cecidisse in terram, et data est illi clavis putei abyssi. ²Et aperuit puteum abyssi, et ascendit fumus ex

13. This passage is a short break before the last three trumpet calls. The lament of the eagle, which may stand for an angel, can be heard all over the world. Its "woe, woe, woe" expresses horror and compassion at the events which follow. This cannot fail to impress the reader; it creates an atmosphere of foreboding.

"Those who dwell on earth": a reference to idolaters (cf. Rev 3:10, who are persecuting Christians. It does not refer to the faithful but only to those who have let themselves be led astray by Christ's enemies (cf. Rev 6:10; 11:10; 13:8, 12, 14; 17:2-8).

9:1 - 11:19. The next two trumpets will impact directly on mankind, producing more horrific effects, in a kind of crescendo. These trumpets follow one after the other (9:1-21), whereas there is a delay before the blowing of the seventh (11:15-19), during which a number of visions occur (10:1 - 11:14) which anticipate later events narrated in chapters 12-22.

1-2. The commonest interpretation of the star fallen from heaven to earth is that it stands for one of the fallen angels, most likely Satan himself, of whom Christ said, "I saw Satan fall like lightning from heaven" (Lk 10:18) and whom the present text later describes as being thrown down to the earth (cf. note on 12:13). Behind this lies the notion that the demons are incarcerated in the bowels of the earth. The writer is trying to convey the idea that, when the fifth trumpet is blown, God is going to let demoniacal forces loose to wreak havoc on those of mankind who refuse to recognize God (cf. v. 4). They will be free to operate only for a limited period and to a limited degree and will have to obey "the angel of the bottomless pit" (v. 11), who would be the same angel as received the key of the shafts of the abyss (v. 9), the prince of the demons. Very near the end of the Apocalypse the writer sees the other side of the coin, as it were—Satan and his followers being shut up once more in the pit, after Christ's victory (cf. 20:1-3).

Ex 10:12, 15
Wis 16:9

Rev 7:3
Ezek 9:4, 6

Job 3:21
Lk 23:30

Joel 2:4

Joel 1:6

Joel 2:5

pit, and from the shaft rose smoke like the smoke of a great furnace, and the sun and the air were darkened with the smoke from the shaft. ³Then from the smoke came locusts on the earth, and they were given power like the power of scorpions of the earth; ⁴they were told not to harm the grass of the earth or any green growth or any tree, but only those of mankind who have not the seal of God upon their foreheads; ⁵they were allowed to torture them for five months, but not to kill them, and their torture was like the torture of a scorpion, when it stings a man. ⁶And in those days men will seek death and will not find it; they will long to die, and death will fly from them.

⁷In appearance the locusts were like horses arrayed for battle; on their heads were what looked like crowns of gold; their faces were like human faces, ⁸their hair like women's hair, and their teeth like lions' teeth; ⁹they had scales like

---

puteo sicut fumus fornacis magnae, et obscuratus est sol et aer de fumo putei. ³Et de fumo exierunt locustae in terram, et data est illis potestas, sicut habent potestatem scorpiones terrae. ⁴Et dictum est illis, ne laederent fenum terrae neque omne viride neque omnem arborem, nisi tantum homines, qui non habent signum Dei in frontibus. ⁵Et datum est illis, ne occiderent eos, sed ut cruciarentur mensibus quinque; et cruciatus eorum ut cruciatus scorpii, cum percutit hominem. ⁶Et in diebus illis quaerent homines mortem et non invenient eam; et desiderabunt mori, et fugit mors ab ipsis. ⁷Et similitudines locustarum similes equis paratis in proelium, et super capita earum tamquam coronae similes auro, et facies earum sicut facies hominum, ⁸et habebant capillos sicut

---

3-6. In order to describe the demons and the havoc they create, St John evokes the eighth plague of Egypt, the plague of locusts (cf. Ex 10:14ff), making it clear, however, that this plague is much more horrific and on another level altogether. It will do such grievous harm to men that they will wish they were dead, but they will have to endure it for a fixed amount of time: the "five months", the life-time of the locust, conveys the idea that these afflictions will last for a limited time.

7-12. The description of the locusts is designed to show how terrifying demons are; cf. the prophet Joel's description of the invading army (Joel 1:2 - 2:17). The crowns of gold identify them as conquerors; their faces, as creatures with intelligence; their hairiness and lions' teeth symbolize ferocity; their iron breastplates show them to be fully armed warriors; and the noise they create and their scorpion tails show their extreme cruelty. They obey a leader, Satan, whose name (Abaddon, Apollyon) denotes destruction and extermination. His name contrasts with that of Jesus, which means "Yahweh saves".

iron breastplates, and the noise of their wings was like the noise of many chariots with horses rushing into battle. ¹⁰They have tails like scorpions, and stings, and their power of hurting men for five months lies in their tails. ¹¹They have as king over them the angel of the bottomless pit; his name in Hebrew is Abaddon, and in Greek he is called Apollyon.[b]

Rev 9:19
Rev 9:1

¹²The first woe has passed; behold, two woes are still to come.

Rev 8:13

¹³Then the sixth angel blew his trumpet, and I heard a voice from the four horns of the golden altar before God, ¹⁴saying to the sixth angel who had the trumpet, "Release the four angels who are bound at the great river Euphrates." ¹⁵So the four angels were released, who had been held ready for the hour, the day, the month, and the year, to kill a third of mankind. ¹⁶The number of the troops of cavalry was twice ten thousand times ten thousand; I heard their number. ¹⁷And this was how I saw the horses in my vision: the riders wore breastplates the colour of fire and of sapphire[c] and of sulphur, and the heads of the horses were

Ex 30:1-3
Rev 16:12
Rev 8:7-12

---

capillos mulierum, et dentes earum sicut leonum erant, ⁹et habebant loricas sicut loricas ferreas, et vox alarum earum sicut vox curruum equorum multorum currentium in bellum. ¹⁰Et habent caudas similes scorpionibus et aculeos, et in caudis earum potestas earum nocere hominibus mensibus quinque. ¹¹Habent super se regem angelum abyssi, cui nomen Hebraice Abaddon et Graece nomen habet Apollyon. ¹²Vae unum abiit. Ecce veniunt adhuc duo vae post haec. ¹³Et sextus angelus tuba cecinit. Et audivi vocem unam ex cornibus altaris aurei, quod est ante Deum, ¹⁴dicentem sexto angelo, qui habebat tubam: "Solve quattuor angelos, qui alligati sunt super flumen magnum Euphraten." ¹⁵Et soluti sunt quattuor angeli, qui parati erant in horam et diem et mensem et annum, ut occiderent tertiam partem hominum. ¹⁶Et numerus equestris exercitus vicies

---

13-19. As before, God permits the angels of evil to have their way; he uses them to inflict just punishment and offer the rest of mankind a chance to repent of their sins (vv. 20-21). The golden altar standing before the throne of God is shaped like the altar of the temple of Jerusalem (cf. Ex 37:26; Amos 3:14), with its four prominent corners and four horns; from the midst of the horns comes the voice which sets these punishments in motion.

The inspired writer now describes a new and dreadful vision. The vast size of the cavalry shows the scale of the evil in the world. The river Euphrates (in a sense the frontier of the world of the Bible) was the direction from which invasions of Israel usually came (cf. Is 7:20; Jer 46:10; etc.). At the time of

[b] Or *Destroyer*   [c] Greek *hyacinth*

like lions' heads, and fire and smoke and sulphur issued from their mouths. [18]By these three plagues a third of mankind was killed, by the fire and smoke and sulphur issuing from their mouths. [19]For the power of the horses is in their mouths and in their tails; their tails are like serpents, with heads, and by means of them they wound.

[20]The rest of mankind, who were not killed by these plagues, did not repent of the works of their hands nor give up worshipping demons and idols of gold and silver and bronze and stone and wood, which cannot either see or hear or walk; [21]nor did they repent of their murders or their sorceries or their immorality or their thefts.

Rev 9:10

Is 2:8, 20; 17:8
Dan 5:4, 23
Ps 115:4; 135:15
1 Cor 10:20

---

milies dena milia; audivi numerum eorum. [17]Et ita vidi equos in visione et, qui sedebant super eos, habentes loricas igneas et hyacinthinas et sulphureas; et capita equorum erant tamquam capita leonum, et de ore ipsorum procedit ignis et fumus et sulphur. [18]Ab his tribus plagis occisa est tertia pars hominum, de igne et fumo et sulphure, qui procedebat ex ore ipsorum. [19]Potestas enim equorum in ore eorum est et in caudis eorum, nam caudae illorum similes serpentibus habentes capita, et in his nocent. [20]Et ceteri homines, qui non sunt occisi in his plagis neque paenitentiam egerunt de operibus manuum suarum, ut non adorarent daemonia et *simulacra aurea et argentea et aerea et lapidea et lignea, quae neque videre* possunt *neque audire neque ambulare,* [21]et non egerunt paenitentiam ab homicidiis suis neque a veneficiis suis neque a fornicatione sua neque a furtis suis.

---

writing it was the region from which the Parthians mounted their threat to the Roman empire.

Some of the details of the vision are reminiscent of other descriptions of ruin and desolation (cf. Gen 19:24-28) and of monstrous animals (cf. Job 41:11). Fire, smoke and sulphur all indicate that this army of monsters originates in hell.

20-21. In the last analysis, as shown here, all the punishments described in the Book of Revelation are designed to move people to repentance. That was also the thrust of the letters to the seven churches (cf. Rev 2:5, 16, 21; 3:3; etc). But the author shows that people persist in turning away from God to worship idols, which are really only scarecrows compared with Yahweh, the living God (cf. e.g., Ps 113; Jer 10:3-5).

In the last analysis idolatry is the root of all other sins: by turning his back on God man comes under the control of the forces of evil (forces within him as well as outside him) which push him to commit all kinds of sins and perversions. St Paul deals with the same idea in his Letter to the Romans where he says that by cutting themselves off from God men are given over to their own passions and commit most abominable sins (cf. Rom 1:18-32).

10

The author is given the little scroll to eat

¹Then I saw another mighty angel coming down from   Rev 5:2; 4:3
heaven, wrapped in a cloud, with a rainbow over his head,
and his face was like the sun, and his legs like pillars of fire.
²He had a little scroll open in his hand. And he set his right

---

¹Et vidi alium angelum fortem descendentem de caelo amictum nube, et iris
super caput, et facies eius erat ut sol, et pedes eius tamquam columnae ignis,
²et habebat in manu sua libellum apertum. Et posuit pedem suum dexterum

---

God inflicts punishment in order to bring about the conversion of sinners. Sometimes, however, the end result is that they become more obdurate. That was the case with Pharaoh; when the plagues struck Egypt, far from repenting, he persecuted the Israelites more bitterly than ever. Divine punishment, then, has a medicinal and exemplary purpose and is good for everyone without exception. In the Gospel Jesus tells us that the Galileans whom Pilate put to death, and the people who perished when the tower collapsed on them in Siloam, were not more blameworthy than other people, and therefore we too will perish unless we repent (cf. Lk 13:1-5).

1. After the events following the sixth trumpet call (cf. 9:13-21) and before the seventh (cf. 11:15), we are shown a new vision (as an aside, as it were). The seer is once again back on earth, as he was when the seven letters were being despatched (cf. 10:4; 1:4 - 3:22), whereas he sees the "trumpet" visions from the vantage point of heaven (chaps. 4-9 and 12). This shows that we are dealing here with an aside which is designed to prepare the reader for the seventh and final trumpet blast.

In this "out of sequence" vision St John reminds us of his prophetic role by bringing in the symbolic action of eating a little scroll (cf. 10:8-11) and recalling the testimony of the ancient prophets, who are represented by the two witnesses (cf. 11:1-13).

Although the angel is not named, he may be Gabriel: he is described as "mighty" (*geber*, in Hebrew), and Gabriel (*gabri'el*, in Hebrew) means "strength of God" or "man of God" (cf. Dan 8:15) or "God shows his strength". Be that as it may, Gabriel is the name given to the angel charged with explaining the messianic prophecies to Daniel and with communicating divine messages to Zechariah (cf. Lk 1:19) and to the Blessed Virgin (cf. Lk 1:26). He performed a function parallel to that of the angel who appears in 8:3-5 and who is usually identified as St Michael. The way he is described emphasizes his heavenly character and his strength.

2. The open scroll carried by the angel is different from the sealed scroll in the vision recounted in Revelation 5:2. It is more like the scroll described by the prophet Ezekiel (cf. Ezek 2:9 - 3:1) which was also meant to be eaten by

Hos 11:10
Amos 1:2, 3:8
Ps 29:3-9
Jer 25:30
Dan 8:26; 12:4, 9
Rev 22:10

Deut 32:40
Dan 12:7

Neh 9:6
Ex 20:11
Rev 6:11

Acts 3:21
Amos 3:7
Dan 9:10
Rom 16:25

foot on the sea, and his left foot on the land, ³and called out with a loud voice, like a lion roaring; when he called out, the seven thunders sounded. ⁴And when the seven thunders had sounded, I was about to write, but I heard a voice from heaven saying, "Seal up what the seven thunders have said, and do not write it down." ⁵And the angel whom I saw standing on sea and land lifted up his right hand to heaven ⁶and swore by him who lives for ever and ever, who created heaven and what is in it, the earth and what is in it, and the sea and what is in it, that there should be no more delay, ⁷but that in the days of the trumpet call to be sounded by the seventh angel, the mystery of God, as he announced to his servants the prophets, should be fulfilled.

supra mare, sinistrum autem super terram, ³et clamavit voce magna, quemadmodum cum leo rugit. Et cum clamasset, locuta sunt septem tonitrua voces suas. ⁴Et cum locuta fuissent septem tonitrua, scripturus eram; et audivi vocem de caelo dicentem: "Signa, quae locuta sunt septem tonitrua, et noli ea scribere." ⁵Et angelus, quem vidi stantem supra mare et supra terram, *levavit manum suam dexteram ad caelum* ⁶*et iuravit per Viventem in saecula* saeculorum, qui creavit caelum et ea, quae in illo sunt, et terram et ea, quae in ea sunt, et mare et ea, quae in eo sunt: "Tempus amplius non erit, ⁷sed in diebus vocis septimi angeli, cum coeperit tuba canere, et consummatum est mysterium

the seer. The fact that it is open indicates that its content is not secret. The eating of the scroll symbolizes that what the prophet has to say after he eats it is really the word of God. It also indicates that God speaks through the medium of a written text. So, this imagery helps to strengthen people's faith in the divine inspiration of sacred writings, that is, the Bible, and to recognize them for what they are—holy books because they are the very word of God which reaches the Church in written form via inspired authors: by reading these books publicly the Church is in fact proclaiming their divine inspiration.

We are not told what this little scroll contains; so, the only reason the writer brings in this symbol is to make it clear that he is a prophet. He wants people to be in no doubt about the fact that his prophecies apply to all creation—both heaven and earth (v. 6).

3-7. Like the voice of God in the Old Testament, the angel's voice is here compared to the roar of a lion (cf. Hos 11:10; Amos 1:2; 3:8) and to thunder (cf. Is 29:6) which strikes fear into men.

According to the text each peal of thunder carries a message of its own; and the fact of there being seven means that they carry everything God wishes to reveal. However, the content of this revelation is not to be communicated further and will only be made known at the end of time. The sealing of the scroll

⁸Then the voice which I had heard from heaven spoke to me again, saying, "Go, take the scroll which is open in the hand of the angel who is standing on the sea and on the land." ⁹So I went to the angel and told him to give me the little scroll; and he said to me, "Take it and eat; it will be bitter to your stomach, but sweet as honey in your mouth." ¹⁰And I took the little scroll from the hand of the angel and ate it; it was sweet as honey in my mouth, but when I had eaten it my stomach was made bitter. ¹¹And I was told,

Rev 10:2

Ezek 2:8; 3:1

Ezek 3:3

Dan 3:4

Dei, sicut evangelizavit servis suis prophetis." ⁸Et vox, quam audivi de caelo, iterum loquentem mecum et dicentem: "Vade, accipe librum apertum de manu angeli stantis supra mare et supra terram." ⁹Et abii ad angelum dicens ei, ut daret mihi libellum. Et dicit mihi: "Accipe et devora illum; et faciet amaricare ventrem tuum, sed in ore tuo erit dulcis tamquam mel." ¹⁰Et accepi libellum de manu angeli et devoravi eum, et erat in ore meo tamquam mel dulcis; et cum

---

shows that this revelation is to be kept secret and that there is no point in anyone trying to discover it. It is part of the mystery which God chooses to keep hidden—in the same way as we do not know when our Lord's second coming and the end of the world will be (cf. Mt 24:36).

The angel's gesture and solemn oath assured the seer that the definitive establishment of the Kingdom of God will come about when there will be "no more delay", no more time, for the world in its present form. However, as to the timing, all that is said is that it will happen when the mystery of God (his plan of salvation) has reached its final climax, when the harvest-time has come (cf. Mt 13:24-30) and good and evil—wheat and weeds—will be clear for all to see (cf. 2 Thess 2:6ff).

In the Apocalypse, the end of time is signalled by the blowing of the seventh trumpet (described later: cf. 11:15) which signals that the "three woes" are over (cf. 8:13; 9:13). The point being made here is that this outcome is certain—which is a motive of hope for the Church and a call to conversion for all mankind: "But do not ignore this one fact, beloved, that with the Lord one day is as a thousand years, and a thousand years as one day. The Lord is not slow about his promise as some count slowness, but is forbearing toward you, not wishing that any should perish, but that all should reach repentance" (2 Pet 3:8-9).

8-11. Cf. note on 10:2. The book described by Ezekiel 2:8 - 3:3 was sweet as honey when eaten; but when Ezekiel began to prophesy, his heart was filled with bitterness (cf. Ezek 3:14). The same symbolism of the two kinds of taste is used here—no doubt to indicate that the prophecy contains grace and blessing, and also judgment and condemnation. The sweetness can also be interpreted as reflecting the triumph of the Church, and the bitterness its afflictions.

"You must again prophesy about many peoples and nations and tongues and kings."

11

The death and resurrection of the two witnesses

Ezek 40:3
Zech 2:5
Is 63:18
Ps 79:1
Dan 7:25; 8:14
Lk 21:24
Rev 12:6, 14;
13:5

[1]Then I was given a measuring rod like a staff, and I was told: "Rise and measure the temple of God and the altar and those who worship there, [2]but do not measure the court outside the temple; leave that out, for it is given over to the

devorassem eum, amaricatus est venter meus. [11]Et dicunt mihi: "Oportet te iterum prophetare super populis et gentibus en linguis et regibus multis."
[1]Et datus est mihi calamus similis virgae dicens: "Surge et metire templum Dei

Although nothing is said about what is written on the scroll John is given to eat, it is reasonable to suppose that it has to do with the passage about the two witnesses which now follows, before the blowing of the seventh trumpet; this would make it a prophetic oracle, brought in here as a preview of the final eschatological battles, to show that evil apparently triumphs on earth.

1-13. The prophecy connected with what is on the scroll (11:1-13) acts as a preamble to the events that follow the blowing of the seventh and last trumpet (11;15ff). It has to do with the tribulation suffered by the Church (the Church is symbolized by the temple of Jerusalem and its altar). The ultimate cause of this suffering is the forces of evil, that is, the beast (antichrist) which makes its appearance in the Holy City (cf. 11:7). In the course of a limited period, that is, the history of mankind, there are moments when the forces of evil prevail and many people transgress God's law. The witnesses of the true God come forward to preach penance 11:3-6) and are martyred to the great delight of their adversaries (cf. 11:7-10). But God intervenes on behalf of these martyrs, taking them up into heaven and decimating their foes; the terrified survivors submit to God (cf. 11:11-13).

This prophetic teaching echoes what we are told in the Second Letter to the Thessalonians: "Let no one deceive you in any way; for that day will not come, unless the rebellion comes first, and the man of lawlessness is revealed, the son of perdition, who opposes and exalts himself against every so-called god or object of worship, so that he takes his seat in the temple of God, proclaiming himself to be God" (2 Thess 2:3-4). Using Old Testament imagery and language the author of Revelation is pointing out, as Jesus did (cf. Mk 13:14-32), that the destruction of Jerusalem and the catastrophes which accompany it are a sign and symbol of the end of the world and a warning to everyone (particularly the Jewish people) who are called as the Jews are, to share in the salvation brought by Christ (cf. Rom 11:25-26).

nations, and they will trample over the holy city for forty-two months. ³And I will grant my two witnesses power to prophesy for one thousand two hundred and sixty days, clothed in sackcloth."

et altare et adorantes in eo. ²Atrium autem, quod est foris templum, eice foras et ne metiaris illud, quoniam datum est gentibus, et civitatem sanctam calcabunt mensibus quadraginta duobus. ³Et dabo duobus testibus meis, et prophetabunt

1-2. The image of the measuring rod is taken from the prophet Ezekiel but it is used in a different way: it shows God is going to preserve part of the Holy City from the destructive power of the Gentiles. This part stands for the Church, the community of those who worship God in spirit and in truth (cf. Jn 4:23).

Jerusalem was trampled under foot by the Gentiles in the time of Antiochus Epiphanes, who profaned the temple and installed in it a statue of Zeus Olympus (cf. 1 Mac 1:54;); worse destruction still was done by the Romans, who destroyed both temple and city, leaving not a stone upon a stone (Mt 24:21; Mk 13:14-23; Lk 21:20-24). Taking his cue from these events, St John prophesies that the Church will never suffer the same fate, for God protects it from the power of its enemies (cf. Mt 16:16-18). Christians may suffer persecution in one way or another, but physical or moral violence cannot overpower the Church, because God protects it. "The Church, 'like a stranger in a foreign land, presses forward amid the persecutions of the world and the consolations of God' (St Augustine, *The City of God*, 18, 51), announcing the cross and death of the Lord until he comes (cf. 1 Cor 11:26). But by the power of the risen Lord it is given strength to overcome, in patience and in love, its sorrows and its difficulties, both those that are from within and those that are from without, so that it may reveal in the world, faithfully, however darkly, the mystery of its Lord until, in the consummation, it shall be manifested in full light" (Vatican II, *Lumen gentium*, 8).

The forty-two months established as the period during which the Gentiles will trample on the Holy City stand for the length of the persecution. This is a symbolic number equivalent to three and a half years or "a time, times and half a time" (12:13), that is, "a half week of years"—half seven—which stands for an incomplete, that is, limited, period of time. Perfect, complete time is symbolized by the figure seven (cf. Gen 1:2 - 2:3) or by seventy (cf. Dan 9:24). The prophet Daniel uses the same symbolism to indicate the duration of persecution (cf. Dan 7:25; 12:7); the author of the Apocalypse puts it to the same purpose here and in the next verse, where the same period is expressed in terms of days (one thousand two hundred and sixty): the period stands for the duration of the Church's sufferings in the course of history (cf. Rev 12:6, 14; 13:5): this period is of limited duration, merely a prelude to the definitive victory of Christ and his Church.

3-6. The period of tribulation coincides with the length of time the two witnesses prophesy. They call people to penance (symbolized by their use of

Zech 4:3, 11-14

2 Kings 1:10
Jer 5:14
Lk 9:54f
2 Sam 22:9
1 Kings 17:1
Ex 7:17
Jas 5:17

4These are the two olive trees and the two lampstands which stand before the Lord of the earth. 5And if any one would harm them, fire pours from their mouth and consumes their foes; if any one would harm them, thus he is doomed to be killed. 6They have power to shut the sky, that no rain may fall during the days of their prophesying, and they have power over the waters to turn them into blood, and to smite the earth with every plague, as often as they

---

diebus mille ducentis sexaginta amicti saccis." *4Hi sunt duae olivae et duo candelabra in conspectu Domini terrae stantes. 5Et si quis eis vult nocere, ignis exit de ore illorum et devorat inimicos eorum; et si quis voluerit eos laedere, sic oportet eum occidi. 6Hi habent potestatem claudendi caelum, ne pluat pluvia*

sackcloth). God protects them in a very special way; and yet he does not spare them death or suffering; in the end, however, they will be glorified in heaven. In the Apocalypse the identity of the two witnesses is not given; they are referred to as "olive trees"—the same language as used of Zerubbabel, a prince of the line of David, and Joshua, the high priest (cf. Zech 3:3-14). But they are assigned features of Elijah, who brought about a drought (cf. 1 Kings 17:1-3; 18:1), and Moses, who turned the Nile to blood (cf. Ex 7:14-16). The enemies of Elijah and Moses were also devoured by fire from heaven (cf. 2 Kings 1:10; Num 16:35). However, because the two witnesses testify to Jesus Christ and die martyrs, tradition identifies them with St Peter and St Paul, who suffered martyrdom in Rome, the city which the Book of Revelation later mentions symbolically. Some early commentators (e.g. Ticonius and St Bede) saw the two witnesses as standing for the Old and New Testaments; but this interpretation has had little following. St Jerome (*Epist.* 59) say that they are Elijah and Enoch, and St Gregory the Great and others give that interpretation (*Moralia*, 9, 4).

What St John is doing is using a theme which occurs fairly frequently in apocalyptic writings where Elijah and Enoch or other combinations of prominent figures are portrayed as opponents of antichrist. His two witnesses do have features of Elijah and Moses, both of whom bore witness to Christ at the Transfiguration (cf. Mt 17:1-8 and par.). However, the duration of the trial they undergo, and the entire context of the passage, point rather to them standing for the prophetic witness of the Church, symbolized by certain more outstanding witnesses, who were present at the death of Christ, which took place in Jerusalem, and who were also witnesses of his glorious resurrection. However, it is the entire Church, right through the course of its history, that has been given the prophetic role of calling men to repentance in the midst of harassment and hostility: "The holy People of God shares also in Christ's prophetic office: it spreads a broad and living witness to him, especially by a life of faith and love and by offering to God a sacrifice of praise, the fruit of lips praising his name (cf. Heb 13:15)" (Vatican II, *Lumen gentium*, 12). "The Church an-

desire. [7]And when they have finished their testimony, the beast that ascends from the bottomless pit will make war upon them and conquer them and kill them, [8]and their dead bodies will lie in the street of the great city which is allegorically[d] called Sodom and Egypt, where their Lord

Dan 7:3, 7, 21
Rev 13:1, 7

---

diebus prophetiae ipsorum, et potestatem habent super aquas convertendi eas in sanguinem et percutere terram omni plaga, quotienscumque voluerint. [7]Et cum finierint testimonium suum, bestia, quae ascendit de abysso, faciet adversus illos bellum et vincet eos et occidet illos. [8]Et corpus eorum in platea civitatis magnae, quae vocatur spiritaliter Sodoma et Aegyptus, ubi et Dominus

---

nounces the good tidings of salvation [. . .], so that all men may believe the one true God and Jesus Christ whom he has sent and may be converted from their ways, doing penance (cf. Jn 17:3; Lk 24:27; Acts 2:38)" (Vatican II, *Sacrosanctum Concilium*, 9).

7-10. The prophet Daniel used four beasts to symbolize the empires of the world as enemies of the people of Israel. In the Apocalypse the beast stands for the enemy of the Church and the enemy of God. Further on it will develop this theme and link the beasts to the dragon or Satan (cf. 13:2), and describe their defeat by Christ, the Lamb of God (cf. 14:1; 19:19-21).

The symbol of the beast is brought forward in this passage to show that there will be a point, or various points, before the End when the forces of evil will apparently win victory. Martyrdom silences the voices of the witnesses of Jesus Christ who preach repentance; many will rejoice over this and even deride those whose words or actions they find uncomfortable, despite the fact that when a Christian bears witness to the salvation that comes from Jesus he is motivated purely by love. "Since Jesus, the Son of God, showed his love by laying down his life for us, no one has greater love than he who lays down his life for him and for his brothers (cf. 1 Jn 3:16; Jn 15:13). Some Christians have been called from the beginning, and will always be called, to give this greatest testimony of love to all, especially to persecutors. Martyrdom makes the disciple like his Master, who willingly accepted death for the salvation of the world, and through it he is conformed to Him by the shedding of blood. Therefore the Church considers it the highest gift and supreme test of love. And while it is given to few, all however must be prepared to confess Christ before men and to follow him along the way of the cross amidst the persecutions which the Church never lacks" (*Lumen gentium*, 42).

"The great city", whose name is not given, seems to be Jerusalem, which in Isaiah 1:10 is called Sodom because it has turned its back on God. However, when the writer tells us that it is "allegorically called Sodom and Egypt, where their Lord was crucified" (v. 8), we may take Jerusalem here to stand for any city or even any nation where perversity holds sway (cf. Wis 19:14-17, which alludes to Sodom and Egypt) and where Christians are persecuted and hunted

[d]Greek *spiritually*

was crucified. [9]For three days and a half men from the peoples and tribes and tongues and nations gaze at their dead bodies and refuse to let them be placed in a tomb, [10]and those who dwell on the earth will rejoice over them and make merry and exchange presents, because these two prophets had been a torment to those who dwell on the earth. [11]But after the three and a half days a breath of life from God entered them, and they stood up on their feet, and great fear fell on those who saw them. [12]Then they heard a loud voice from heaven saying to them, "Come up hither!"

Ezek 35:5, 10

2 Kings 2:11

---

eorum crucifixus est; [9]et vident de populis et tribubus et linguis et gentibus corpus eorum per tres dies et dimidium, et corpora eorum non sinunt poni in monumento. [10]Et inhabitantes terram gaudent super illis et iucundantur et munera mittent invicem, quoniam hi duo prophetae cruciaverunt eos, qui inhabitant super terram. [11]Et post dies tres et dimidium spiritus vitae a Deo intravit in eos, et steterunt super pedes suos; et timor magnus cecidit super eos,

---

down (cf. Acts 9:5). Thus, St Jerome (*Epist.* 17) interpreted the names of Sodom and Egypt as having a mystical or figurative meaning, referring to the entire world seen as the city of the devil and of evildoers.

Further on, St John will identify the Rome of his time with this "great city" (cf. 17:9).

Evil will triumph for only a limited period. Its reign is fixed to last "three days and a half", to show its brevity and temporary character as compared with the one thousand two hundred and sixty days (three years and a half) for which the prophetic witness endures (cf. note on 11:1-2).

11-13. Those who have given their lives to bear witness to Jesus will also, through the power of the Holy Spirit, share in his resurrection and ascension into heaven. The writer describes this by various references to the Old Testament, references rich in meaning. The breath of life which causes the witnesses to stand up, that is, to be resurrected, reveals the power of the Spirit of God, which is also described by the prophet Ezekiel in his vision of the dry bones which become living warriors (cf. Ezek 37:1-14). The voice which calls them up to heaven reminds us of what happened to Elijah at the end of his life (cf. 2 Kings 2:11), and to certain other Old Testament saints like Enoch (cf. Gen 5:24; Sir 44:16); according to certain Jewish traditions (cf. Flavius Josephus, *Jewish Antiquities*, IV, 8, 48), all of these men were carried up into heaven at the end of their days on earth.

The exaltation of the witnesses is in sharp contrast with the punishment meted out to their enemies, a punishment designed to move men to conversion. The earthquake indicates that the chastisement is sudden and unexpected; the number of those who die symbolizes a great crowd (thousands) embracing all types (seven).

And in the sight of their foes they went up to heaven in a cloud. ¹³And at that hour there was a great earthquake, and a tenth of the city fell; seven thousand people were killed in the earthquake, and the rest were terrified and gave glory to the God of heaven.

Ezek 38:19, 20

¹⁴The second woe has passed; behold, the third woe is soon to come.

Rev 8:13; 9:12

The sounding of the seventh trumpet

Dan 2:44; 7:14, 27
Zech 14:9
Ezek 15:18

¹⁵Then the seventh angel blew his trumpet, and there

Ps 2:2; 22:9

qui videbant eos. ¹²Et audierunt vocem magnam de caelo dicentem illis: "Ascendite huc"; et ascenderunt in caelum in nube, et viderunt illos inimici eorum. ¹³Et in illa hora factus est terraemotus magnus, et decima pars civitatis cecidit, et occisi sunt in terraemotu nomina hominum septem milia, et reliqui in timorem sunt missi et dederunt gloriam Deo caeli. ¹⁴Vae secundum abiit; ecce vae tertium venit cito. ¹⁵Et septimus angelus tuba cecinit, et factae sunt

The prophecy of the two witnesses is a call to the Christian to bear witness to Christ in the midst of persecution, even to the point of martyrdom. It makes it quite clear that God does not abandon those who boldly take his side. If the prophets of the Old Testament suffered martyrdom, the same will happen in the new, only more so: the messianic times have begun, persecution will grow in strength, but the end of the world is approaching.

14. The tribulations connected with the blowing of the last three trumpets are thrown into sharp and terrible relief by the three "woes" announced from heaven (cf. 8:13), which are a kind of loud lamentation. The second "woe" has been described as something that has already taken place, and the third one is announced. Thus, after the parenthesis of 10:1 - 11:13, the thread of the narrative (following the successive trumpet blasts) is taken up again, and our attention is drawn to the importance of what follows.

15. The seventh trumpet opens a new section which will tell us, first, about the climax of the confrontation between Satan and the powers of evil, and Christ and the Church (cf. 12:1 - 16:16), and then go on to describe the last battles, with Christ triumphing as Lord of all for ever (cf. 16:17 - 22:5). All this is prefaced by an introduction which tells us that his kingdom will come and will endure forever (cf. 11:15-19).

The description of the confrontation between Christ and Satan begins with the war between the dragon and the beasts, on the one hand, and the Messiah, the woman and her children, on the other (cf. 12:1 - 13:18). Then the Lamb appears, Christ in glory, and the moment of judgment is announced (cf. 14:1-20). This is depicted by the seven bowls or plagues (cf. 15:1 - 16:16); when the seventh plague is released, the contenders are introduced again, and the account of the last battles follows (cf. 16:17).

93

were loud voices in heaven, saying, "The kingdom of the world has become the kingdom of our Lord and of his Rev 4:10; 7:11 Christ, and he shall reign for ever and ever." [16]And the twenty-four elders who sit on their thrones before God fell on their faces and worshipped God, [17]saying,

---

voces magnae in caelo dicentes: "Factum est regnum huius mundi Domini nostri et Christi eius, et regnabit in saecula saeculorum." [16]Et viginti quattuor seniores, qui in conspectu Dei sedent in thronis suis, ceciderunt super facies suas et adoraverunt Deum [17]dicentes: "Gratias agimus tibi, Domine, Deus

---

As announced earlier (cf. 10:17), the blowing of the seventh trumpet means that God's mysterious design has been fully implemented. The voices from heaven (11:15) proclaim the revelation of this mystery: that divine design which makes Christ reign forever has taken effect. As elsewhere in the New Testament (cf. Acts 4:25-28), this passage of the Apocalypse also teaches that Christ's complete dominion fulfils the prophetic words of Psalm 2. The climax of human history is the full installation of Christ's Kingdom; the Apocalypse, given its perspective, views this as a present event. It thereby offers Christians a great message of hope and consolation, for the Church "is on earth the seed and the beginning of that kingdom. While it slowly grows to maturity, the Church longs for the completed kingdom and, with all its strength, hopes and desires to be united in glory with its king" (Vatican II, *Lumen gentium*, 5).

Jesus himself teaches us to pray constantly to the Father, "Thy Kingdom come."

16-18. In response to this revelation from God, his people (represented by the twenty-four elders: cf. 4:4) hasten to adore him and thank him. Although all this is placed in a celestial context, it also represents the Church's response to its Redeemer's victorious struggle, which will culminate in his second coming. At that point almighty God will establish his absolute sovereignty; that period will come to an end in which God in his infinite patience permitted man to rebel against him; and all men who ever existed will be judged. This is the faith the Church professes when it proclaims its belief in Jesus Christ, "who will come again in glory to judge the living and the dead" (*Nicene-Constantinopolitan Creed*).

The author of the Apocalypse carries us forward to that final moment when God's action in human history reaches its climax. That is why it no longer speaks of God with reference to the future (as it previously did)—he "who is and who was and who is to come": cf. Rev 1:4, 8; 4:8—but rather in relation to the present and the past—"who art and who wast" (v. 17).

At this final point in history God's justice is fully revealed. Insofar as it involves the condemnation of those who oppose him it is referred to as his "anger" or "wrath" (cf. Rom 1:18). Only God has the power to establish enduring justice or righteousness, as Psalms 96 and 98 tell us.

"We give thanks to thee, Lord God Almighty, who art
and who wast,
that thou hast taken thy great power and begun to reign.
¹⁸The nations raged, but thy wrath came,
and the time for the dead to be judged,
for rewarding thy servants, the prophets and saints,
and those who fear thy name, both small and great,
and for destroying the destroyers of the earth."
¹⁹Then God's temple in heaven was opened, and the ark

Ez 3:14
Rev 1:4; 4:8; 19:6

Ps 2:1, 5; 46:7;
99:1; 115:13
Amos 3:7

Ex 19:16; 25:8-10
Rev 15:5; 4:5
2 Mac 2:5-8

omnipotens, qui es et qui eras, quia accepisti virtutem tuam magnam et regnasti. ¹⁸Et iratae sunt gentes, et advenit ira tua, et tempus mortuorum iudicari et reddere mercedem servis tuis prophetis et sanctis et timentibus nomen tuum, pusillis et magnis, et exterminare eos, qui exterminant terram." ¹⁹Et apertum

Mankind is divided into two groups—those who are rewarded and those who are destroyed; cf. how our Lord describes the Last Judgment in Matthew 25:31-46. The first group consists of those who, down the centuries (in the times of both the Old and the New Covenants) have borne witness to Christ (the prophets), those who have been sanctified by Baptism and have striven for holiness (the saints), and all people great and small who have sought God with sincerity of heart. The second group consists of those who have not kept the law of God (impressed on Creation itself) and who by their sins have helped to corrupt the world by serving the powers of evil (cf. Rev 19:2). When it says that God will destroy them that does not mean that he will annihilate them but rather that he will make them incapable of doing any more evil and will punish them as they deserve. On the Last Judgment, see the notes on Matthew 25:31-46.

19. The seer introduces the heavenly temple (the location *par excellence* of God's presence), paralleling the earlier mention of the temple of Jerusalem (cf. 11:1-2). The opening of the temple and the sight of the Ark of the Covenant show that the messianic era has come to an end and God's work of salvation has been completed. The ark was the symbol of Israel's election and salvation and of God's presence in the midst of his people. According to a Jewish tradition, reported in 2 Maccabees 2:4-8, Jeremiah placed the ark in a secret hiding place prior to the destruction of Jerusalem, and it would be seen again when the Messiah came. The author of the Apocalypse uses this to assure us that God has not forgotten his covenant: he has sealed it definitively in heaven, where the ark is located.

Many early commentators interpreted the ark as a reference to Christ's sacred humanity, and St Bede explains that just as the manna was kept in the original ark, so Christ's divinity lies hidden in his sacred body (cf. *Explanatio Apocalypsis*, 11, 19).

The heavenly covenant is the new and eternal one made by Jesus Christ (cf.

of his covenant was seen within his temple; and there were flashes of lightning, loud noises, peals of thunder, an earthquake, and heavy hail.

12

The woman fleeing from the dragon

_{Gen 37:9} ¹And a great portent appeared in heaven, a woman clothed with the sun, with the moon under her feet, and on her head

---

est templum Dei in caelo, et visa est arca testamenti eius in templo eius; et facta sunt fulgura et voces et terraemotus et grando magna.

¹Et signum magnum apparuit in caelo: mulier amicta sole, et luna sub pedibus

---

Mt 26:26-29 and par.) which will be revealed to all at his second coming when the Church will triumph, as the Apocalypse goes on to describe. The presence of the ark in the heavenly temple symbolizes the sublimity of the messianic kingdom, which exceeds anything man could create. "The vigilant and active expectation of the coming of the Kingdom is also the expectation of a finally perfect justice for the living and the dead, for people of all times and places, a justice which Jesus Christ, installed as supreme Judge, will establish (cf. Mt 24:29-44, 46; Acts 10:42; 2 Cor 5:10). This promise, which surpasses all human possibilities, directly concerns our life in this world. For true justice must include everyone; it must explain the immense load of suffering borne by all generations. In fact, without the resurrection of the dead and the Lord's judgment, there is no justice in the full sense of the term. The promise of the resurrection is freely made to meet the desire for true justice dwelling in the human heart" (SCDF, *Libertatis conscientia*, 60).

The thunder and lightning which accompany the appearance of the ark are reminiscent of the way God made his presence felt on Sinai; they reveal God's mighty intervention (cf. Rev 4:5; 8:5) which is now accompanied by the chastisement of the wicked, symbolized by the earthquake and hailstones (cf. Ex 9:13-35).

1-17. We are now introduced to the contenders in the eschatological battles which mark the final confrontation between God and his adversary, the devil. The author uses three portents to describe the leading figures involved, and the war itself. The first is the woman and her offspring, including the Messiah (12:1-2); the second is the dragon, who will later transfer his power to the beasts (12:3); the third, the seven angels with the seven bowls (15:1).

Three successive confrontations with the dragon are descibed—1) that of the Messiah to whom the woman gives birth (12:1-6); 2) that of St Michael and his angels (12:7-12); and 3) that of the woman and the rest of her offspring (12:13-17). These confrontations should not be seen as being in chronological

a crown of twelve stars; ²she was with child and she cried

eius, et super caput eius corona stellarum duodecim; ²et in utero habens, et

order. They are more like three distinct pictures placed side by side because they are closely connected: in each the same enemy, the devil, does battle with God's plans and with those whom God uses to carry them out.

1-2. The mysterious figure of the woman has been interpreted ever since the time of the Fathers of the Church as referring to the ancient people of Israel, or the Church of Jesus Christ, or the Blessed Virgin. The text supports all of these interpretations but in none do all the details fit. The woman can stand for the people of Israel, for it is from that people that the Messiah comes, and Isaiah compares Israel to "a woman with child, who writhes and cries out in her pangs, when she is near her time" (Is 26:17).

She can also stand for the Church, whose children strive to overcome evil and to bear witness to Jesus Christ (cf. v. 17). Following this interpretation St Gregory wrote: "The sun stands for the light of truth, and the moon for the transitoriness of temporal things; the holy Church is clothed like the sun because she is protected by the splendour of supernatural truth, and she has the moon under her feet because she is above all earthly things" (*Moralia*, 34, 12).

The passage can also refer to the Virgin Mary because it was she who truly and historically gave birth to the Messiah, Jesus Christ our Lord (cf. v. 5). St Bernard comments: "The sun contains permanent colour and splendour; whereas the moon's brightness is unpredictable and changeable, for it never stays the same. It is quite right, then, for Mary to be depicted as clothed with the sun, for she entered the profundity of divine wisdom much much further than one can possibly conceive" (*De B. Virgine*, 2).

In his account of the Annunciation, St Lukes sees Mary as representing the faithful remnant of Israel; the angel greets her with the greeting given in Zephaniah 3:15 to the daughter of Zion (cf. notes on Lk 1:26-31). St Paul in Galatians 4:4 sees a woman as the symbol of the Church, our mother; and non-canonical Jewish literature contemporary with the Book of Revelation quite often personifies the community as a woman. So, the inspired text of the Apocalypse is open to interpreting this woman as a direct reference to the Blessed Virgin who, as mother, shares in the pain of Calvary (cf. Lk 2:35) and who was earlier prophesied in Isaiah 7:14 as a "sign" (cf. Mt 1:22-23). At the same time the woman can be interpreted as standing for the people of God, the Church, whom the figure of Mary represents.

The Second Vatican Council has solemnly taught that Mary is a "type" or symbol of the Church, for "in the mystery of the Church, which is itself rightly called mother and virgin, the Blessed Virgin stands out in eminent and singular fashion as exemplar both of virgin and mother. Through her faith and obedience she gave birth on earth to the very Son of the Father, not through the knowledge of man but by the overshadowing of the Holy Spirit, in the manner of a new Eve who placed her faith, not in the serpent of old but in God's messenger,

Is 66:7
Mic 4:10

Dan 7:7

Dan 8:10

out in her pangs of birth, in anguish for delivery. ³And another portent appeared in heaven; behold, a great red dragon, with seven heads and ten horns, and seven diadems upon his heads. ⁴His tail swept down a third of the stars of

clamat parturiens et cruciatur, ut pariat. ³Et visum est aliud signum in caelo: et

without wavering in doubt. The Son whom she brought forth is he whom God placed as the first-born among many brethren (cf. Rom 8:29), that is, the faithful, in whose generation and formation she cooperates with a mother's love" (Vatican II, *Lumen gentium*, 63).

The description of the woman indicates her heavenly glory, and the twelve stars of her victorious crown symbolize the people of God—the twelve patriarchs (cf. Gen 37:9) and the twelve apostles. And so, independently of the chronological aspects of the text, the Church sees in this heavenly woman the Blessed Virgin, "taken up body and soul into heavenly glory, when her earthly life was over, and exalted by the Lord as Queen over all things, that she might be the more fully conformed to her Son, the Lord of lords (cf. Rev 19:16) and conqueror of sin and death" (*Lumen gentium*, 59). The Blessed Virgin is indeed the great sign, for, as St Bonaventure says, "God could have made none greater. He could have made a greater world and a greater heaven; but not a woman greater than his own mother" (*Speculum*, 8).

3-4. In his description of the devil (cf. v. 9), St John uses symbols taken from the Old Testament. The dragon or serpent comes from Genesis 3:1-24, a passage which underlies all the latter half of this book. Its red colour and seven heads with seven diadems show that it is bringing its full force to bear to wage this war. The ten horns in Daniel 7:7 stand for the kings who are Israel's enemies; in Daniel a horn is also mentioned to refer to Antiochus IV Epiphanes, of whom Daniel also says (to emphasize the greatness of Antiochus' victories) that it cast stars down from heaven onto the earth (cf. Dan 8:10). Satan drags other angels along with him, as the text later recounts (Rev 12:9). All these symbols, then, are designed to convey the enormous power of Satan. "The devil is described as a serpent", St Cyprian writes, "because he moves silently and seems peaceable and comes by easy ways and is so astute and so deceptive [...] that he tries to have night taken for day, poison taken for medicine. So, by deceptions of this kind, he tries to destroy truth by cunning. That is why he passes himself off as an angel of light" (*De unitate Ecclesiae*, I-III).

After the fall of our first parents war broke out between the serpent and his seed and the woman and hers: "I will put enmity between you and the woman, between your seed and her seed; he shall bruise your head, and you shall bruise his heel" (Gen 3:15). Jesus Christ is the woman's descendant who will obtain victory over the devil (cf. Mk 1:23-26; Lk 4:31-37; etc.). That is why the power of evil concentrates all his energy on destroying Christ (cf. Mt 2:13-18) or deflecting him from his mission (cf. Mt 4:1-11 and par.). By relating this enmity to the beginnings of the human race St John paints a very vivid picture.

heaven, and cast them to the earth. And the dragon stood before the woman who was about to bear a child, that he might devour her child when she brought it forth; [5]she brought forth a male child, one who is to rule all the nations with a rod of iron, but her child was caught up to God and to his throne, [6]and the woman fled into the wilderness, where she has a place prepared by God, in which to be nourished for one thousand two hundred and sixty days.

Is 66:7
Ps 2:9
Rev 2:27

Hos 2:16

ecce draco rufus magnus, habens capita septem et cornua decem, et super capita sua septem diademata; [4]et cauda eius trahit tertiam partem stellarum caeli et misit eas in terram. Et draco stetit ante mulierem, quae erat paritura, ut, cum peperisset, filium eius devoraret. [5]Et peperit filium, masculum, qui *recturus est* omnes *gentes in virga ferrea*; et raptus est filius eius ad Deum et ad thronum eius. [6]Et mulier fugit in desertum, ubi habet locum paratum a Deo, ut ibi pascant

5. The birth of Jesus Christ brings into operation the divine plan announced by the prophets (cf. Is 66:7) and by the Psalms (cf. Ps 2:9), and marks the first step in ultimate victory over the devil. Jesus' life on earth, culminating in his passion, resurrection and ascension into heaven, was the key factor in achieving this victory. St John emphasises the triumph of Christ as victor, who, as the Church confesses, "sits at the right hand of the Father" (*Nicene-Constantino-politan Creed*).

6. The figure of the woman reminds us of the Church, the people of God. Israel took refuge in the wilderness to escape from Pharaoh, and the Church does the same after the victory of Christ. The wilderness stands for solitude and intimate union with God. In the wilderness God took personal care of his people, setting them free from their enemies (cf. Ex 17:8-16) and nourishing them with quail and manna (cf. Ex 16:1-36). The Church is given similar protection against the powers of hell (cf. Mt 16:18) and Christ nourishes it with his body and his word all the while it makes its pilgrimage through the ages; it has a hard time (like Israel in the wilderness) but there will be an end to it: it will take one thousand two hundred and sixty days (cf. notes on 11:3).

Although the woman, in this verse, seems to refer directly to the Church, she also in some way stands for the particular woman who gave birth to the Messiah, the Blessed Virgin. As no other creature has done, Mary has enjoyed a very unique type of union with God and very special protection from the powers of evil, death included. Thus, as the Second Vatican Council teaches, "in the meantime [while the Church makes its pilgrim way on earth], the Mother of Jesus in the glory which she possesses in body and soul in heaven is the image and beginning of the Church as it is to be perfected in the world to come. Likewise she shines forth on earth, until the day of the Lord shall come (cf. 2 Pet 3:10), a sign of certain hope and comfort to the pilgrim people of God" (*Lumen gentium*, 68).

Dan 10:31, 21; 12:1

Jn 12:31

[7]Now war arose in heaven, Michael and his angels fighting against the dragon; and the dragon and his angels fought, [8]but they were defeated and there was no longer any place for them in heaven. [9]And the great dragon was thrown

---

illam diebus mille ducentis sexaginta. [7]Et factum est proelium in caelo, Michael et angeli eius, ut proeliarentur cum dracone. Et draco pugnavit et angeli eius, [8]et non valuit, neque locus inventus est eorum amplius in caelo. [9]Et proiectus est draco ille magnus, serpens antiquus, qui vocatur Diabolus et Satanas, qui seducit universum orbem; proiectus est in terram, et angeli eius cum illo proiecti

7-9. The war between the dragon with his angels, and Michael and his, and the defeat of the former, are depicted as being closely connected with the death and glorification of Christ (cf. vv. 5, 11). The reference to Michael and the "ancient" serpent, and also the result of the battle (being cast down from heaven), reminds us of the origin of the devil. Once a most exalted creature, according to certain Jewish traditions (cf. *Latin Life of Adam and Eve*, 12-16) he became a devil because when God created man in his own image and likeness (cf. Gen 1:26; 2:7), he refused to acknowledge the dignity granted to man: Michael obeyed, but the devil and some other angels rebelled against God because they regarded man as beneath them. As a result the devil and his angelic followers were cast down to earth to be imprisoned in hell, which is why they ceaselessly tempt man, trying to make him sin so as to deprive him of the glory of God.

In the light of this tradition, the Book of Revelation emphasizes that Christ, the new Adam, true God and true man, through his glorification merits and receives the worship that is his due—which spells the total rout of the devil. God's design embraces both creation and redemption. Christ, "the image of the invisible God, the first-born of all creation; for in him all things were created" (Col 1:15-16), defeats the devil in a war which extends throughout human history; but the key stage in that war was the incarnation, death and glorification of our Lord: "Now is the judgment of this world," Jesus says, referring to those events; "now shall the ruler of this world be cast out; and I, when I am lifted up from earth, will draw all men to myself" (Jn 12:31-33). And, when his disciples come to him to tell him that demons were subject to his name, he exclaimed, "I saw Satan fall like lightning from heaven" (Lk 10:18).

In Daniel 10:13 and 12:1 we are told that it is the archangel Michael who defends the chosen people on God's behalf. His name means "Who like God?" and his mission is to guard the rights of God against those who would usurp them, be they human tyrants or Satan himself, who tried to make off with the body of Moses according to the Letter of St Jude (v. 9). This explains why St Michael appears in the Apocalypse as the one who confronts Satan, the ancient serpent, although the victory and punishment is decided by God or Christ. The Church, therefore, invokes St Michael as its guardian in adversity and its protector against the snares of the devil (cf. *The Liturgy of the Hours*, 29 September, office of readings).

down, that ancient serpent, who is called the Devil and Satan, the deceiver of the whole world—he was thrown down to the earth, and his angels were thrown down with him. [10]And I heard a loud voice in heaven, saying, "Now the salvation and the power and the kingdom of our God and the authority of his Christ have come, for the accuser

Lk 10:18
Gen 3:1, 14
Rev 20:2

Job 1:11
Lk 22:31
Mt 28:18
Rev 11:15

sunt. [10]Et audivi vocem magnam in caelo dicentem: "Nunc facta est salus et virtus et regnum Dei nostri et potestas Christi eius, quia proiectus est accusator fratrum nostrorum, qui accusabat illos ante conspectum Dei nostri die ac nocte.

The Fathers of the Church interpret these verses of the Apocalypse as a reference to the battle between Michael and the devil at the dawn of history, a battle which stemmed from the test which angelic spirits had to undergo. And, in the light of the Apocalypse, they interpret as referring to that climactic moment the words which the prophet Isaiah uttered against the king of Babylon: "How you are fallen from heaven, O Day Star, son of Dawn! How you are cut down to the ground, you who laid the nations low!" (Is 14:12). They also see this passage of the Apocalypse as referring to the war Satan wages against the Church throughout history, a war which will take on its most dreadful form at the end of time: "Heaven is the Church," St Gregory writes, "which in the night of this present life, the while it possesses in itself the countless virtues of the saints, shines like the radiant heavenly stars; but the dragon's tail sweeps the stars down to the earth [. . .]. The stars which fall from heaven are those who have lost hope in heavenly things and covet, under the devil's guidance, the sphere of earthly glory" (*Moralia*, 32, 13).

10-12. With the ascension of Christ into heaven the Kingdom of God is established and so all those who dwell in heaven break out into a song of joy. The devil has been deprived of his power over man in the sense that the redemptive action of Christ and man's faith enable man to escape from the world of sin. The text expresses this joyful truth by saying that there is now no place for the accuser, Satan, whose name means and whom the Old Testament teaches to be the accuser of men before God: cf. Job 1:6-12; 2:1-10). Given what God meant creation to be, Satan could claim as his victory anyone who, through sinning, disfigured the image and likeness of God that was in him. However, once the Redemption has taken place, Satan no longer has power to do this, for, as St John writes, "if any one does sin, we have an advocate with the Father, Jesus Christ the righteous; and he is the expiation for our sins, and not for ours only but also for the sins of the whole world" (Jn 2:1-2). Also, on ascending into heaven, Christ sent us the Holy Spirit as "Intercessor and Advocate, especially when men, that is, mankind, find themselves before the judgment of condemnation by that 'accuser' about whom the Book of Revelation says that 'he accuses them day and night before our God'" (John Paul II, *Dominum et Vivificantem*, 67).

of our brethren has been thrown down, who accuses them day and night before our God. [11]And they have conquered him by the blood of the Lamb and by the word of their testimony, for they loved not their lives even unto death.

[12]Rejoice then, O heaven and you that dwell therein! But woe to you, O earth and sea, for the devil has come down to you in great wrath, because he knows that his time is short!"

[13]And when the dragon saw that he had been thrown down to the earth, he pursued the woman who had borne the male child. [14]But the woman was given the two wings

---

[11]Et ipsi vicerunt illum propter sanguinem Agni et propter verbum testimonii sui; et non dilexerunt animam suam usque ad mortem. [12]Propterea laetamini, caeli et qui habitatis in eis. Vae terrae et mari, quia descendit Diabolus ad vos habens iram magnam, sciens quod modicum tempus habet!" [13]Et postquam vidit draco quod proiectus est in terram, persecutus est mulierem, quae peperit masculum. [14]Et datae sunt mulieri duae alae aquilae magnae, ut volaret in

---

Although Satan has lost this power to act in the world, he still has time left, between the resurrection of our Lord and the end of history, to put obstacles in man's way and frustrate Christ's action. And so he works ever more frenetically, as he sees time run out, in his effort to distance everyone and society itself from the plans and commandments of God.

The author of the Book of Revelation uses this celestial chant to warn the Church of the onset of danger as the End approaches.

13-17. In these verses the dragon's onslaught is seen in terms of the Church which suffers it. The woman who gives birth to a male child is an image of the Mother of the Messiah, the Blessed Virgin, and of the Church, who "faithfully fulfilling the Father's will, by receiving the word of God in faith becomes herself a mother" (*Lumen gentium*, 64). By means of the Church men become members of Christ and contribute to the growth of his body (cf. note on Eph 4:13). It is in this sense that we can speak of the Church as the woman who gives birth to Christ.

The struggle the Church maintains against the powers of evil is described here in terms of the Exodus (another time of great peril for the people of Israel). God brought the Israelites into the wilderness "on eagle's wings" (Ex 19:4), that is, by ways no man could devise. When the prophet Isaiah announces the liberation from captivity in Babylon he also says that "they shall mount up with wings like eagles" (Is 40:31). Throughout the course of history, the Church enjoys this same divine protection which enables her to have that intimacy with God symbolized by the wilderness. The period of "a time, and times and half a time", that is, three and a half years, is regarded as the conventional duration of any persecution, at least from Daniel 7:25 onwards.

of the great eagle that she might fly from the serpent into the wilderness, to the place where she is to be nourished for a time, and times, and half a time. ¹⁵The serpent poured water like a river out of his mouth after the woman, to sweep her away with the flood. ¹⁶But the earth came to the help of the woman, and the earth opened its mouth and swallowed the river which the dragon had poured from his mouth. ¹⁷Then the dragon was angry with the woman, and went off to make war on the rest of her offspring, on those who keep the commandments of God and bear testimony to Jesus. And he stoodᵉ on the sand of the sea.

Ex 19:4
Dan 7:25
Is 40:31

Num 16:32

Gen 3:15
1 Jn 5:10

---

desertum in locum suum, ubi alitur per tempus et tempora et dimidium temporis a facie serpentis. ¹⁵Et misit serpens ex ore suo post mulierem aquam tamquam flumen, ut eam faceret trahi a flumine. ¹⁶Et adiuvit terra mulierem, et aperuit terra os suum et absorbuit flumen, quod misit draco de ore suo. ¹⁷Et iratus est draco in mulierem et abiit facere proelium cum reliquis de semine eius, qui custodiunt mandata Dei et habent testimonium Iesu. ¹⁸Et stetit super arenam maris.

The river of water symbolizes the destructive forces of evil unleashed by the devil. Just as in the wilderness of Sinai the earth swallowed up those who rebelled against God (cf. Num 16:30-34), so will these forces be frustrated in their attack on the Church, for, as our Lord promised, "the powers of death [hell] shall not prevail against it" (Mt 16:18). "This is nothing new," Monsignor Escrivá comments. "Since Jesus Christ our Lord founded the Church, this Mother of ours has suffered constant persecution. In times past the attacks were delivered openly. Now, in many cases, persecution is disguised. But today, as yesterday, the Church continues to be buffeted from many sides" (*In Love with the Church*, 18).

The Church is holy, but those who make it up—Christians, "the rest of her offspring"—suffer the onslaught of the Evil One, who is unrelenting in his efforts to seduce them. That is why "the Christian is certainly bound both by need and by duty to struggle with evil through many afflictions and to suffer death; but, as one who has been made a partner in the paschal mystery, and as one who has been configured to the death of Christ he will go forward, strengthened by hope, to the resurrection" (Vatican II, *Gaudium et spes*, 22).

18. Most Greek manuscripts, but not the most important ones, give this verse in the first person singular: "And I stood" (cf. RSV note below), referring to the seer. The New Vulgate, however, prefers the third person, in which case the phrase refers to the dragon, who is thus depicted as causing the powers of evil (in the form of the beasts: 13:1) to emerge.

ᵉOther ancient authorities read *And I stood*, connecting the sentence with 13:1

13

The beasts given authority by the dragon

Rev 11:7; 17:3, 9, 12
Dan 7:3, 7
Dan 7:4-6

¹And I saw a beast rising out of the sea, with ten horns and seven heads, with ten diadems upon its horns and a blasphemous name upon its heads. ²And the beast that I saw was like a leopard, its feet were like a bear's, and its mouth was like a lion's mouth. And to it the dragon gave his power

---

¹Et vidi de mari bestiam ascendentem habentem cornua decem et capita septem, et super cornua eius decem diademata, et super capita eius nomina blasphemiae. ²Et bestia, quam vidi, similis erat pardo, et pedes eius sicut ursi, et os eius sicut

1-18. Satan, the ancient serpent, launches his attack via the beasts, whom he endows with his power (cf. vv. 2, 12). The beasts stand for those who in the course of history have embodied the powers of evil in one way or another. The first beast (vv. 1-10) symbolizes political power taken to such an extreme that it supplants God; the second (vv. 11-12), those forces of evil who defend, justify and propagate that deification of power by giving it an acceptable face. These beasts are, first, a reference to the Roman empire, but that empire is seen in turn as being the tool of a diabolical power which forever hovers over mankind and will become more virulent as the End approaches.

In his war against the woman's children, the devil in addition to himself attacking them one by one also avails of socio-political and cultural factors which usurp the position of the one true God: "Unfortunately, the resistance to the Holy Spirit which St Paul emphasizes in the *interior and subjective dimension* as tension, struggle and rebellion taking place in the human heart finds in every period and especially in the modern era its *external dimension*, which takes concrete form as the content of culture and civilization, as a *philosophical system, an ideology, a programme* for action and for the shaping of human behaviour. It reaches its clearest expression in *materialism*, both in its theoretical form—as a system of thought—and in its practical form—as a method of interpreting and evaluating facts, and likewise as a programme of corresponding conduct. The system which has developed most and carried to its extreme practical consequences this form of thought, ideology and praxis is dialectical and historical materialism, which is still recognized as the essential core of Marxism" (John Paul II, *Dominum et Vivificantem*, 56).

1-4. In his description of the first beast St John employs symbols used by the prophet Daniel to describe the various empires which overran Israel, particularly the successors of Alexander the Great (notably Antiochus Epiphanes); they are symbolized in the fourth beast of the prophet's vision (cf. Dan 7:7-8). In Jewish and Christian circles at the time when the Apocalypse was written, the fourth beast in the Book of Daniel was already bring reinterpreted as the Roman empire; and the author of the Book of Revelation

and his throne and great authority. ³One of its heads seemed
to have a mortal wound, but its mortal wound was healed,
and the whole earth followed the beast with wonder. ⁴Men
worshipped the dragon, for he had given his authority to the
beast, and they worshipped the beast, saying, "Who is like
the beast, and who can fight against it?"
    ⁵And the beast was given a mouth uttering haughty and
blasphemous words, and it was allowed to exercise authority for forty-two months; ⁶it opened its mouth to utter

Rev 17:8

Rev 12:7
2 Thess 2:4

Dan 7:8, 11, 25
Rev 11:2

---

os leonis. Et dedit illi draco virtutem suam et thronum suum et potestatem
magnam. ³Et unum de capitibus suis quasi occisum in mortem, et plaga mortis
eius curata est. Et admirata est universa terra post bestiam, ⁴et adoraverunt
draconem, quia dedit potestatem bestiae, et adoraverunt bestiam dicentes:
"Quis similis bestiae, et quis potest pugnare cum ea?" ⁵Et datum est ei os
loquens magna et blasphemias, et data est illi potestas facere menses quadra-

---

himself does this more explicitly when he says later that the seven heads and
ten horns are so many other emperors and kings (cf. Rev 17:9-12).

The wound on one of the heads may be a reference to some particular
political crisis, like the assassination of Julius Caesar or the disturbances which
followed the death of Nero and in the event came to nothing. The majority of
the Fathers see the beast as representing antichrist; St Irenaeus, for example,
writes: "The beast that rises up is the epitome of evil and falsehood, so that the
full force of apostasy which it embodies can be cast into the fiery furnace"
(*Against heresies*, 5, 29).

In any event, the sacred text is denouncing the sin of idolizing political
authority, as if it had divine attributes. The exclamation "Who is like the beast?"
is a kind of rejoinder to the meaning of the archangel Michael's name, "Who
like God?" It makes sense, then, that the description of the head of the beast is
the same as that of the serpent (cf. 12:3), showing they are undoubtedly
connected with one another. "Idolatry is an extreme form of disorder produced
by sin. The replacement of adoration of the living God by worship of created
things falsifies the relationships between individuals and brings with it various
kinds of oppression" (SCDF, *Libertatis conscientia*, 39).

5-8. The beast's blasphemous language and acts of violence show that his
power derives from Satan. He is active throughout the course of history—
forty-two months or three and a half years—and is present the world over. Only
those who by the grace of God acknowledge and follow Christ can avoid
worshipping the beast, that is, can resist political absolutism which has no place
for God or his law.

Christian faith is the great guarantor of true freedom: "The reality of the
depth of freedom has always been known to the Church, above all through the
lives of a multitude of the faithful, especially among the little ones and the poor.

blasphemies against God, blaspheming his name and his
Rev 11:7
Dan 7:21
dwelling, that is, those who dwell in heaven. [7]Also it was
allowed to make war on the saints and to conquer them.[f]
And authority was given it over every tribe and people and
Ps 69:29
Is 53:7
Rev 3:5
tongue and nation, [8]and all who dwell on earth will worship
it, every one whose name has not been written before the
foundation of the world in the book of life of the Lamb that
Mt 13:9
was slain. [9]If any one has an ear, let him hear:
Jer 15:2
Mt 26:52
Rev 14:12
[10]If any one is to be taken captive, to captivity he goes;
if any one slays with the sword, with the sword must he
be slain.

---

ginta duos. [6]Et aperuit os suum in blasphemias ad Deum, blasphemare nomen eius et tabernaculum eius, eos, qui in caelo habitant. [7]Et datum est illi bellum facere cum sanctis et vincere illos, et data est ei potestas super omnem tribum et populum et linguam et gentem. [8]Et adorabunt eum omnes, qui inhabitant terram, cuiuscumque non est scriptum nomen in libro vitae Agni, qui occisus est, ab origine mundi. [9]Si quis habet aurem, audiat: [10]*Si quis in captivitatem, in captivitatem* vadit; *si quis in gladio debet occidi*, oportet eum *in gladio* occidi.

In their faith, these latter know that they are the object of God's infinite love. Each of them can say: 'I live by faith in the Son of God, who loved me and gave himself for me' (Gal 2:20b). Such is the dignity which none of the powerful can take away from them: such is the liberating joy present in them" (SCDF, *Libertatis conscientia*, 21). And so it is that the Church, in the socio-political context, is "the sign and the safeguard of the transcendental dimension of the human person" (Vatican II, *Gaudium et spes*, 76).

9-10. Here, in an aside, St John addresses the reader directly, inviting him to recognize the contemporary truth of what he is revealing at God's command. The people to whom the book was originally addressed could see for themselves what happened when Satan's power was unleashed against the Church (it was the time of Domitian's persecution: A.D. 95-96). However, his invitation is addressed to everyone who reads the book, irrespective of what period of history they live in. We well know that "our age has seen the birth of totalitarian systems and forms of tyranny which would not have been possible in the time before the technological leap forward. On the one hand, technical expertise has been applied to acts of genocide. On the other, various minorities try to hold in thrall whole nations by the practice of terrorism. Today control can penetrate into the innermost life of individuals, and even the forms of dependence created by early-warning systems can represent potential threats of oppression" (SCDF, *Libertatis conscientia*, 14).

The Book of Revelation, using the words which Jeremiah addressed to

---

[f]Other ancient authorities omit this sentence

Here is a call for the endurance and faith of the saints.

The beast rising from out of the earth

[11]Then I saw another beast which rose out of the earth; it had two horns like a lamb and it spoke like a dragon. [12]It exercises all the authority of the first beast in its presence, and makes the earth and its inhabitants worship the first beast, whose mortal wound was healed. [13]It works great signs, even making fire come down from heaven to earth in the sight of men; [14]and by the signs which it is allowed to work in the presence of the beast, it deceives those who dwell on earth, bidding them make an image for the beast which was wounded by the sword and yet lived; [15]and it

Mt 7:15
Rev 16:13
Rev 13:3

Mt 24:24
2 Thess 2:9-10

Deut 13:2-4
Rev 19:20

Dan 3:5f

Hic est patientia et fides sanctorum. [11]Et vidi aliam bestiam ascendentem de terra, et habebat cornua duo similia agni, et loquebatur sicut draco. [12]Et potestatem prioris bestiae omnem facit in conspectu eius. Et facit terram et inhabitantes in ea adorare bestiam primam, cuius curata est plaga mortis. [13]Et facit signa magna, ut etiam ignem faciat de caelo descendere in terram in conspectu hominum. [14]Et seducit habitantes terram propter signa, quae data sunt illi facere in conspectu bestiae, dicens habitantibus in terra, ut faciant imaginem bestiae, quae habet plagam gladii et vixit. [15]Et datum est illi, ut daret

evildoers (cf. Jer 15:2; 43:11), applies them to the last times. St John thereby exhorts Christians to stiffen their resistance despite what persecution brings—to call on their resources of faith. "Suffering", says John Paul II commenting on Romans 5:3, "as it were contains a special *call to the virtue* which man must exercise on his own part. And this is the virtue of perseverance in bearing whatever disturbs and causes harm. In doing this, the individual unleashes hope, which maintains in him the conviction that suffering will not get the better of him, that it will not deprive him of his dignity as a human being" (*Salvific doloris*, 23).

11-17. Further on (cf. 16:13; 19:20 and notes), this second beast is identified with the false prophet because his role consists in leading men astray, getting them to worship the first beast. Because he has real (but evil) power he is able to work wonders similar to those performed by the prophets (for example, Elijah, who brought fire down from heaven: cf. 1 Kings 18:38) and can even seem to vie with the power of the life-giving Spirit by breathing life into the images of the beast. He is despotic in the extreme, depriving people of subsistence unless they submit to him and bear his mark. "The beast that rises from the earth stands for pride in earthly glory; and the fact that it has two horns like a lamb means that its hypocritical sanctity makes it appear to have wisdom, whereas only the Lord has true wisdom" (St Gregory the Great, *Moralia*, 33, 20).

was allowed to give breath to the image of the beast so that
the image of the beast should even speak, and to cause those
who would not worship the image of the beast to be slain.
[16]Also it causes all, both small and great, both rich and poor,
both free and slave, to be marked on the right hand or the
forehead, [17]so that no one can buy or sell unless he has the
mark, that is, the name of the beast or the number of its
name. [18]This calls for wisdom: let him who has under-
standing reckon the number of the beast, for it is a human
number, its number is six hundred and sixty-six.[g]

spiritum imagini bestiae, ut et loquatur imago bestiae et faciat, ut quicumque
non adoraverint imaginem bestiae, occidantur. [16]Et facit omnes pusillos et
magnos et divites et pauperes et liberos et servos accipere characterem in
dextera manu sua aut in frontibus suis, [17]et ne quis possit emere aut vendere,
nisi qui habet characterem, nomen bestiae aut numerum nominis eius. [18]Hic

We do not know if the author is referring to a specific individual (such as
the Asiarch who was charged with the fostering of emperor worship in Asia
Minor) or a group (such as the pagan priests who exercised and propagated that
cult). There is little doubt but that this beast is introduced in order to draw
attention to the political-religious implications of emperor worship and its consequences for Christians. Basically the beast is a symbol for regimes which
reject God and put man on a pedestal. Nowadays emperor worship is seldom a
problem but militant atheism has been a modern parallel whether in the form
of atheistic secularism or of dialectic materialism. St Hippolytus describes the
mark and seal of the beast in these words: "I reject the Creator of heaven and
earth; I reject Baptism; I refuse to worship God. To you [Beast] I adhere; in
you I believe" (*De consummat.*).

Materialism works in the same deceptive way as the beast does, for although
"it sometimes also speaks of the 'spirit' and of 'questions of the spirit', as for
example in the fields of culture or morality, it does so only insofar as it considers
certain facts as derived from matter (*epiphenomena*), since according to this
system matter is the one and only form of being. It follows, according to this
interpretation, that religion can only be understood as a kind of 'idealistic
illusion', to be fought with the most suitable means and methods according to
circumstances of time and place, in order to eliminate it from society and from
man's very heart" (John Paul II, *Dominum et Vivificantem*, 56).

18. The author of the Apocalypse here uses a method (called *gematria* in
Greek) to reveal the name of the beast in a numerical form. In both Hebrew and
Latin letters of the alphabet were also used as numbers. The figure 666 fits with
the name Caesar Nero in Hebrew. Some manuscripts gave the number as 616,
which fits Caesar Nero in Greek. However, Tradition does not provide an exact
interpretation and various other names have in fact been suggested.

[g]Other ancient authorities read *six hundred and sixteen*

14

The Lamb and his companions

¹Then I looked, and lo, on Mount Zion stood the Lamb, and with him a hundred and forty-four thousand who had his name and his Father's name written on their foreheads. ²And I heard a voice from heaven like the sound of many waters and like the sound of loud thunder; the voice I heard was like the sound of harpers playing on their harps, ³and

Ezek 9:4
Joel 3:5
Rev 7:4-5

Ezek 1:24; 43:2
Rev 1:15

---

sapientia est: qui habet intellectum, computet numerum bestiae; numerus enim hominis est: et numerus eius est sescenti sexaginta sex.
¹Et vidi: et ecce Agnus stans supra montem Sion, et cum illo centum quadraginta

---

14:1 - 16:21 The book now turns to the Lamb and to divine judgment (anticipating the victory of the Lamb). It stays with this theme up to chapter 17, at which point the powers of evil appear again (in various symbolic forms) and are subjected to the judgment of God. First we are shown the Lamb and his entourage (cf. 14:1-5); immediately after this the Last Judgment is proclaimed and a preliminary description given (14:6-20); the glory of the Lamb is again extolled (cf. 15:1-4) and the unleashing of the wrath of God is further described in terms of the pouring out of the seven bowls (cf. 15:5 - 16:21).

In opposition to the powers of evil and the active hostility to God and the Church caused by the machinations of Satan stand the risen Christ and his followers, who sing in praise of his glory and triumph. These followers are those who have attained redemption; the salvation will reach its climax when the Kingdom of God is fully established (the marriage of the Lamb, and the heavenly Jerusalem: chaps. 21-22). In the meantime, although the Church has to do battle with the forces of evil, it can contemplate Christ "as an innocent lamb (who) merited life for us by his blood which he freely shed. In him God reconciled us to himself and to one another, freeing us from the bondage of the devil and of sin, so that each one of us could say with the Apostle: the Son of God 'loved me and gave himself for me' (Gal 2:20)" (Vatican II, *Gaudium et spes*, 22).

1-3. It is highly significant that the Lamb stands on Mount Zion, in Jerusalem, which was where God dwelt among men according to the Old Testament (cf. Ps 74:1; 132:14; etc.) and where, according to certain Jewish traditions, the Messiah would appear, to join all his followers. The assembly, then, is an idealization of the Church, protected by Christ and gathered about him. It includes all those who belong to Christ and to the Father and who therefore bear their mark, which shows them to be children of God. They are so many that it is impossible to count them, but their number is complete: they are given a symbolic number which is 12 (the tribes of Israel) by 12 (the Apostles) by 1000 (a number indicating a huge scale): cf. Rev 7:3ff.

Ps 33:3; 40:4;
98:1; 144:9;
149:1
Is 42:10
Rev 5:9

Jas 1:18
1 Cor 7;24
Rev 5:9

Ps 32:2
Is 53:9
Zeph 3:13

they sing a new song before the throne and before the four living creatures and before the elders. No one could learn that song except the hundred and forty-four thousand who had been redeemed from the earth. [4]It is these who have not defiled themselves with women, for they are chaste;[h] it is these who follow the Lamb wherever he goes; these have been redeemed from mankind as first fruits for God and the Lamb, [5]and in their mouth no lie was found, for they are spotless.

quattuor milia, habentes nomen eius et nomen Patris eius scriptum in frontibus suis. [2]Et audivi vocem de caelo tamquam vocem aquarum multarum et tamquam vocem tonitrui magni; et vox, quam audivi, sicut citharoedorum citharizantium in citharis suis. [3]Et cantant quasi canticum novum ante thronum et ante quattuor animalia et seniores. Et nemo poterat discere canticum nisi illa centum quadraginta quattuor milia, qui empti sunt de terra. [4]Hi sunt qui cum mulieribus

The one hundred and forty-four thousand are not yet in heaven (for the loud noise comes from heaven); they are on earth, but they have been rescued from the power of the beast (cf. 13:13-14). The voice from heaven symbolizes the strength and power of God; and the heavenly voice speaks with the gentleness of liturgical music. It is a new song, for it now sings of the salvation wrought by Christ (cf. 15:3-4) in the same style as the Old Testament chants the praises of God (cf., e.g., Ps 33:3; 40:2; 96:1). Only those who belong to Christ can join in this song and be associated with the heavenly liturgy: "It is especially in the sacred liturgy that our union with the heavenly Church is best realized; in the liturgy, through the sacramental signs, the power of the Holy Spirit acts on us, and with community rejoicing we celebrate together the praise of the divine majesty; when all those of every tribe and tongue and people and nation (cf. Rev 5:9) who have been redeemed by the blood of Christ and gathered together into one Church glorify, in one common song of praise, the one and triune God" (*Lumen gentium*, 50).

4-5. The text refers to those who are properly disposed to take part in the marriage supper of the Lamb (cf. 19:9; 21:2) because they have not been stained by idolatry but have kept themselves undefiled for him. St Paul compares every Christian to a chaste virgin (cf. 2 Cor 11:2) and describes the Church as the spouse of Christ (cf. Eph 5:21-32). The author of the Apocalypse is referring to all the members of the Church insofar as they are holy, that is, called to holiness; but the symbolism he uses also draws attention to the fact that virginity and celibacy for the sake of the Kingdom of heaven is a special expression and clear sign of the Church as Bride of Christ. Referring to the chastity practised by religious, the Second Vatican Council teaches that in this way they "recall that wonderful marriage made by God, which will be fully manifested in the

[h]Greek *virgins*

Proclamation and symbols of the Judgment

⁶Then I saw another angel flying in midheaven, with an eternal gospel to proclaim to those who dwell on earth, to every nation and tribe and tongue and people; ⁷and he said with a loud voice, "Fear God and give him glory, for the hour of his judgment has come; and worship him who made heaven and earth, the sea and the fountains of water."

Rev 8:13

Ex 20:11
Mt 10:28

non sunt coinquinati, virgines enim sunt. Hi qui sequuntur Agnum, quocumque abierit. Hi empti sunt ex hominibus primitiae Deo et Agno; ⁵et in ore ipsorum non est inventum mendacium: sine macula sunt. ⁶Et vidi alterum angelum volantem per medium caelum, habentem evangelium aeternum ut evangelizaret super sedentes in terra et super omnem gentem et tribum et linguam et populum,

future age, and in which the Church has Christ for her only spouse" (*Perfectae caritatis*, 12).

The one hundred and forty-four thousand are also those who have identified themselves fully with Christ, dead and risen, by denying themselves and devoting all their energies to apostolate (cf. Mt 10:38). They also stand for those whom Christ, by the shedding of his blood, has made his own and his Father's property (like Israel, the first fruits of Yahweh: cf. Jer 2:3), that is, those who constitute a holy people like that remnant of Israel described in Zephaniah 3:13: "they shall do no wrong and utter no lies, nor shall there be found in their mouth a deceitful tongue." The prophet's words refer to people who have not invoked false gods, but the Apocalypse applies them to those who are fully committed to Christ.

6-20. Christ comes in victory at the end of time (the Parousia) to judge all mankind. In this passage, which is a general call to conversion, that judgment is solemnly announced in a scenario in which seven personages appear—three angels who proclaim the judgment (cf. vv. 6, 8, 9), the Son of man who delivers it (v. 14), and three more angels charged with implementing it (vv. 15, 17, 19): God's decision is final and it affects all mankind.

The Church warns us that "since we know neither the day nor the hour, we should follow the advice of the Lord and watch constantly so that, when the single course of our earthly life is completed (cf. Heb 9:27), we may merit to enter with him into the marriage feast and be numbered among the blessed (cf. Mt 25:31-46) [. . .]. Before we reign with Christ in glory we must all appear 'before the judgment seat of Christ, so that each one may receive good or evil, according to what he has done in the body' (2 Cor 5:10), and at the end of the world 'they will come forth, those who have done good, to the resurrection of life, and those who have done evil, to the resurrection of judgment' (Jn 5:29; cf. Mt 25:46)" (*Lumen gentium*, 48).

6-7. "Another angel": this tells us that this angel is not one of those who blew the trumpets (cf. 11:15), and yet is one of the same series of divine

111

Dan 4:27
Jer 51:7, 8
Is 21:9
Rev 18:2-3

Rev 13:15-17

Is 51:17
Ps 75:9
Gen 19:24
Ezek 38:22
Jer 25:15
Rev 16:19; 19:20

⁸Another angel, a second, followed, saying, "Fallen, fallen is Babylon the great, she who made all nations drink the wine of her impure passion."

⁹And another angel, a third, followed them, saying with a loud voice, "If any one worships the beast and its image, and receives a mark on his forehead or on his hand, ¹⁰he also shall drink the wine of God's wrath, poured unmixed into the cup of his anger, and he shall be tormented with fire and brimstone in the presence of the holy angels and in the presence of the Lamb. ¹¹And the smoke of their torment

---

⁷dicens magna voce: "Timete Deum et date illi gloriam, quia venit hora iudicii eius, et adorate eum, qui fecit caelum et terram et mare et fontes aquarum." ⁸Et alius angelus secutus est dicens: "Cecidit, cecidit Babylon illa magna, quae a vino irae fornicationis suae potionavit omnes gentes!" ⁹Et alius angelus tertius secutus est illos dicens voce magna: "Si quis adoraverit bestiam et imaginem eius et acceperit characterem in fronte sua aut in manu sua, ¹⁰et hic bibet de vino irae Dei, quod mixtum est mero in calice irae ipsius, et cruciabitur igne et sulphure in conspectu angelorum sanctorum et ante conspectum Agni. ¹¹Et

---

messengers that will be sent at the last times. He delivers his message from "midheaven" so that it can be heard by all who dwell on earth. It is a call to acknowledge and worship God as Creator of all things; this presupposes, therefore, that man can "know and love his creator" (*Gaudium et spes*, 12). And the proclamation is described as "an eternal Gospel" because man's acknowledgment of God will be ratified and rewarded on the Day of Judgment and will therefore be valid for ever (cf. Acts 14:15ff; 1 Thess 1:9).

8. Viewed from the perspective of the end of time, the downfall of the Church's enemy is seen as an accomplished fact. Absolutist and pagan Rome insisted on everyone worshipping the emperor; those who conformed earned God's anger. Rome is called "Babylon the great" because ever since the deportation of the Jews to that ancient city in 587 B.C. it had symbolized pagan power hostile to the people of God.

9-11. This passage predicts and describes the punishment to be inflicted on those who worship the beast, that is, those who submit to false gods. The "fire and brimstone", deriving from Genesis 19:24, indicates the horrific nature of the punishment: it will be like that suffered by Sodom and Gomorrah but it will be everlasting and will take place in the presence of the Lamb and his angels.

Eternal punishment of the damned and eternal reward of the elect is a dogma of faith, solemnly defined by the Magisterium in the Fourth Lateran Council: "[Christ] will come at the end of the world; he will judge the living and the dead; and he will reward all, both the damned and the elect, according to their works. And all these will rise from their own bodies which they now have so

goes up for ever and ever; and they have no rest, day or night, these worshippers of the beast and its image, and whoever receives the mark of its name." Is 34:9-10 Rev 19:3; 13:16

¹²Here is a call for the endurance of the saints, those who keep the commandments of God and the faith of Jesus. Rev 12:17

¹³And I heard a voice from heaven saying, "Write this:

---

fumus tormentorum eorum in saecula saeculorum ascendit, nec habent requiem die ac nocte, qui adoraverunt bestiam et imaginem eius, et si quis acceperit characterem nominis eius." ¹²Hic patientia sanctorum est, qui custodiunt mandata Dei et fidem Iesu. ¹³Et audivi vocem de caelo dicentem: "Scribe: Beati

---

that they may receive according to their works, whether good or bad; the wicked, a perpetual punishment with the devil; the good, eternal glory with Christ" (*De fide catholica*, chap. 1).

The punishment suffered in hell will be both spiritual (permanent unhappiness) and physical (pain), because man is made up of spirit and matter. We do not know what form hell takes; however, from what the Book of Revelation says here and from other passages of Sacred Scripture (cf., e.g. Mt 25:41) we can deduce that it involves both pain of loss (of God and eternal happiness) and physical suffering.

12. As in Revelation 13:10, the faithful are exhorted to stand firm in the midst of tribulation, confident in the hope that God will reward each according to his merits. Patience of that type does not mean that one should retreat before the powers of evil or fail to try to secure and guarantee "the conditions needed for the exercise of an authentic Christian freedom" (SCDF, *Libertatis conscientia*, 31). In this connexion the Second Vatican Council teaches: "Far from diminishing our concern to develop this earth, the expectancy of a new earth should spur us on, for it is here that the body of a new human family grows, foreshadowing in some way the age which is to come" (*Gaudium et spes*, 39).

In this passage of the book Christians are told that, in their efforts to deal with the particular persecution which was going on at the time, they should never answer with violence. This teaching always applies where the kind of liberation one is claiming is a temporal one: "Christ has commanded us to love our enemies (cf. Mt 5:44; Lk 6:27-28, 35). Liberation in the spirit of the Gospel is therefore incompatible with hatred of others, taken individually or collectively, and this includes hatred of one's enemy" (SCDF, *Libertatis conscientia*, 77).

13. God's blessing proclaims the joy of those who stay true to Christ to death. Jewish rabbis taught that "when a man dies, neither silver nor gold, neither precious stones nor pearls, follow him, but rather the law and good works" (*Pirqe Abhoth*, 6, 9). It is not simply that the righteous are rewarded for their works but that these works (in some way) stay with them; as the Church

Is 57:2
Heb 4:10
Mt 11:28-29

Blessed are the dead who die in the Lord henceforth."
"Blessed indeed," says the Spirit, "that they may rest from
their labours, for their deeds follow them!"

The harvest and the vintage

Dan 7:13; 10:16
Mt 13:39, 41

¹⁴Then I looked, and lo, a white cloud, and seated on the
cloud one like a son of man, with a golden crown on his

Joel 4:13
Mk 4:29
Jn 4:35

head, and a sharp sickle in his hand. ¹⁵And another angel
came out of the temple, calling with a loud voice to him
who sat upon the cloud, "Put in your sickle, and reap, for
the hour to reap has come, for the harvest of the earth is
fully ripe." ¹⁶So he who sat upon the cloud swung his sickle
on the earth, and the earth was reaped.

---

mortui, qui in Domino moriuntur amodo. Etiam, dicit Spiritus, ut requiescant
a laboribus suis; opera enim illorum sequuntur illos." ¹⁴Et vidi: et ecce nubem
candidam, et supra nubem sedentem quasi Filium hominis, habentem super
caput suum coronam auream et in manu sua falcem acutam. ¹⁵Et alter angelus
exivit de templo clamans voce magna ad sedentem super nubem: "Mitte falcem
tuam et mete, quia venit hora, ut metatur, quoniam aruit messis terrae." ¹⁶Et
misit, qui sedebat supra nubem, falcem suam in terram, et messa est terra. ¹⁷Et
alius angelus exivit de templo, quod est in caelo, habens et ipse falcem acutam.

---

teaches, "when we have spread on earth the fruits of our nature and our
enterprise—human dignity, brotherly communion, and freedom—according to
the command of the Lord and in his Spirit, we will find them once again,
cleansed this time from the stain of sin, illuminated and transfigured, when
Christ presents to his Father an eternal and universal kingdom of truth and life,
a kingdom of holiness and grace, a kingdom of justice, love and peace"
(*Gaudium et spes*, 39).

Death, understood in this way, is not the end but rather a transition, a step;
St Bernard compares it to Easter: "The unfortunate unbelievers call it death—
this step into life—but how can believers call it anything other than Easter? For
one dies to the world in order to live completely for God. One enters the precinct
of the marvellous tabernacle, the house of God" (*Divini amoris*, chap. 15).

14-20. This preliminary description of the Last Judgment is given in two
scenes—the harvest (cf. 14:14- 16) and the vintage (cf. 14:17-20)—no doubt
following the prophecy of Joel about how God will judge nations hostile to
Israel: "Let the nations bestir themselves, and come up to the valley of
Jehoshaphat; for there I shall sit to judge all the nations round about. Put in the
sickle, for the harvest is ripe. Go in, tread, for the wine press is full" (Joel
3:12-13).

In the first scene Christ himself appears, described as "son of man" (cf. Dan

[17]And another angel came out of the temple in heaven, and he too had a sharp sickle. [18]Then another angel came out from the altar, the angel who has power over fire, and he called with a loud voice to him who had the sharp sickle, "Put in your sickle, and gather the clusters of the vine of the earth, for its grapes are ripe." [19]So the angel swung his sickle on the earth and gathered the vintage of the earth, and threw it into the great wine press of the wrath of God; [20]and the wine press was trodden outside the city, and blood flowed from the wine press, as high as a horse's bridle, for one thousand six hundred stadia.[i]

Rev 6:9; 8:3-5
Joel 4:13

Rev 19:15

Is 63:3

---

[18]Et alius angelus de altari, habens potestatem supra ignem, et clamavit voce magna ad eum, qui habebat falcem acutam, dicens: "Mitte falcem tuam acutam et vindemia botros vineae terrae, quoniam maturae sunt uvae eius." [19]Et misit angelus falcem suam in terram et vindemiavit vineam terrae et misit in lacum irae Dei magnum. [20]Et calcatus est lacus extra civitatem, et exivit sanguis de lacu usque ad frenos equorum per stadia mille sescenta.

7:13); it is he who will deliver the judgment (symbolized by the harvest), as in the parable of the wheat and the weeds (cf. Mt 13:24-30). In the second it is an angel sent by God who gathers the grapes and puts them in the press to be trodden on either by God (in keeping with the prophecy of Isaiah 63:3, which says, "I have trodden the wine press alone") or by Christ (as we are told later in Revelation 19:15). In either case we are being told that Jesus Christ, true God and true man, has been empowered to perform the General Judgment which, according to Jewish tradition, will take place at the gates of Jerusalem (cf., e.g., Zech 14:4) and which involves a huge bloodbath (cf. Rev 14:20).

In both scenes, an angel has the prominent role of giving the order (cf. vv. 15, 18). The fact that he comes out from the temple and the altar shows that the outcome is linked to the prayers of the saints and martyrs, which stir Christ to take action (cf. Rev 8:3-4). So it is that the moment Christ is made present on the altar through the consecration of the bread and wine the Church calls for him to come again—calls for his second coming, the Parousia, which will make his victory complete: "When we eat this bread and drink this cup, we proclaim your death, Lord Jesus, until you come in glory" (*Roman Missal*, eucharistic acclamation).

[i]About two hundred miles

15

The hymn of the saved

Lev 26:21
Rev 16:17

¹Then I saw another portent in heaven, great and wonderful, seven angels with seven plagues, which are the last, for with them the wrath of God is ended.

Rev 13:15, 18

²And I saw what appeared to be a sea of glass mingled with fire, and those who had conquered the beast and its image and the number of its name, standing beside the sea of glass with harps of God in their hands. ³And they sing

---

¹Et vidi aliud signum in caelo magnum et mirabile: angelos septem habentes plagas septem novissimas, quoniam in illis consummata est ira Dei. ²Et vidi tamquam mare vitreum mixtum igne et eos, qui vicerunt bestiam et imaginem illius et numerum nominis eius, stantes supra mare vitreum, habentes citharas Dei. ³Et cantant canticum Moysis servi Dei et canticum Agni dicentes: "Magna

---

1. The third portent (cf. the first two in 12:1, 3) is of special significance—it is "great and wonderful"—for it heralds the final outcome of the contention between the beasts and the followers of the Lamb, between the powers of evil and the Church of Jesus Christ. That this is the denouement is shown by the use of the figure seven for a third time, after the seven seals (5:1) and the seven trumpets (cf. Rev 8:2). This is the last word: "the wrath of God is ended."

As in the case of the two earlier groups of seven, the author first announces the sevenfold nature of the sign. It consists of seven plagues—which immediately recall the punishments God inflicted on Pharaoh in Egypt prior to the Exodus. Then follows a very liturgical type of scene (15:2-8) which as it were encourages and calls for the divine judgments which follow (cf. 16:1-17). The last of these plagues acts as an introduction to the account of the last battles and total victory of the Church (cf. chaps. 17-22).

2-4. The image of the sea of glass mixed with fire is somewhat reminiscent of the passage of the Red Sea during the Exodus. On that occasion, according to the Book of Wisdom (cf. Wis 19:6-22), natural elements were changed to enable the Israelites to walk on water: the water became as hard as glass for the Israelites whereas for the Egyptians it was unable to protect them from the fire sent to punish them. The sea of glass may also be evocative of the molten sea (used for the cleansing of those going to take part in temple rites) which was positioned in front of the Holy of Holies (cf. note on Rev 4:6-7). In any event, the author depicts the saved as giving thanks and praising God while entoning a hymn which fuses the salvation of the Israelites with the Redemption wrought by Christ. The latter is the full realization of the former, and God's plan is seen to embrace all men and all nations (cf. v. 4; Eph 3:4-7). For this reason some early Christian writers (Primasius, for example) interpret the sea

the song of Moses, the servant of God, and the song of the
Lamb, saying,

   "Great and wonderful are thy deeds,
   O Lord God the Almighty!
   Just and true are thy ways,
   O King of the ages!ʲ
   ⁴Who shall not fear and glorify thy name, O Lord?
   For thou alone art holy.
   All nations shall come and worship thee,
   for thy judgments have been revealed."

The seven bowls of plagues

⁵After this I looked, and the temple of the tent of witness in heaven was opened, ⁶and out of the temple came the

---

et mirabilia opera tua, Domine, Deus omnipotens; iustae et verae viae tuae, Rex gentium! ⁴Quis non timebit, Domine, et glorificabit nomen tuum? Quia solus Sanctus, quoniam omnes gentes venient et adorabunt in conspectu tuo, quoniam iudicia tua manifestata sunt." ⁵Et post haec vidi: et apertum est templum tabernaculi testimonii in caelo, ⁶et exierunt septem angeli habentes septem

---

of glass as a symbol of Baptism (prefigured in the Red Sea) which makes Christians pure and transparent. The reference to fire signifies the gift of the Holy Spirit (cf. *Commentariorum super Apoc.*, 15, 2).

Every saving action of God has ultimately a supernatural purpose, even though it may include noble human aims, for when "God rescues his people from hard economic, political and cultural slavery, he does so in order to make them, through the Covenant on Sinai, 'a kingdom of priests and a holy nation' (Ex 19:6). God wishes to be adored by people who are free. All the subsequent liberations of the people of Israel help to lead them to this full liberty that they can only find in communion with their God" (SCDF, *Libertatis conscientia*, 44).

5-8. The text now goes on to describe the divine intervention which is as it were a response to this hymn of praise; its language is very similar to that used in connexion with the blowing of the seventh trumpet (cf. 11:19). This helps to link up the two passages. The difference is that the tent of witness now takes the place of the Ark of the Covenant. Both tent and ark were supposed to remain hidden until the advent of the messianic times (cf. 2 Mac 2:4-8); once they were rediscovered, the glory of God would make itself manifest again, as happened when the temple of Solomon was dedicated. The cloud of smoke (a symbol of the glory of the Lord) meant that the priests were unable to perform their ministry (cf. 1 Kings 8:10-11).

ʲOther ancient authorities read *the nations*

Lev 26:21
Rev 19:8

Rev 14:10

Ex 40:34
1 Kings 8:10
Is 6:4
Ez 44:4

seven angels with the seven plagues, robed in pure bright linen, and their breasts girded with golden girdles. [7]And one of the four living creatures gave the seven angels seven golden bowls full of the wrath of God who lives for ever and ever; [8]and the temple was filled with smoke from the glory of God and from his power, and no one could enter the temple until the seven plagues of the seven angels were ended.

---

plagas de templo, vestiti lino mundo candido et praecincti circa pectora zonis aureis. [7]Et unum ex quattuor animalibus dedit septem angelis septem phialas aureas plenas iracundiae Dei viventis in saecula saeculorum. [8]Et impletum est templum fumo de gloria Dei et de virtute eius, et nemo poterat introire in templum, donec consummarentur septem plagae septem angelorum.

The appearing of the tent signals that God's design is about to be fully realized. The author is telling us that the Parousia is imminent; he will describe it further on.

Because the seven golden bowls are used to cast the plagues on the earth, they are said to be full of the wrath of God: in other words, they are filled with divine justice, as will now be made manifest to all. The bowls, then, symbolize both the prayers of the saints (which have caused God to intervene: cf. note on 5:8) and the effects of those prayers—the victory of good and the punishment of evil. Strictly speaking the *bowls* symbolize the prayers of the saints; their *content* is not the plagues as such but the outcome of prayer—action on God's part which serves to console the righteous (the perfume of incense) and punish the followers of the beast, those who work iniquity (the wrath of God).

16

¹Then I heard a loud voice from the temple telling the seven angels, "Go and pour out on the earth the seven bowls of the wrath of God."

Is 66:6
Ps 69:25
Jer 10:25
Rev 8:6-12

---

¹Et audivi vocem magnam de templo dicentem septem angelis: "Ite et effundite

---

1. The events which result from the pouring out of the seven bowls of the wrath of God are depicted in the same kind of system as used in connexion with the seven trumpet blasts. In both cases the imagery is inspired by the plagues of Egypt; the first four actions have to do with the elements of nature (cf. 16:2-9, paralleling 8:6-12), the fifth and sixth with historical forces (cf. 16:10-16 and 9:1-21), and the seventh with the final climax. The main difference lies in the fact that whereas previously only a third of everything was affected, here it is everything—signifying that divine intervention is on the increase right up to the End.

The fury of God's anger expresses itself in various evils which overtake mankind; God is not their direct cause; he allows them to occur, in the hope that men will turn back to him. These evils are the result of sin, and God's wrath expresses itself in fact by his allowing men to follow the desires of their idolatrous hearts (as St Paul explains in Romans 1:18-32). As history advances, the signs are that sin is on the increase; sin is the ultimate cause of the new plagues which can be seen in the world today. "It must be added", John Paul II writes, "that on the horizon of contemporary civilization—especially in the form that is most developed in the technical and scientific sense—*the signs and symptoms of death* have become particularly present and frequent. One has only to think of the arms race and of its inherent danger of nuclear self-destruction. Moreover, everyone has become more and more aware of the grave situation of vast areas of our planet, marked by death-dealing poverty and famine. It is a question of problems that are not only economic but also and above all ethical. But on the horizon of our era there are gathering ever darker 'signs of death': a custom has become widely established—in some places it threatens to become almost an institution—of taking the lives of human beings even before they are born, or before they reach the natural point of death" (*Dominum et Vivificantem*, 57).

2-9. The author uses the plagues of Egypt writ large to show how terrifying are the evils which will overtake mankind because of its failure to turn to God. Creation itself, through the words of the angel, acknowledges the justice of this punishment, as do the true worshippers of God symbolized by the altar (cf. vv. 5-7).

The whole scenario shows how nature turns against man to threaten him with total destruction. Although the imagery and language used here seem somewhat strange to us, the text does act as a warning for all generations,

Ex 9:10-11
Deut 28:35
Rev 13:15-17

²So the first angel went and poured his bowl on the earth, and foul and evil sores came upon the men who bore the mark of the beast and worshipped its image.

Ex 7:19-24
Rev 8:8

³The second angel poured his bowl into the sea, and it became like the blood of a dead man, and every living thing died that was in the sea.

Rev 8:10
Ps 78:44

⁴The third angel poured his bowl into the rivers and the fountains of water, and they became blood. ⁵And I heard

Ps 119:137;
145:17
Ex 3:14

the angel of water say,

"Just art thou in these thy judgments, thou who art and wast, O Holy One.

Ps 79:3
Rev 18:24

⁶For men have shed the blood of saints and prophets, and thou hast given them blood to drink.
It is their due!"

Ps 19:10;
119:137
Rev 19:2

⁷And I heard the altar cry,
"Yea, Lord God the Almighty,
true and just are thy judgments!"

⁸The fourth angel poured his bowl on the sun, and it was

Rev 9:20-21
Amos 4:11

allowed to scorch men with fire; ⁹men were scorched by the fierce heat, and they cursed the name of God who had power over these plagues, and they did not repent and give him glory.

---

septem phialas irae Dei in terram." ²Et abiit primus et effudit phialam suam in terram; et factum est vulnus saevum ac pessimum in homines, qui habebant characterem bestiae, et eos, qui adorabant imaginem eius. ³Et secundus effudit phialam suam in mare; et factus est sanguis tamquam mortui, et omnis anima vivens mortua est, quae est in mari. ⁴Et tertius effudit phialam suam in flumina et in fontes aquarum; et factus est sanguis. ⁵Et audivi angelum aquarum dicentem: "Iustus es, qui es et qui eras, Sanctus, quia haec iudicasti, ⁶quia sanguinem sanctorum et prophetarum fuderunt, et sanguinem eis dedisti bibere: digni sunt!" ⁷Et audivi altare dicens: "Etiam, Domine, Deus omnipotens, vera et iusta iudicia tua!" ⁸Et quartus effudit phialam suam in solem; et datum est

---

including our own. Thus, as John Paul II points out, the "second half of our century, in its turn, brings with it—*as though in proportion to the mistakes and transgressions* of our contemporary civilization—such a horrible threat of nuclear war that we cannot think of this period except in terms of *an incomparable accumulation of sufferings*, even to the possible self-destruction of humanity" (*Salvifici doloris*, 8).

The Book of Revelation views these events from the vantage-point of the end of time: God has already intervened radically, making himself manifest once and for all (this is why he is called "thou who art and wast"), performing

¹⁰The fifth angel poured his bowl on the throne of the beast, and its kingdom was in darkness; men gnawed their tongues in anguish ¹¹and cursed the God of heaven for their pain and sores, and did not repent of their deeds.

¹²The sixth angel poured his bowl on the great river Euphrates, and its water was dried up, to prepare the way for the kings from the east. ¹³And I saw, issuing from the mouth of the dragon and from the mouth of the beast and from the mouth of the false prophet, three foul spirits like

Ex 10:21
Is 8:21-22

Gen 15:18
Deut 1:7
Josh 1:4
Rev 9:14

Ex 8:3
Rev 12:9; 13:1, 11

---

illi aestu afficere homines in igne. ⁹Et aestuaverunt homines aestu magno et blasphemaverunt nomen Dei habentis potestatem super has plagas et non egerunt paenitentiam, ut darent illi gloriam. ¹⁰Et quintus effudit phialam suam super thronum bestiae; et factum est regnum eius tenebrosum, et commanducaverunt linguas suas prae dolore ¹¹et blasphemaverunt Deum caeli prae doloribus suis et vulneribus suis et non egerunt paenitentiam ex operibus suis. ¹²Et sextus effudit phialam suam super flumen illud magnum Euphratem; et exsiccata est aqua eius, ut praepararetur via regibus, qui sunt ab ortu solis. ¹³Et

---

prodigious actions and giving men the opportunity of conversion. The panorama provides no room for superficial optimism; it gives a stark warning of what will happen to those who are unfaithful and who fail to respond to grace (cf. v. 9).

10-11. The beast is the same "star fallen from heaven to earth" and now shut up in the depths of the abyss as first appeared at the blowing of the fifth trumpet (cf. note on Rev 9:1-2). The meaning of human life which the beast proposes, the savagery with which it vents its fury on the Church, is now exposed as total meaninglessness which leads man to despair. As time goes on, it becomes clearer and clearer that when "man wishes to free himself from the moral law and become independent of God, far from gaining his freedom he destroys it. Escaping the measuring rod of truth, he falls prey to the arbitrary; fraternal relations between people are abolished and give place to terror, hatred and fear" (SCDF, *Libertatis conscientia*, 19).

12-16. The kings from the east, the Parthians, were the great threat to the Roman empire in John's time; here, paralleling the description of the sixth trumpet blast (cf. Rev 9:14) they stand for immense, terrifying power. Joining forces with the kings the world over, they will be marshalled by the powers of evil which derive from Satan (the dragon), the beast and the false prophet. These "three foul spirits" (v. 13) constitute a kind of blasphemous counterpoint to the Blessed Trinity.

The assembling of the kings of the whole world marks the climax of the final victory of Christ, which will take place when the seventh bowl is poured out; at that point his enemies will be routed in reverse order—first the kings (cf.

Rev 13:13;
19:19

1 Thess 5:2
Rev 3:3, 18

2 Kings 23:29
Zech 12:11

Is 66:6
Rev 21:6

frogs; [14]for they are demonic spirits, performing signs, who go abroad to the kings of the whole world, to assemble them for battle on the great day of God the Almighty. [15]("Lo, I am coming like a thief! Blessed is he who is awake, keeping his garments that he may not go naked and be seen exposed!") [16]And they assembled them at the place which is called in Hebrew Armageddon.

[17]The seventh angel poured his bowl into the air, and a

vidi de ore draconis et de ore bestiae et de ore pseudoprophetae spiritus tres immundos velut ranas: [14]sunt enim spiritus daemoniorum facientes signa, qui procedunt ad reges universi orbis congregare illos in proelium diei magni Dei omnipotentis. [15]Ecce venio sicut fur. Beatus, qui vigilat et custodit vestimenta sua, ne nudus ambulet, et videant turpitudinem eius. [16]Et congregavit illos in locum, qui vocatur Hebraice Harmagedon. [17]Et septimus effudit phialam suam

19:18), then the beast and the false prophet (cf. 19:20), and finally the Devil (cf. 20:10). Then the words of Psalm 2 will find their complete fulfilment: "The kings of the earth set themselves, and the rulers take counsel together, against the Lord and his anointed [. . .]. You shall break them with a rod of iron, and dash them to pieces like a potter's vessel" (Ps 2:3, 9). "That is a strong promise, and it is God who makes it. We cannot tone it down. Not for nothing is Christ the Redeemer of the world; he rules as sovereign, at the right hand of the Father. It is a terrifying announcement of what awaits each man when life is over—for over it will be. When history comes to an end, it will be the lot of all those whose hearts have been hardened by evil and despair" (J. Escrivá, *Christ is passing by*, 186).

In the middle of the prophecy the author breaks off into an exhortation to vigilance and faithfulness (v. 15), as he did in 3:1-3, 18, for "God, although he can conquer, prefers to convince people" (*Christ is passing by*, 186), as can be seen from what Psalm 2 itself says: "Therefore, O kings, be wise; be warned, O rulers of the earth . . ." (Ps 2:10).

The name Armageddon means "the mountain of Megiddo", the place where King Josiah suffered defeat (cf. 2 Kings 23:21f) and which now symbolizes defeat for the assembled armies (cf. 12:11).

17. The symbolic action of pouring the seventh and last bowl into the air means that it affects the entire world. What is now happening is final and irreversible: this is proclaimed by the heavenly voice which, coming as it does from the temple and the centre of heaven, makes it plain that God is Lord of all, that the prayers of the saints have been answered and that nothing can reverse God's intervention in human history.

The episode of the seventh bowl introduces the final scene of the book, in which are described the last battles, the victory of Christ and the absolute establishment of his kingship. The scene is a triptych: first we are shown the

great voice came out of the temple, from the throne, saying, "It is done!" [18]And there were flashes of lightning, loud noises, peals of thunder, and a great earthquake such as had never been since men were on the earth, so great was that earthquake. [19]The great city was split into three parts, and the cities of the nations fell, and God remembered great Babylon, to make her drain the cup of the fury of his wrath. [20]And every island fled away, and no mountains were to be found; [21]and great hailstones, heavy as a hundredweight, dropped on men from heaven, till men cursed God for the plague of the hail, so fearful was that plague.

Ex 19:16
Dan 12:1
Mk 13:19

Jer 25:15
Rev 14:8-10

Rev 6:14

Ex 9:23

---

in aerem; et exivit vox magna de templo a throno dicens: "Factum est!" [18]Et facta sunt fulgura et voces et tonitrua, et terraemotus factus est magnus, qualis numquam fuit, ex quo homo fuit super terram, talis terraemotus sic magnus. [19]Et facta est civitas magna in tres partes, et civitates gentium ceciderunt. Et Babylon magna venit in memoriam ante Deum dare ei calicem vini indignationis irae eius. [20]Et omnis insula fugit, et montes non sunt inventi. [21]Et grando magna sicut talentum descendit de caelo in homines; et blasphemaverunt homines Deum propter plagam grandinis, quoniam magna est plaga eius nimis.

---

harlot (*porne*), or Babylon (cf. 16:19; 17:5; 18:8, 10, 25), already mentioned (cf. 14:8), and her trial, condemnation and destruction by fire (cf. chaps. 17-18). Then, in the centre, comes the victory of Christ, the Lamb, "Lord of lords and King of kings" (17:14), and his battles are described and lauded (cf. chaps. 19-20). The third part of the triptych shows the exaltation of the Bride (*nymphe*) and spouse of the Lamb (cf. 19:7), the Church or heavenly Jerusalem (cf. chaps. 21-22).

18-21. God's intervention is described in terms of a great storm, as in the theophany on Sinai (cf. Ex 19:16) and earlier passages of the Apocalypse (cf. 4:5; 8:5; 11:9). In this instance the storm is compounded by an earthquake, its unique character underlined by words of the prophet Daniel: there had never been the like before (cf. Dan 12:1). This is designed to show that God's intervention has reached its climax; sea as well as land suffers upheaval. The enormous hailstones recall the seventh plague of Egypt (cf. Ex. 9:24) and show how drastic the punishment is. The great city, Rome, whose ruin has already been decreed, is singled out for special treatment.

These events are the last call to conversion—a useless call, for, instead of turning to God, men in their fury curse his name.

17

The great harlot and the beast

Jer 51:13
Ezek 16

Is 23:27
Nahum 3:4

Dan 7:7
Is 21:1f

Rev 13:1

[1]Then one of the seven angels who had the seven bowls came and said to me, "Come, I will show you the judgment of the great harlot who is seated upon many waters, [2]with whom the kings of the earth have committed fornication, and with the wine of whose fornication the dwellers on earth have become drunk." [3]And he carried me away in the Spirit into a wilderness, and I saw a woman sitting on a scarlet beast which was full of blasphemous names, and it

---

[1]Et venit unus de septem angelis, qui habebant septem phialas, et locutus est mecum dicens: "Veni, ostendam tibi damnationem meretricis magnae, quae sedet super aquas multas, [2]cum qua fornicati sunt reges terrae, et inebriati sunt, qui inhabitant terram, de vino prostitutionis eius." [3]Et abstulit me in desertum in spiritu. Et vidi mulierem sedentem super bestiam coccineam, plenam nominibus blasphemiae, habentem capita septem et cornua decem. [4]Et mulier erat circumdata purpura et coccino et inaurata auro et lapide pretioso et

17:1 - 19:10. This first section of the final scene begins with the depiction of the city of Rome (described as the great harlot, the great city, great Babylon), its punishment, and its connexion with the beast (the symbol of absolutist antichristian power personified by certain emperors: cf. 13:18). This takes up chapter 17. The vision then goes on to depict the fall of Rome as an accomplished fact, followed on the one hand by lamentation (cf. chap. 18) and the other by hymns of praise sung by the righteous (cf. chap. 19).

1-6. An angel joins the seer to explain the vision to him. Again the imagery used is very evocative of the Old Testament: the great harlot recalls the cities of Tyre and Nineveh, which Isaiah and Nahum described as harlots (cf. Is 23:16-17; Nah 3:4). As explained in 17:15, the "many waters" are the peoples ruled by the great harlot. Some commentators have interpreted this as a reference to their ultimate downfall, which would precipate the collapse of the ancient world.

The metaphor of prostitution is used in the Old Testament to refer to idolatry and also alliances with foreign powers (cf. Ezek 16:15, 23-24; 23:1-20). In the present case, the power and influence of Rome was practically universal, given the extent of the Empire. It is called Babylon because Babylon was the prototype of cities hostile to God (cf. v. 5; Is 21:9; Jer 51:1-19). It is characterized by its wealth, its immoral influence (v. 4) and its horrendous crimes against the Christian martyrs (cf. v. 6), who, according to the Roman historian Tacitus, "were abused in various ways: they were covered with hides to be set upon by dogs, or nailed to crosses, or burned alive and used as torches to light up the darkness" (*Annals*, 15, 44).

had seven heads and ten horns. [4]The woman was arrayed in purple and scarlet, and bedecked with gold and jewels and pearls, holding in her hand a golden cup full of abominations and the impurities of her fornication; [5]and on her forehead was written a name of mystery: "Babylon the great, mother of harlots and of earth's abominations." [6]And I saw the woman, drunk with the blood of the saints and the blood of the martyrs of Jesus.

Jer 51:7

2 Thess 2:7
Rev 14:8

Rev 18:24

When I saw her I marvelled greatly. [7]But the angel said to me, "Why marvel? I will tell you the mystery of the woman, and of the beast with seven heads and ten horns that carries her. [8]The beast that you saw was, and is not, and is to ascend from the bottomless pit and go to perdition; and the dwellers on earth whose names have not been written in the book of life from the foundation of the world, will marvel to behold the beast, because it was and is not and is

Rev 13:1-5

---

margaritis, habens poculum aureum in manu sua plenum abominationibus et immunditiis fornicationis eius, [5]et in fronte eius nomen scriptum, mysterium: "Babylon magna, mater fornicationum et abominationum terrae." [6]Et vidi mulierem ebriam de sanguine sanctorum et de sanguine martyrum Iesu. Et miratus sum, cum vidissem illam, admiratione magna. [7]Et dixit mihi angelus: "Quare miraris? Ego tibi dicam mysterium mulieris et bestiae, quae portat eam, quae habet capita septem et decem cornua: [8]bestia, quam vidisti, fuit et non est, et ascensura est de abysso et in interitum ibit. Et mirabuntur inhabitantes terram, quorum non sunt scripta nomina in libro vitae a constitutione mundi, videntes

The figure of the great harlot, and the influence she wields, is also interpreted as referring to impurity; St John of the Cross, for example, explains the passage as follows: "This phrase 'have become drunk' should be noted. For, however little a man may drink of the wine of this rejoicing, it at once takes hold of the heart, as wine does to those who have been corrupted by it. So, if some antidote is not at once taken against this poison, to expel it quickly, the life of the soul is put in jeopardy" (*Ascent of Mount Carmel*, 3, 22).

7-8. The angel explains the meaning of the beast (v. 8), its seven heads (v. 9) and its ten horns (v. 12), and then reveals the identity of the great harlot (v. 18). However, what he says is still enigmatic, in keeping with the style of apocalyptic texts, which are written in a kind of code to protect the writer from being sought out and punished.

The phrase "was, and is not" (v. 8) is a kind of counter and parody of "him who is and was and is to come" (Rev 1:4). It identifies the antichrist who is headed for perdition (v. 11); St Paul also calls him "the son of perdition" (2 Thess 2:3). When it speaks of the beast reappearing ("is to come"), this refers,

Rev 13:18to come. ⁹This calls for a mind with wisdom: the seven heads are seven hills on which the woman is seated; ¹⁰they are also seven kings, five of whom have fallen, one is, the other has not yet come, and when he comes he must remain only a little while. ¹¹As for the beast that was and is not, it is an eighth but it belongs to the seven, and it goes to perdition. ¹²And the ten horns that you saw are ten kings who have not yet received royal power, but they are to receive authority as kings for one hour, together with the beast. ¹³These are of one mind and give over their power and authority to the beast; ¹⁴they will make war on the Lamb, and the Lamb will conquer them, for he is Lord of

Rev 17:8; 19:20

Dan 7:20, 24
Rev 13:1

Deut 10:17
Dan 2:47

---

bestiam, quia erat et non est et aderit. ⁹Hic est sensus, qui habet sapientiam. Septem capita septem montes sunt, super quos mulier sedet. Et reges septem sunt: ¹⁰quinque ceciderunt, unus est, alius nondum venit et, cum venerit, oportet illum breve tempus manere. ¹¹Et bestia, quae erat et non est, et is octavus est et de septem est et in interitum vadit. ¹²Et decem cornua, quae vidisti, decem reges sunt, qui regnum nondum acceperunt, sed potestatem tamquam reges una hora

---

according to some commentators, to the legend about Nero returning at the head of the Parthians to avenge himself on his enemies in Rome. However, what the sacred writer really means is that the beast, which had disappeared, will return to wage war on Christians (cf. Rev 11:7; 13:1ff).

9-15. In v. 9 St John warns the reader that what he is writing has a deeper, hidden meaning, rich in wisdom. He is inviting the reader to interpret what he is reading, to discern an implicit, concealed meaning: the harlot is the city of Rome (cf. 13:18 on the name of the emperor), as is fairly plain from the reference to the seven hills on which the harlot is seated. Pliny the Elder describes Rome as "complexa septem montes" (*Historia naturalis*, 3, 9), nestling on seven hills.

The beast's seven heads (cf. 17:3) also stand for seven kings. From what the author says we can deduce that he is referring to seven emperors. The sixth, alive when St John is writing, would be Domitian, and the first five would be Caligula (37-41), Claudius (41-54), Nero (54-68), Vespasian (69-78) and Titus (79-81); with Nerva (96-98) as the seventh. The beast is number eight, though it can also be taken as one of the seven, for it will be as cruel as one of them—Nero. The ten kings (v. 12) stand for those whom Rome established as kings in the nations it conquered, rulers subject to the emperor.

The description of Christ as the Lamb (cf. 5:6) forms a contrast here with the beast. Through his death and resurrection, this humble figure has been made King and Lord of the entire universe (cf. Acts 2:32-36) and already truly reigns in the hearts of Christians. Therefore his victory over the powers of evil, no

lords and King of kings, and those with him are called and Rev 19:14, 16, 19 chosen and faithful." 1 Tim 6:15

[15]And he said to me, "The waters that you saw, where Jer 51:13 the harlot is seated, are peoples and multitudes and nations and tongues. [16]And the ten horns that you saw, they and the Rev 18:8 beast will hate the harlot; they will make her desolate and Ezek 16:39-41 naked, and devour her flesh and burn her up with fire, [17]for God has put it into their hearts to carry out his purpose by being of one mind and giving over their royal power to the beast, until the words of God shall be fulfilled. [18]And the Ps 2:2 woman that you saw is the great city which has dominion Rev 11:8 over the kings of the earth."

---

accipiunt cum bestia. [13]Hi unum consilium habent et virtutem et potestatem suam bestiae tradunt. [14]Hi cum Agno pugnabunt; et Agnus vincet illos, quoniam Dominus dominorum est et Rex regum, et qui cum illo sunt vocati et electi et fideles." [15]Et dicit mihi: "Aquae, quas vidisti, ubi meretrix sedet, populi et turbae sunt et gentes et linguae. [16]Et decem cornua, quae vidisti, et bestia, hi odient fornicariam et desolatam facient illam et nudam, et carnes eius manducabunt et ipsam igne concremabunt; [17]Deus enim dedit in corda eorum, ut faciant, quod illi placitum est, et faciant unum consilium et dent regnum suum bestiae, donec consummentur verba Dei. [18]Et mulier, quam vidisti, est civitas magna, quae habet regnum super reges terrae."

---

matter how strong they be, is assured. As Pius XI rightly put it "it has long been a common custom to give Christ the metaphorical title of 'king', because of the high degree of perfection whereby he excels all creatures [. . .]. He is king of our hearts, too, by reason of his charity 'which surpasses knowledge' (Eph 3:19) and his mercy and kindness, which draw all men to him; for there never was, nor ever will be a man loved so much and so universally as Jesus Christ" (*Quas primas*, 6).

16-18. With words taken from Ezekiel's prophecy of the destruction of Jerusalem (by the very kingdoms with which Judah had made idolatrous alliances instead of trusting in Yahweh: cf. 16:30-41; 23:25-29), St John now predicts the punishment which will befall Rome, at the hands too of those nations which, like Rome and under her influence, serve the beast, that is, have fallen into idolatrous absolutism, which prevents the exercise of freedom of conscience. God makes use of the forces of evil to punish those very people who follow evil ways.

The fall of Babylon proclaimed

Ezek 43:2

[1]After this I saw another angel coming down from heaven, having great authority; and the earth was made bright with his splendour. [2]And he called out with a mighty voice,

Rev 14:8
Is 13:21; 21:9;
34:11, 14
Jer 50:39; 51:8

"Fallen, fallen is Babylon the great!
It has become a dwelling place of demons,
a haunt for every foul spirit,
a haunt of every foul and hateful bird;

Jer 25:15; 51:7
Nahum 3:4

[3]for all nations have drunk[k] the wine of her impure
passion,
and the kings of the earth have committed fornication
with her,
and the merchants of the earth have grown rich with the
wealth of her wantonness."

---

[1]Post haec vidi alium angelum descendentem de caelo, habentem potestatem magnam, et terra illuminata est a claritate eius. [2]Et clamavit in forti voce dicens: "Cecidit, cecidit Babylon magna et facta est habitatio daemoniorum et custodia omnis spiritus immundi et custodia omnis bestiae immundae et odibilis, [3]quia de vino irae fornicationis eius biberunt omnes gentes, et reges terrae cum illa fornicati sunt, et mercatores terrae de virtute deliciarum eius divites facti sunt!"

1-3. These verses describing the downfall of Rome follow the prophetical style of foretelling a future event by reporting it as something that has already happened. First the fall of the city is proclaimed (vv. 1-3). Then the people of God are exhorted to leave the city and escape the terrible punishment soon to befall it (vv. 4-8). This is followed by the lament of the kings who were allied to Rome (vv. 9-10), of the merchants who prospered by trading with her (v. 11-17a) and of the sailors (17b-19). Finally we are shown the joy of those who suffered under her yoke and now see justice done.

In words reminiscent of Old Testament passages foretelling the destruction of hostile cities (cf. Is 13:21-22; 21:9; Jer 50:30; Ezek 43:3-5), St John describes the fate of Rome in the last days before its desolation. Among the sins which have brought about its ruin is unbridled sexual indulgence (cf. also vv. 7 and 12-14). Such behaviour leads to the degradation and self-destruction of a society, as witness the history of civilization and contemporary experience. Consumerism, self-indulgence and greed for possessions, clearly features of our time, were denounced by Pius XI when he said that "the disease of the modern age, and the main source of the evils we all deplore, is that lack of reflection, that continuous and quite feverish pursuit of external things, that immoderate desire for wealth and pleasure, which gradually causes the heart

[k]Other ancient authorities read *fallen by*

⁴Then I heard another voice from heaven saying,
"Come out of her, my people,
lest you take part in her sins,
lest you share in her plagues;
⁵for her sins are heaped high as heaven, and God has
remembered her iniquities.
⁶Render to her as she herself has rendered,
and repay her double for her deeds;
mix a double draught for her in the cup she mixed.
⁷As she glorified herself and played the wanton,
so give her a like measure of torment and mourning.
Since in her heart she says, 'A queen I sit,
I am no widow, mourning I shall never see,'
⁸so shall her plagues come in a single day,
pestilence and mourning and famine,
and she shall be burned with fire;
for mighty is the Lord God who judges her."

Is 48:20; 52:11
Jer 50:8; 51:6, 9, 45
2 Cor 6:17

Gen 18:20-21
Jer 51:9

Ps 137:8
Jer 50:15, 29
2 Thess 1:6

Jer 50:29
Is 47:8

Is 47:9
Rev 17:16

---

⁴Et audivi aliam vocem de caelo dicentem: "Exite de illa, populus meus, ut ne comparticipes sitis peccatorum eius et de plagis eius non accipiatis, ⁵quoniam pervenerunt peccata eius usque ad caelum, et recordatus est Deus iniquitatum eius. ⁶Reddite illi, sicut et ipsa reddidit, et duplicate duplicia secundum opera eius; in poculo, quo miscuit, miscete illi duplum. ⁷Quantum glorificavit se et in deliciis fuit, tantum date illi tormentum et luctum. Quia in corde suo dicit: 'Sedeo regina et vidua non sum et luctum non videbo', ⁸ideo in una die venient plagae eius, mors et luctus et fames, et igne comburetur, quia fortis est Dominus

---

to lose sight of its nobler ideals, drowning them in a sea of impermanent, earthly things, and preventing them from contemplating higher, eternal things" (*Mens nostra*, 6).

4-8. St John is inserting here the scene in which Jeremiah prophesies the punishment of Babylon and God protects his people by ordering them to leave the city before it falls (cf. Jer 51:6, 45). The verses also echo the flight of Lot from Sodom (cf. Gen 19:12ff) and the advice Jesus gave his followers on what to do when the fall of Jerusalem came (cf. Mt 24:16ff).

The idea of the sins heaped as high as heaven (cf. Gen 18:20) is a way of saying that sin is something very grave because it is above all an offence to the Godhead, and so "is linked to the *sense* of God, since it derives from man's conscious relationship with God as his Creator, Lord and Father" (John Paul II, *Reconciliatio et Paenitentia*, 18). When one's perception of the greatness of God becomes vague, one loses the sense of sin; as John Paul II adds, "my predecessor Pius XII one day declared, in words that have almost become proverbial, that 'the sin of the century is the loss of the sense of sin'" (*ibid.*).

Ezek 26:16;
27:30, 33, 35
Is 23:17

Ezek 26:17
Rev 18:17

Ezek 37:36

Ezek 27:12, 13,
22

9And the kings of the earth, who committed fornication and were wanton with her, will weep and wail over her when they see the smoke of her burning; 10they will stand far off, in fear of her torment, and say,

"Alas! alas! thou great city,
thou mighty city, Babylon!
In one hour has thy judgment come."

11And the merchants of the earth weep and mourn for her, since no one buys their cargo any more, 12cargo of gold, silver, jewels and pearls, fine linen, purple, silk and scarlet, all kinds of scented wood, all articles of ivory, all articles of costly wood, bronze, iron and marble, 13cinnamon, spice, incense, myrrh, frankincense, wine, oil, fine flour and wheat, cattle and sheep, horses and chariots, and slaves, that is, human souls.

14"The fruit for which thy soul longed has gone from thee,
and all thy dainties and thy splendour are lost to thee,
never to be found again!"

Deus, qui iudicavit illam." 9Et flebunt et plangent se super illam reges terrae, qui cum illa fornicati sunt et in deliciis vixerunt, cum viderint fumum incendii eius, 10longe stantes propter timorem tormentorum eius, dicentes: "Vae, vae, civitis illa magna, Babylon, civitas illa fortis, quoniam una hora venit iudicium tuum!" 11Et negotiatores terrae flent et lugent super illam, quoniam mercem eorum nemo emit amplius: 12mercem, auri et argenti et lapidis pretiosi et margaritarum, et byssi et purpurae et serici et cocci, et omne lignum thyinum et omnia vasa eboris et omnia vasa de ligno pretiosissimo et aeramento et ferro et marmore, 13et cinnamomum et amomum et odoramenta et unguenta et tus, et vinum et oleum et similam et triticum, et iumenta et oves et equorum et raedarum, et mancipiorum et animas hominum. 14Et fructus tui, desiderium

---

The punishment ordained by God and carried out by his agents is related to the scale of the offence; the word "double" does not refer to any particular amount but to the severity of the punishment (as in Is 40:2; Jer 16:18; etc.).

Using this passage as his basis, St John of Avila teaches that in order to overcome strong temptation it is very helpful to reflect on the love we should have for God; but "if that does not get rid of the temptation, turn your thoughts to hell and see how ferociously that fire burns" (*Audi, filia*, 10).

9-19. To describe the punishment inflicted on Rome, the author of the Book of Revelation seems to be borrowing from the oracles of Ezekiel about the fall of Tyre. In both cases we have the lament of the kings (cf. Ezek 26:15-18) and

[15]The merchants of these wares, who gained wealth from Rev 18:3
her, will stand far off, in fear of her torment, weeping and
mourning aloud,

[16]"Alas, alas, for the great city that was clothed in fine Rev 17:4
linen, in purple and scarlet,
bedecked with gold, with jewels, and with pearls!
[17]In one hour all this wealth has been laid waste." Ezek 27:27-29

And all shipmasters and seafaring men, sailors and all
whose trade is on the sea, stood far off [18]and cried out as
Ezek 27:32
Is 34:10
they saw the smoke of her burning,
"What city was like the great city?"

[19]And they threw dust on their heads, as they wept and Ezek 27:30-34
mourned, crying out,
"Alas, alas, for the great city where all who had ships at
sea grew rich by her wealth!
In one hour she has been laid waste.
[20]Rejoice over her, O heaven, Deut 32:43
Is 44:23
Rev 19:1-2
O saints and apostles and prophets,

---

animae, discesserunt a te, et omnia pinguia et clara perierunt a te, et amplius
illa iam non invenient. [15]Mercatores horum, qui divites facti sunt ab ea, longe
stabunt propter timorem tormentorum eius flentes ac lugentes, [16]dicentes: "Vae,
vae, civitas illa magna, quae amicta erat byssino et purpura et cocco, et deaurata
auro et lapide pretioso et margarita, [17]quoniam una hora desolatae sunt tantae
divitiae!" Et omnis gubernator et omnis, qui in locum navigat, et nautae et,
quotquot maria operantur, longe steterunt [18]et clamabant, videntes fumum
incendii eius, dicentes: "Quae similis civitati huic magnae?" [19]Et miserunt
pulverem super capita sua et clamabant, flentes et lugentes, dicentes: "Vae, vae,
civitas illa magna, in qua divites facti sunt omnes, qui habent naves in mari, de
opibus eius, quonium una hora desolata est! [20]Exsulta super eam, caelum, et

---

the complaint of merchants and sailors, who see it as meaning financial ruin
(cf. Ezek 27:9-36). Each of these three groups, from different standpoints of
time, will lament over the city—the kings in the future (cf. v. 10), the merchants
in the present (cf. v. 11) and the sailors in the past (v. 18). This style of writing
makes for a very vivid narrative and depicts the punishment as both forth-
coming and already executed.

20-24. In sharp contrast with the previous lamentation is this invitation to
rejoice—the reply to which comes in 19:1-8, where we are told that the elect
joyfully intone songs in praise of God almighty. The throwing of the millstone
into the sea is an instance of "prophetic action"; it comes from Jeremiah
51:60-64, which uses this device to prophesy the total downfall of Babylon.

for God has given judgment for you against her!"

Jer 51:63-64
Ezek 26:21

²¹Then a mighty angel took up a stone like a great millstone and threw it into the sea, saying,

"So shall Babylon the great city be thrown down with violence,

Is 24:8

and shall be found no more;

Ezek 26:13
Jer 25:10

²²and the sound of harpers and minstrels, of flute players and trumpeters,

shall be heard in thee no more;

and a craftsman of any craft shall be found in thee no more;

and the sound of the millstone shall be heard in thee no more;

Jer 25:10; 7:34;
16:9
Is 23:8; 47:9

²³and the light of a lamp shall shine in thee no more;

and the voice of bridegroom and bride shall be heard in thee no more;

for thy merchants were the great men of the earth,

and all nations were deceived by thy sorcery.

Mt 23:35-37
Jer 51:49
Rev 6:10; 17:6;
19:2

²⁴And in her was found the blood of prophets and of saints,

and of all who have been slain on earth."

---

sancti et apostoli et prophetae, quoniam iudicavit Deus iudicium vestrum de illa!" ²¹Et sustulit unus angelus fortis lapidem quasi molarem magnum et misit in mare dicens: "Impetu sic mittetur Babylon magna illa civitas et ultra iam non invenietur. ²²Et vox citharoedorum et musicorum et tibia canentium et tuba non audietur in te amplius, et omnis artifex omnis artis non invenietur in te amplius, et vox molae non audietur in te amplius, ²³et lux lucernae non lucebit tibi amplius, et vox sponsi et sponsae non audietur in te amplius, quia mercatores tui erant magnates terrae, quia in veneficiis tuis erraverunt omnes gentes, ²⁴et in ea sanguis prophetarum et sanctorum inventus est et omnium, qui interfecti sunt in terra!"

The millstone also appears in Luke 17:2 and par. as a symbol of disgrace and shame.

The sepulchral silence and darkness of the city are described in detail. The reason for this terrible punishment was its opulence, its idolatry and the fact that it was where the Christian martyrs were tortured and put to death. Like Jerusalem it is called "city of blood" (cf. Ezek 24:6), and just as the ancient capital of Israel was accused by Jesus of murdering the prophets and messengers of God and was told that all the blood it had spilt would come back upon it (cf. Mt 23:35), so will Rome be punished for martyring the saints.

19

Songs of victory in heaven

¹After this I heard what seemed to be the mighty voice of
a great multitude in heaven, crying,

> "Hallelujah! Salvation and glory and power belong to
> our God,
> ²for his judgments are true and just;
> he has judged the great harlot who corrupted the earth
> with her fornication,
> and he has avenged on her the blood of his servants."

³Once more they cried,

> "Hallelujah! The smoke from her goes up for ever and
> ever."

⁴And the twenty-four elders and the four living creatures
fell down and worshipped God who is seated on the throne,

Rev 7:10

Ps 19:10
Rev 16:7; 11:18
Deut 32:43
2 Kings 9:7

Is 34:10
Rev 14:11

Rev 4:6, 10

---

¹Post haec audivi quasi vocem magnam turbae multae in caelo dicentium:
"Alleluia! Salus et gloria et virtue Deo nostro, ²quia vera et iusta iudicia eius;
quia iudicavit de meretrice magna, quae corrupit terram in prostitutione sua, et
vindicavit sanguinem servorum suorum de manibus eius!" ³Et iterum dixerunt:
"Alleluia! Et fumus eius ascendit in saecula saeculorum!" ⁴Et ceciderunt
seniores viginti quattuor et quattuor animalia et adoraverunt Deum sedentem
super thronum dicentes: "Amen, Alleluia." ⁵Et vox de throno exivit dicens:
"Laudem dicite Deo nostro, omnes servi eius et qui timetis eum, pusilli et
magni!" ⁶Et audivi quasi vocem turbae magnae et sicut vocem aquarum
multarum et sicut vocem tonitruum magnorum dicentium: "Alleluia, quoniam
regnavit Dominus, Deus noster omnipotens. ⁷Gaudeamus et exsultemus et
demus gloriam ei, quia venerunt nuptiae Agni, et uxor eius praeparavit se. ⁸Et
datum est illi, ut cooperiat se byssino splendenti mundo: byssinum enim

---

1-4. The righteous rejoice to see their enemy overwhelmed; the praises they
sing of God end in three loud "Hallelujahs". In the following passage (vv. 6-8),
they welcome the establishment of the Kingdom of God and the imminent
marriage of the Lamb.

This is the first and only time the word "Hallelujah" appears in the New
Testament. It is a Hebrew term (*hallelu-yah*) meaning "Praise Yahweh" used
especially in the psalms (cf., e.g., Ps 111; 114; 115). The Church uses it,
unchanged, usually to express to God its joy and praise at the resurrection of
Christ. It is used particularly at Eastertide and also on many other days, both
in the divine office and in the celebration of the Eucharist.

These shouts of praise are motivated by the salvation which comes from
God and by the rightness of his judgments as evidenced by the punishment
inflicted on the great harlot who is turned into a fire which burns forever.

133

Ps 115:13; 134:1 saying, "Amen. Hallelujah!" [5]And from the throne came a voice crying,

"Praise our God, all you his servants,
you who fear him, small and great."

Ezek 1:24; 43:2
Ps 93:1; 97:1;
99:1
Rev 11:17

[6]Then I heard what seemed to be the voice of a great multitude, like the sound of many waters and like the sound of mighty thunderpeals, crying,

"Hallelujah! For the Lord our God the Almighty reigns.

Ps 118:24
Rev 21:2, 9

[7]Let us rejoice and exult and give him the glory,
for the marriage of the Lamb has come,
and his Bride has made herself ready;

Is 61:10
Ps 45:14-15

[8]it was granted her to be clothed with fine linen, bright and pure"—
for the fine linen is the righteous deeds of the saints.

---

iustificationes sunt sanctorum." [9]Et dicit mihi: "Scribe: Beati, qui ad cenam nuptiarum Agni vocati sunt!" Et dicit mihi: "Haec verba Dei vera sunt." [10]Et cecidi ante pedes eius, ut adorarem eum. Et dicit mihi: "Vide, ne feceris!

5-8. This further invitation to praise God is very reminiscent of the Psalms; in fact it contains some direct quotations from them (cf. Ps 93:1; 97:1; 115:2; 135:1, 20). The response is on a grand scale, like a choral symphony involving all the elect. This particular chant praises not only the destruction and defeat of evil but the definitive establishment of the Kingdom of God; his is a Kingdom of love, as symbolized by a marriage feast. In the Old Testament Yahweh was sometimes likened to a bridegroom (cf., e.g., Is 54:6: Jer 2:2; Ezek 16:7-8; Hos 2:16) and in the New Testament the Church is depicted as the Bride of Christ (cf. Eph 5:22-23). Thus, the Second Vatican Council says that the Church "is described as the spotless spouse of the spotless lamb (Rev 19:7; 21:2, 9; 22:17). It is she whom Christ 'loved and for whom he delivered himself up that he might sanctify her' (Eph 5:26). It is she whom he unites to himself by an unbreakable alliance, and whom he constantly 'nourishes and cherishes' (Eph 5:29). It is she whom, once purified, he willed to be joined to himself, subject in love and fidelity (cf. Eph 5:24), and whom, finally, he filled with heavenly gifts for all eternity" (*Lumen gentium*, 6). And so, John Paul II teaches, "*redemptive love* is transformed, I might say, into *spousal love*. Christ, on giving himself to the Church, by that very act of redemption has made himself one with her for ever, as husband and wife" (*Address*, 18 July 1982).

This singing of the praises of the marriage of the Lamb from the vantage-point of the end of time also depicts the Church down the ages; it shows us, too, the destiny that awaits every Christian and the form his or her every day should take—weaving the wedding garment by doing good works, by praising God and by living a holy life, so as to be ready to attend the marriage feast. Those who live well away from idolatry, unbridled sensuality and all the sins

⁹And the angel said[1] to me, "Write this: Blessed are those who are invited to the marriage supper of the Lamb." And he said to me, "These are true words of God." ¹⁰Then I fell down at his feet to worship him, but he said to me, "You must not do that! I am a fellow servant with you and your brethren who hold the testimony of Jesus. Worship God." For the testimony of Jesus is the spirit of prophecy.

Rev 1:3
Mt 22:1-14

Acts 10:25-26
Rev 22:8-9

Conservus tuus sum et fratrum tuorum habentium testimonium Iesu. Deum adora. Testimonium enim Iesu est spiritus prophetiae." ¹¹Et vidi caelum apertum: et ecce equus albus; et, qui sedebat super eum, vocabatur Fidelis et Verax, et in iustitia iudicat et pugnat. ¹²Oculi autem eius sicut flamma ignis, et in capite eius diademata multa, habens nomen scriptum, quod nemo novit nisi ipse, ¹³et vestitus veste aspersa sanguine, et vocatur nomen eius Verbum Dei. ¹⁴Et exercitus, qui sunt in caelo, sequebantur eum in equis albis, vestiti byssino albo mundo. ¹⁵Et de ore ipsius procedit gladius acutus, ut in ipso percutiat

---

of the "great city" can already celebrate their victory by joining in the praises sung by the choirs of heaven. Here again we can see the intimate connexion between the heavenly and earthly liturgies. By taking part in the liturgy of the Church, especially the Mass, we are already entering the sphere of things divine. And so the Second Vatican Council tells us that "the liturgy is the summit toward which the activity of the Church is directed; it is also the fount from which all her power flows. For the goal of apostolic endeavour is that all who are made children of God by faith and Baptism should come together to praise God in the midst of his Church, to take part in the Sacrifice and to eat the Lord's Supper" (*Sacrosanctum Concilium*, 10). For his part, John Paul II exhorts us: "Nourish yourselves with this eucharistic Bread, which will enable you to make your way through the paths of the world ever united in the faith of your fathers, always faithful to God and his Church, ever active in building the kingdom of God, and feeling privileged if at any time the Lord should allow your faith to be put severely to the test. Only he who perseveres will be worthy to share in the marriage supper of the Lamb" (*Radio message*, 22 July 1984).

9. On the instructions of the angel who is explaining the vision to him (cf. 17:1), St John tells Christians to count themselves blessed (v. 9); God guarantees the truth of this assurance. At Mass the priest makes a similar proclamation just before distributing Holy Communion: "Happy are those who are called to his [the Lord's] supper." This shows that the Eucharist truly is "a pledge of future glory".

10. The angel apparently leaves at this point and St John again reminds Christians that they have a prophetic mission—to bear witness to Jesus by spreading his teaching by word and deed.

[1]Greek *he said*

The first battle: the beast is destroyed

Is 11:4-5
2 Mac 3:25
Rev 1:5; 3:7, 14

Rev 1:14; 2:18;
19:16

Is 63:1f
Jn 1:1

[11]Then I saw heaven opened, and behold, a white horse! He who sat upon it is called Faithful and True, and in righteousness he judges and makes war. [12]His eyes are like a flame of fire, and on his head are many diadems; and he has a name inscribed which no one knows but himself. [13]He is clad in a robe dipped in[m] blood, and the name by which he is called is The Word of God. [14]And the armies of

---

gentes, et ipse *reget eos in virga ferrea*; et ipse calcat torcular vini furoris irae

---

19:11 - 20:15. The prophetic narrative (given in the form of a proclamation) of the fall of Babylon (Rome) is now followed by a depiction of Christ as endowed with power (vv. 11-16) permanently and decisively to conquer the forces of evil which sustained the great city. Their defeat is narrated in reverse order to that given earlier in the book: the first to be conquered are the kings of the earth (who first allied themselves with the great city and then rebelled against it: vv. 17-18) and the beast and the false prophet to whom the kings gave over their royal power (vv. 20-21; cf. 17:16-17). Then, in a second eschatological battle, Christ defeats the ancient serpent, Satan, the one who originally gave power to the beast (cf. 20:1-10; 13:2). Not until this happens will the general judgment take place (20:11-15).

The Apocalypse in this way points to the origin of evil and its later manifestations. The most immediate manifestation of evil, and the first to be destroyed, is the world of opulence, unbridled sexuality and power, and idolatry—that society which persecuted and martyred the Christians. Pagan Rome, the symbol of that world, draws its strength from absolutist divinized forces intolerant of human freedom and dignity (and especially hostile to religion), and from atheistic and materialistic ideologies which make for absolutism. These forces are the beast and the false prophet. However, at a deeper and more mysterious level lies the ultimate source of these sociological phenomena—Satan (symbolized by the dragon or ancient serpent). The message of Revelation is that Christ towers above all these forces, and his victory (which began with his death and resurrection) will reach its climax at the end of time, although it will be manifested to a degree over the course of history by the holiness of the Church.

11-16. This vision of the glorious and conquering Christ is similar to the way he is portrayed at the start of the book: by focusing attention on parts of his body (through not in any systematic way: cf. Rev 1:5, 12-16), he seems to be the same person as the rider on the white horse mentioned when the first seal was broken (cf. 6:2). White is the symbol of victory, and the narrative is now going to describe that victory. Christ is portrayed first in a "static" fashion(vv. 11-14) and then in a "dynamic" one, in terms of his actions (vv. 15-16).

[m]Other ancient authorities read *sprinkled with*

heaven, arrayed in fine linen, white and pure, followed him on white horses. [15]From his mouth issues a sharp sword with which to smite the nations, and he will rule them with a rod of iron; he will tread the wine press of the fury of the wrath of God the Almighty. [16]On his robe and on his thigh he has a name inscribed, King of kings and Lords of lords.

[17]Then I saw an angel standing in the sun, and with a loud voice he called to all the birds that fly in midheaven, "Come, gather for the great supper of God, [18]to eat the flesh of kings, the flesh of captains, the flesh of mighty men, the flesh of horses and their riders, and the flesh of all men, both free and slave, both small and great." [19]And I saw the

---

Dei omnipotentis. [16]Et habet super vestimentum et super femur suum nomen scriptum: Rex regum et Dominus dominorum. [17]Et vidi unum angelum stantem in sole, et clamavit voce magna dicens omnibus avibus, quae volabant per medium caeli: "Venite, congregamini ad cenam magnam Dei, [18]ut manducetis carnes regum et carnes tribunorum et carnes fortium et carnes equorum et sedentium in ipsis et carnes omnium liberorum ac servorum et pusillorum ac

---

The two titles "Faithful" and "True" are closely connected. In the Old Testament Yahweh is frequently described as "faithful" (cf. Deut 32:4; Ps 145:13; Ps 117:2). When this title is applied to Christ in the New Testament it suggests his divinity (cf. 1 Thess 5:24; Rev 1:5; 3:14) and shows that, through Christ, God has been faithful to the promises he made in the Old Testament. The name "which no one knows but himself" (v. 12) is an allusion to his divinity, which is something sublime, mysterious and beyond man's grasp.

Another title is "The Word of God". St John is the only one to use this name (cf. Jn 1:1-18), which is a reference to Jesus as the Revealer, the Word of the Father (cf. Jn 1:18). Regarding the titles "King of Kings" and "Lord of lords", see the note on Revelation 17:14. The "thigh" may well mean "standard", because both words are similar in Hebrew, or else it refers to that part of his tunic which covered his thigh.

The blood on the Victor's robe refers not to his passion but to his victory over his enemies, whom he treads as in a wine press. This imagery is used by the Old Testament prophets (cf., e.g., Is 63:1-6; Joel 4:13). The sword coming out of his mouth is a reference to the word of God (cf. Heb 4:12). It is a way of referring to divine omnipotence and judgment.

17-21. After describing Christ and his army, the text deals with preparations for the last battle, and its outcome. The angel's call to the birds is reminiscent of the passage in Ezekiel (39:17-20) which tells who the vanquished will be. Here they include people of every type and description who followed the beast and the false prophet, that is, who served the forces of evil they represent.

Dan 7:11, 26

Rev 13:1, 13-17;
20:10, 14

Ezek 39:17, 20

beast and the kings of the earth with their armies gathered
to make war against him who sits upon the horse and against
his army. [20]And the beast was captured, and with it the false
prophet who in its presence had worked the signs by which
he deceived those who had received the mark of the beast
and those who worshipped its image. These two were
thrown alive into the lake of fire that burns with brimstone.
[21]And the rest were slain by the sword of him who sits upon
the horse, the sword that issues from his mouth; and all the
birds were gorged with their flesh.

---

magnorum." [19]Et vidi bestiam et reges terrae et exercitus eorum congregatos
ad faciendum proelium cum illo, qui sedebat super equum, et cum exercitu eius.
[20]Et apprehensa est bestia et cum illa pseudopropheta, qui fecit signa coram
ipsa, quibus seduxit eos, qui acceperunt characterem bestiae et qui adorant
imaginem eius; vivi misi sunt hi duo in stagnum ignis ardentis sulphure. [21]Et
ceteri occisi sunt in gladio sedentis super equum, qui procedit de ore ipsius, et
omnes aves saturatae sunt carnibus eorum.

The lake of fire and brimstone, which will appear again in 20:10, 14 as the
final destination of the powers of evil, is hell, called *gehenna* elsewhere in the
New Testament (cf., e.g., Mt 5:22; 10:28; Mk 9:42; Lk 12:5). It is also where
those men will end up who earn damnation in the eyes of God (cf. Rev 20:15),
although now the writer focuses attention only on the physical death their
punishment involves (v. 21; cf. Mt 10:28 and note).

The fact that they are thrown alive into the fire emphasizes the horrific nature
of their punishment. This physical torment is a terrible one, but far more painful
is the eternal loss of God, which is what hell essentially involves. As St John
Chrysostom puts it, "the pain of hell is indeed insufferable. But even if one
were to imagine ten thousand hells, this suffering would be nothing compared
to the pain caused by the loss of heaven and by being rejected by Christ" (*Hom.
on St Matthew*, 28).

The thousand-year reign of Christ and his people

¹Then I saw an angel coming down from heaven, holding in his hand the key of the bottomless pit and a great chain. ²And he seized the dragon, that ancient serpent, who is the Devil and Satan, and bound him for a thousand years, ³and threw him into the pit, and shut it and sealed it over him, that he should deceive the nations no more, till the thousand years were ended. After that he must be loosed for a little while.

Jude 6

Gen 3:1
Rev 12:9

2 Thess 2:8

---

¹Et vidi angelum descendentem de caelo habentem clavem abyssi et catenam magnam in manu sua. ²Et apprehendit draconem, serpentem antiquum, qui est diabolus et Satanas, et ligavit eum per annos mille ³et misit eum in abyssum et clausit et signavit super illum, ut non seducat amplius gentes, donec consummentur mille anni; post haec oportet illum solvi modico tempore. ⁴Et vidi thronos, et sederunt super eos, et iudicium datum est illis; et animas decollatorum propter testimonium Iesu et propter verbum Dei, et qui non adoraverunt bestiam neque imaginem eius nec acceperunt characterem in frontibus et in manibus suis; et vixerunt et regnaverunt cum Christo mille annis. ⁵Ceteri mortuorum non vixerunt, donec consummentur mille anni. Haec est resurrectio prima. ⁶Beatus et sanctus, qui habet partem in resurrectione prima! In his

---

1-3. The victory of the Lamb is manifested by the fact that Rome, the great harlot, has been destroyed (chap. 18); then the beast and its prophet are overcome (chap. 19); there remains the dragon whom we saw in chapter 12 and whose defeat marks the final outcome of the war referred to in that chapter.

The battle between Satan and God is described in two scenes; the first tells of how Satan is brought under control and deprived of his power for a time (vv. 1-3); the second describes his last assault on the Church and what happens to him in the end (vv. 7-10). Between these two scenes comes the reign of Christ and his followers for a thousand years (vv. 4-6). At the end of the second scene comes the General Judgment, with the reprobate being damned (vv. 11-18) and a new world coming into being (21:1-8).

The bottomless pit, or abyss, refers to a mysterious place, different from the lake of fire, or hell. Satan is also called the "ancient serpent" because it was he who seduced our first parents at the dawn of history (cf. Gen 3:1-19).

The period during which Satan is held captive coincides with the reign of Christ and his saints—one thousand years (cf. v. 4)—and contrasts with the "little while" during which he is given further scope to act. This contrast is very significant and it may simply be a symbolic way of showing that Christ's power is vastly greater than Satan's and that the devil's power is doomed to perish even though on occasions it may emerge with unsuspected force.

Dan 7:9, 22, 27
1 Cor 6:9
Rev 5:10; 13:16

⁴Then I saw thrones, and seated on them were those to whom judgment was committed. Also I saw the souls of those who had been beheaded for their testimony to Jesus and for the word of God, and who had not worshipped the beast or its image and had not received its mark on their foreheads or their hands. They came to life, and reigned with Christ a thousand years. ⁵The rest of the dead did not come to life until the thousand years were ended. This is the first resurrection. ⁶Blessed and holy is he who shares in the first resurrection! Over such the second death has no power, but they shall be priests of God and of Christ, and they shall reign with him a thousand years.

1 Cor 15:21-27

Is 61:6
Rev 5:10; 1:3

---

secunda mors non habet potestatem, sed erunt sacerdotes Dei et Christi et

---

4-6. The power to judge belongs to Jesus Christ in his own right because he has been given it by the Father (cf., e.g., Jn 5:22; 9:39; Acts 10:42). However, our Lord gives a share in his power to the Apostles, whom he promised would sit on twelve thrones judging the tribes of Israel (cf. Mt 19:28). All other Christians will also share in Christ's power (cf. 1 Cor 6:2-3).

Various interpretations have been offered for this "thousand years". The "millenarian" interpretation, supported by some early writers, takes the passage literally and says that after the resurrection of the dead Christ will reign on earth for a thousand years; the Church has never accepted this interpretation. Like the other numbers mentioned in the Book of Revelation, the number of one thousand should be taken as more symbolic than arithmetic. It may be a reference to the period that runs from the incarnation of Christ to the end of time. It is also possible to see this millenium as a reference to a world of the future after the second coming of Christ; or simply as a symbolically long time contrasting with the "little while". It could also be that the author is fusing two notions current in Judaism in his time—one which saw the end of time as a messianic kingdom on earth, and the other which saw that End as a future which transcends this world, when a new heaven and a new earth would appear.

Our Lord Jesus Christ depicts the establishment of the messianic Kingdom as happening in two stages—his first coming, in which he demonstrates his power over the devil and inaugurates the Kingdom of God; and his second coming at the end of time, when that kingdom will be established in its full, finished form. That is why we see St Augustine's explanation of the millenium as the most satisfactory. According to him, this millenium covers the time between the incarnation of the Son of God and his coming at the end of the world. During this period the activity of the devil is to some degree restricted; he is in some way enchained. Christ reigns fully in the Church triumphant and he reigns in the Church militant in an incomplete way. The power of the devil is no longer sovereign, which means that man is able to elude him. So, although

The second battle: Satan is overthrown

[7]And when the thousand years are ended, Satan will be loosed from his prison [8]and will come out to deceive the nations which are at the four corners of the earth, that is, Gog and Magog, to gather them for battle; their number is like the sand of the sea. [9]And they marched up over the broad earth and surrounded the camp of the saints and the beloved city; but fire came down from heaven[n] and consumed them, [10]and the devil who had deceived them was

Ezek 7:2; 38:2, 9, 15

Ps 78:68
2 Kings 1:10
Gen 19:24
Lk 21:24

---

regnabunt cum illo mille annis. [7]Et cum consummati fuerint mille anni, solvetur Satanas de carcere suo [8]et exibit seducere gentes, quae sunt in quattuor angulis terrae, Gog et Magog, congregare eos in proelium, quorum numerus est sicut arena maris. [9]Et ascenderunt super latitudinem terrae et circumierunt castra sanctorum et civitatem dilectam. Et descendit ignis de caelo et devoravit eos; [10]et Diabolus, qui seducebat eos, missus est in stagnum ignis et sulphuris, ubi

---

"he desires to do us harm, he cannot do so because his power is subject to another's power [. . .]. He who gives him the ability to tempt, also gives his mercy to the one who is tempted. He has restricted the devil's ability to tempt people" (St Augustine, *De Serm. Dom. in monte*, II, 9, 34). In fact, the Curé of Ars used to say, "the devil is a big dog on a chain, who threatens and makes a lot of noise but who only bites those who go too near him" (*Selected Sermons*, First Sunday of Lent).

According to this interpretation, the "first resurrection" should be understood in a spiritual sense; it is Baptism, which regenerates man and gives him new life by freeing him from sin and making him a son of God. The second resurrection is the one which will take place at the end of time, when the body is brought back to life and the human being, body and soul, enters into everlasting joy. The "rest of the dead" are those who did not receive Baptism. They too will rise again on the last day, to be judged according to their deeds.

On the priesthood referred to in v. 6, see the note on 1:6.

7-10. God will give the devil a particularly free rein during the last days. Our Lord also said that they would be marked by great tribulation the like of which had never been seen (cf. Mt 24:21-22). And St Paul refers to "the man of lawlessness" who will take his seat in the temple and proclaim himself to be God (cf. 2 Thess 2:3-8).

The writer once again draws on Ezekiel (chaps. 38-39) to describe the final eschatological battle. Gog and Magog are names connected with the nations of the north near the Black Sea, whose invasion of Israel was so devastating that it became the prototype of the worst kind of invasion. Ezekiel describes how they advance through the plan of Esdraelon, scene of so many battles, till they

[n]Other ancient authorities read *from God, out of heaven,* or *out of heaven from God*

thrown into the lake of fire and brimstone where the beast and the false prophet were, and they will be tormented day and night for ever and ever.

The Last Judgment of the living and dead

[11]Then I saw a great white throne and him who sat upon it; from his presence earth and sky fled away, and no place was found for them. [12]And I saw the dead, great and small, standing before the throne, and books were opened. Also another book was opened, which is the book of life. And the dead were judged by what was written in the books, by what they had done. [13]And the sea gave up the dead in it, Death and Hades gave up the dead in them, and all were judged by what they had done. [14]Then Death and Hades

Ezek 38:22
Rev 19:20

Dan 7:9
Ps 114:3
Mt 25:31-46
2 Pet 3:7, 10, 13
Rev 21:1
Ps 62:13
Jer 17:10
Dan 7:10
Rev 3:5; 13:8
Jn 5:28-29
1 Cor 15:26, 54
Rev 14:10; 2:11

---

et bestia et pseudopropheta, et cruciabuntur die ac nocte in saecula saeculorum. [11]Et vidi thronum magnum candidum et sedentem super eum, a cuius aspectu fugit terra et caelum, et locus non est inventus eis. [12]Et vidi mortuos, magnos et pusillos, stantes in conspectu throni; et libri aperti sunt. Et alius liber apertus est, qui est vitae; et iudicati sunt mortui ex his, quae scripta erant in libris secundum opera ipsorum. [13]Et dedit mare mortuos, qui in eo erant, et mors et

---

reach the mountains of Judea, on one of whose hills Jerusalem sits, the symbol of the beloved city, the Church. However, the progress of this destructive force is suddenly brought to a halt by the overwhelming might of God.

Once the devil is thrown into the lake of fire and brimstone evil ceases to act in the world. In that fire the impious, along with the beast and the false prophet, will suffer eternal torment. Scripture's teaching on the everlasting duration of divine punishment is yet again confirmed (cf., e.g., Mt 18:8; 25:41, 46; Mk 4:43, 48).

11-15. Now that the devil, the root of all evil, is removed from the scene, we are shown (as we were after the previous battle) the resurrection of the dead and the General Judgment. The white throne symbolizes the power of God, who judges the living and the dead. Other New Testament texts tell us that the supreme Judge is Christ, who has been charged with this task by the Father (cf., e.g., Mt 16:27; 25:31-46; Acts 17:31; 2 Cor 5:10). The "flight of earth and sky" mean that they disappear (for even non-rational created things have been contaminated by sin: cf. Rom 8:19ff) to make way for a new heaven and a new earth (21:1; cf. 2 Pet 3:13; Rom 8:23).

The author then turns his attention to the resurrection, when all men will be judged according to their works. He describes this by using the metaphor of two books. One of these records the actions of men (as in Daniel 7:10 and other passages of the Old Testament, cf., e.g., Is 65:6; Jer 22:30). The second book contains the names of those predestined to eternal life (an idea inspired by

were thrown into the lake of fire. This is the second death, the lake of fire; [15]and if any one's name was not found written in the book of life, he was thrown into the lake of fire.

Ps 69:29

---

infernus dederunt mortuos, qui in ipsis erant; et iudicati sunt singuli secundum opera ipsorum. [14]Et mors et infernus missi sunt in stagnum ignis. Haec mors secunda est, stagnum ignis. [15]Et si quis non est inventus in libro vitae scriptus, missus est in stagnum ignis.

Daniel 12:1: cf. also, e.g., Ex 32:32). This is a way of showing that man cannot attain salvation by his own efforts alone: it is God who saves him; however, he needs to act in such a way that he responds to the destiny God has marked out for him; if he fails to do that he runs the risk of having his name blotted out of the book of life (cf. Rev 3:5), that is, of being damned. By using this metaphor, the author of Revelation is teaching us two truths which are always mysteriously connected—1) that we are free and 2) that there is a grace of predestination.

Regarding Hades or hell, it should be pointed out that this does not refer to hell in the strict sense, but to *sheol*, the name the Jews gave to the gloomy abode of the dead.

The Last Judgment is a truth of faith concerning which Paul VI says: "He ascended to heaven, and he will come again, this time in glory, to judge the living and the dead—each according to his merits; those who have responded to the love and compassion of God going to eternal life, those who have refused them to the end going to the fire that is not extinguished [. . .]. We believe in the life eternal. We believe that the souls of all those who die in the grace of Christ, whether they must still be purified in purgatory, or whether from the moment they leave their bodies Jesus takes them to paradise as he did for the Good Thief, are the people of God in the eternity beyond death, which will be finally conquered on the day of the Resurrection when these souls will be reunited with their bodies" (*Creed of the People of God*, 12 and 28).

A new world comes into being. The New Jerusalem

Is 65:17; 68:22
2 Pet 3:13
Rom 8:19-23
Rev 20:11
Is 52:1; 61:10
Gal 4:26
Heb 11:10, 16
Rev 19:7, 8
Is 7:14
Ezek 37:37
2 Chron 6:18

¹Then I saw a new heaven and a new earth; for the first heaven and the first earth had passed away, and the sea was no more. ²And I saw the holy city, new Jerusalem, coming down out of heaven from God, prepared as a bride adorned for her husband; ³and I heard a great voice from the throne saying, "Behold, the dwelling of God is with men. He will

¹Et vidi caelum novum et terram novam; primum enim caelum et prima terra abierunt, et mare iam non est. ²Et civitatem sanctam Ierusalem novam vidi descendentem de caelo a Deo, paratam sicut sponsam ornatam viro suo. ³Et audivi vocem magnam de throno dicentem: *"Ecce tabernaculum* Dei cum hominibus! *Et habitabit cum eis, et ipsi populi eius erunt, et* ipse Deus cum eis

21:1 - 22:15. Now that all the forces of evil, including death, have been vanquished the author turns to contemplate the establishment of the Kingdom of God in all its fulness. Thus, the climax of the book shows a new world inhabited by a new race—the new Jerusalem (cf. 21:1-4); a world guaranteed by the eternal and almighty Word of God to last forever (cf. 21:5-8).

The focus of attention now becomes the people of God; the new Jerusalem is portrayed as the Bride of the Lamb; a detailed description shows it to be a wonderful city of great beauty ruled over by God the Father and Christ (21:9 -2:6). The contrast between this and the pilgrim Church in its present circumstances is so great that the new city can be discerned only if one puts one's faith in what God's messengers reveal (cf. 22:6-9). Faith is also an effective stimulus to the Christian to continue to strive for holiness and the reward of eternal life (cf. 22:10-15).

1-4. The prophet Isaiah depicted the messianic times as a radical change in the fortunes of the people of Israel—so radical that, as he put it, God was going to create new heavens and a new earth, a new Jerusalem full of joy, where the sound of weeping would never more be heard, where God would make himself plain for all to see and where everything would be as it was in paradise before sin (cf. Is 65:12-25). The author of the Apocalypse uses this same format to describe the future Kingdom of God. The imagery of a new heaven and a new earth (taken in a physical sense) was very much in vogue in Jewish writing around the time of the Apocalypse (cf. 1 Enoch 72:1; 91:16), and is probably reflected also in 2 Peter 3:10-13 and Matthew 19:28. Scripture nowhere indicates what form the new heaven and the new earth will take. However, what is clear is that there will be a radical "renewal" of the present cosmos, contaminated as it is by the sin of man and the powers of evil (cf. Gen 2:8 - 3:24; Rom 8:9-13); through this renewal all creation will be "recapitulated" in Christ (cf. Eph 1:10; Col 1:16:20). No reference is made to the sea, probably

dwell with them, and they shall be his people,[o] and God himself will be with them;[p] [4]he will wipe away every tear from their eyes, and death shall be no more, neither shall there be mourning nor crying nor pain any more, for the former things have passed away."

Jn 1:14
Zech 8:8

Rev 7:17
Is 25:8; 35:10;
65:17, 19

[5]And he who sat upon the throne said, "Behold, I make all things new." Also he said, "Write this, for these words are trustworthy and true." [6]And he said to me, "It is done!

2 Cor 5:17
Is 43:19

Is 55:1

---

erit eorum Deus, [4]*et absterget omnem lacrimam* ab oculis eorum, et mors ultra non erit, neque luctus neque clamor neque dolor erit ultra, quia prima abierunt." [5]Et dixit, qui sedebat super throno: "Ecce nova facio omnia." Et dicit: "Scribe: Haec verba fidelia sunt et vera." [6]Et dixit mihi: "Facta sunt! Ego sum Alpha et Omega, principium et finis. Ego sitienti dabo de fonte aquae vivae gratis. [7]Qui

---

because in Jewish literature it symbolized the abyss, the abode of demonic powers hostile to God.

Those who will inhabit this new world (symbolized by the Holy City, the new Jerusalem) are the entire assembly of the saved, the entire people of God (cf. vv. 12-14)—a holy people disposed to live in loving communion with God (as reflected by the image of the adorned bride: cf. vv. 2, 9). The promise of a new covenant (Ezek 37:27) will be fulfilled to the letter: God will see to it that none of the evil, suffering or pain found in this world will find its way into the new world.

This passage of the Book of Revelation strengthens the faith and hope of the Church—not only St John's own generation but all generations down the ages for as long as the Church makes its way through this valley of tears. The Second Vatican Council says: "We know neither the moment of the consummation of the earth and of man nor the way the universe will be transformed. The form of this world, distorted by sin, is passing away and we are taught that God is preparing a new dwelling and a new earth in which righteousness dwells, whose happiness will fill and surpass all the desires of peace arising in the hearts of men. Then with death conquered the children of God will be raised in Christ and what was sown in weakness and dishonour will put on the imperishable: charity and its works will remain, and all of creation, which God made for man, will be set free from its bondage to decay" (*Gaudium et spes*, 39).

5-8. For the first and only time in the entire book God himself speaks. He does so as absolute Lord of all, to ratify what has just been expounded. While the author and his readers are still in this world of suffering, God affirms that he—even now—is creating a new world. There is, then, a connexion between present human suffering and the future world which is taking shape thanks to the mercy of God.

[o]Other ancient authorities read *peoples*
[p]Other ancient authorities add *and be their God*

Zech 14:8
Rev 1:8; 22:17

2 Sam 7:14
Ps 89:27

Rev 22:15

I am the Alpha and the Omega, the beginning and the end. To the thirsty I will give water without price from the fountain of the water of life. [7]He who conquers shall have this heritage, and I will be his God and he shall be my son. [8]But as for the cowardly, the faithless, the polluted, as for murderers, fornicators, sorcerers, idolaters, and all liars, their lot shall be in the lake that burns with fire and brimstone, which is the second death."

---

vicerit, hereditabit haec, et *ero illi Deus, et ille erit mihi filius.* [8]Timidis autem et incredulis et exsecratis et homicidis et fornicatoribus et veneficis et idolatris

---

Although that new world will emerge in its complete form on the last day, the renewal of all things has already begun; it began with the life, death and resurrection of Christ. "The kingdom of life has begun," St Gregory of Nyssa teaches, "and the empire of death has been undone. Another generation, another life, another way of loving has made its appearance: our very nature is being transformed. What type of generation am I referring to? A generation which results not from blood or carnal love or human love, but from God. Are you wondering how that can be? I shall explain it in a few words. This new creature is begotten by faith; the regeneration of Baptism brings it to birth; the Church, its nurse, weans it by her teaching and institutions and nourishes it with her heavenly bread. This new creature matures through holiness of life; its marriage is marriage with Wisdom; its children, hope; its home, the Kingdom; its inheritance and its riches, the delights of paradise; its final destiny is not death, but eternal and joyful life in the dwelling-place of the saints" (*Oratio I in Christi resurrectionem*). We should remember that "the Kingdom is mysteriously present here on earth; when the Lord comes it will enter into its perfection" (*Gaudium et spes*, 39).

The promise of a world to come is so sure that although that world has not achieved its full perfection, it can be categorically stated that it is a promise *already kept*—"It is done": God himself, the Lord of history guarantees it (cf. note on Rev 1:8).

"To the thirsty": being thirsty refers to the desire man should have for the good things of the Kingdom, which God's loving kindness grants him. The idea of thirst (taken from Isaiah 55:1) here points to that yearning for God and the infinite which can only be satisfied by the grace of Christ, by the Holy Spirit within us (symbolized by St John in the water of life, cf., e.g., Jn 4:10; 7:38).

A Christian who has the grace of Christ and the gifts of the Holy Spirit can consider himself a conqueror, a sharer in our Lord's victory over sin and the powers of evil, and a sharer therefore in the dignity of a son or daughter of God in Christ. And so the title "son of God" (which in 2 Samuel 7:14 is applied, almost with the very same words as here, to the successor of David, and in Psalm 2:7 to the Messiah) is extended by St John to cover all Christians, called as they are to share in Christ's victory.

⁹Then came one of the seven angels who had the seven bowls full of the seven last plagues, and spoke to me, saying, "Come, I will show you the Bride, the wife of the Lamb." ¹⁰And in the Spirit he carried me away to a great,

Rev 15:1, 6, 7; 19:7

Mt 4:8
Ezek 40:2
Rev 21:2

---

et omnibus mendacibus, pars illorum erit in stagno ardenti igne et sulphure, quod est mors secunda." ⁹Et venit unus de septem angelis habentibus septem phialas plenas septem plagis novissimis et locutus est mecum dicens: "Veni, ostendam tibi sponsam uxorem Agni." ¹⁰Et sustulit me in spiritu super montem

---

Contrasting with the beatitudes is the proclamation of the rejection of those who will have no part in the future Kingdom because they are damned for ever due to their persistence in sin. Therefore, we should be vigilant, as St Augustine taught: "Everyone fears physical death; but few fear the death of the soul [...]. Mortal man strives not to die; so, should not the man destined to live eternally strive not to sin?" (*In Ioann. Evang.*, 49, 2).

9-21. In contrast with the punishment visited on the evil city, Babylon, the harlot (cf. 17:1), we are now shown the Holy City, the new Jerusalem, the spouse, coming down from heaven. There is a significant parallel between 17:1ff and 21:9ff.

The author writes with a truly remarkable mastery of language: after the introduction (v. 9), he describes the Holy City using three literary devices which, after giving the measurements of the city, he repeats in more or less reverse order. The description is like the impressions a traveller has as he approaches: first, from afar, he sees its radiance—the city as a whole and the glory of God (vv. 10-11); as he comes closer he can distinguish walls and gates (vv. 12-13), and when closer still its foundation stones (v. 14). Once inside, he realizes its sheer scale (vv. 15-16) and is able to assess the size and richness of its walls (vv. 17-18) and foundation stones and gates (vv. 19-21); and he is spellbound by the brightness that shines from the glory of God (21:22 - 22:5).

The city is given the titles of Bride and Wife (Spouse) which are normally used to designate the Church (cf. 19:7). This is easy to understand in the context of the imagery used: the city represents the Church, the community of the elect viewed in its complete, indissoluble union with the Lamb.

10-14. This vision is rather like the one the prophet Ezekiel had when he saw the New Jerusalem and the temple of the future (cf. Ezek 40-42). However, St John stresses (cf. also 21:2) that the city comes down from heaven: this shows that the full establishment (so long desired) of the messianic kingdom will be brought about by the power of God and in line with his will.

The description of the Holy City begins with the view from outside. This is the first thing that is seen and it is what makes it strong and unassailable. He speaks of walls and gates and foundations. The names of the tribes of Israel and the twelve Apostles show the continuity between the ancient chosen people and

Rev 21:23
Is 58:8; 60:1, 2, 19

Ezek 48:31-35
Rev 7:1-8

Eph 2:20

Ezek 40:3, 5

Ezek 43:16;
48:16f

high mountain, and showed me the holy city Jerusalem coming down out of heaven from God, [11]having the glory of God, its radiance like a most rare jewel, like a jasper, clear as crystal. [12]It had a great, high wall, with twelve gates, and at the gates twelve angels, and on the gates the names of the twelve tribes of the sons of Israel were inscribed; [13]on the east three gates, on the north three gates, on the south three gates, and on the west three gates. [14]And the wall of the city had twelve foundations, and on them the twelve names of the twelve apostles of the Lamb.

[15]And he who talked to me had a measuring rod of gold to measure the city and its gates and walls. [16]The city lies foursquare, its length the same as its breadth; and he measured the city with his rod, twelve thousand stadia;[q] its length and breadth and height are equal. [17]He also measured its wall, a hundred and forty-four cubits by a man's measure,

---

magnum et altum et ostendit mihi civitatem sanctam Ierusalem descendentem de caelo a Deo, [11]habentem claritatem Dei; lumen eius simile lapidi pretiosissimo, tamquam lapidi iaspidi, in modum crystalli; [12]et habebat murum magnum et altum et habebat *portas* duodecim et super portas angelos duodecim et *nomina* inscripta, quae sunt duodecim *tribuum filiorum Israel.* [13]*Ab oriente portae tres et ab aquilone portae tres et ab austro portae tres et ab occasu portae tres*; [14]et murus civitatis habens fundamenta duodecim, et super ipsis duodecim nomina duodecim apostolorum Agni. [15]Et, qui loquebatur mecum, habebat mensuram arundinem auream, ut metiretur civitatem et portas eius et murum eius. [16]Et civitas in quadro posita est, et longitudo eius tanta est quanta et latitudo. Et mensus est civitatem arundine per stadia duodecim milia; longitudo et latitudo et altitudo eius aequales sunt. [17]Et mensus est murum eius

---

the Church of Christ; and yet the point is made that the Church is something quite new which rests on the twelve Apostles of the Lord (cf. Eph 2:20). The arrangement of the gates, in threes facing the four points of the compass, indicates that the Church is universal: all nations must come to it to gain salvation. This is what St Augustine means when he says that "outside the catholic Church one can find everything except salvation" (*Sermo ad Cassar.*, 6).

15-17. The proportions, purely symbolic, convey the idea of the city's solidity and stability: it is depicted as a cube, as high as it is broad and long.

The Holy of Holies (described in 1 Kings 6:19f) was also cubic in form. The numbers are also symbolic: the twelve thousand stadia signify the chosen people with its twelve tribes and also the multitude of nations which make up

[q]About fifteen hundred miles

that is, an angel's. [18]The wall was built of jasper, while the city was pure gold, clear as glass. [19]The foundations of the wall of the city were adorned with every jewel; the first was jasper, the second sapphire, the third agate, the fourth emerald, [20]the fifth onyx, the sixth carnelian, the seventh chrysolite, the eighth beryl, the ninth topaz, the tenth chrysoprase, the eleventh jacinth, the twelfth amethyst. [21]And the twelve gates were twelve pearls, each of the gates made of a single pearl, and the street of the city was pure gold, transparent as glass.

Is 54:11-12
Tob 13:17

centum quadraginta quattuor cubitorum, mensura hominis, quae est angeli. [18]Et erat structura muri eius ex iaspide, ipsa vero civitas aurum mundum simile vitro mundo. [19]Fundamenta muri civitatis omni lapide pretioso ornata; fundamentum primum iaspis, secundus sapphirus, tertius chalcedonius, quartus smaragdus, [20]quintus sardonyx, sextus sardinus, septimus chrysolithus, octavus beryllus, nonus topazius, decimus chrysoprasus, undecimus hyacinthus, duodecimus amethystus. [21]Et duodecim portae duodecim margaritae sunt, et singulae portae erant ex singulis margaritis. Et platea civitatis aurum mundum tamquam vitrum

the new people. The one hundred and forty-four cubits (also a multiple of twelve), the height of the wall, are nothing compared with the towering height of the city; this is making the point that the walls are ornamental rather than defensive. Its enemies have been overthrown and it has no need of fortifications.

The point is made that the measurements are human ones, despite the fact that it is an angel that does the measuring. In any case they are measures which indicate that the heavenly Jerusalem is vast and rich.

18-21. These descriptions recall those of Ezekiel, but they are much more colourful and beautiful. Each one of the precious foundation stones reveals the richness of the Holy City, as do the huge pearls which form its gates. Some Fathers of the Church have seen these descriptions as a reference to all the divine gifts present in some way in the soul in the state of grace.

As usual in the book, the message draws on the Old Testament: Tobit 13:17 speaks of the rebuilding of Jerusalem with precious stones such as sapphires and emeralds, which in turn are reminiscent of the ornamentation on the high priest's breastplate (cf. Ex 28:17-20) and the raiment of the prince of Tyre (Ezek 28:13). Thus, the precious stones identify the priestly and royal features of the City.

21b-27. After taking us up to the walls and through the gates of the City, the author brings us right inside, to its very centre; this also is amazingly rich. However, surprisingly, there is no temple. This makes it different from the Jerusalem described by Ezekiel, for the centre of that city was the temple (cf. Ezek 40-42). The temple in Jerusalem and the tent of the tabernacle in the wilderness symbolized the fact that God dwelt there; it was the visible sign of

Jn 2:19-21
Is 24:23; 60:1, 19
Rev 22:5
Is 60:3, 5
Is 60:11
Rev 22:5
Is 60:11
Is 52:1
2 Pet 3:13
Zech 13:1-2

[22]And I saw no temple in the city, for its temple is the Lord God the Almighty and the Lamb. [23]And the city has no need of sun or moon to shine upon it, for the glory of God is its light, and its lamp is the Lamb. [24]By its light shall the nations walk; and the kings of the earth shall bring their glory into it, [25]and its gates shall never be shut by day—and there shall be no night there; [26]they shall bring into it the glory and the honour of the nations. [27]But nothing unclean shall enter it, nor any one who practises abomination or falsehood, but only those who are written in the Lamb's book of life.

---

perlucidum. [22]Et templum non vidi in ea: Dominus enim, Deus omnipotens, templum illius est, et Agnus. [23]Et civitas non eget sole neque luna, ut luceant ei, nam claritas Dei illuminavit eam, et lucerna eius est Agnus. [24]Et ambulabunt gentes per lumen eius, et reges terrae afferunt gloriam suam in illam; [25]et portae eius non claudentur per diem, nox enim non erit illic; [26]et afferent gloriam et divitias gentium in illam. [27]Nec intrabit in ea aliquid coinquinatum et faciens abominationem et mendacium, nisi qui scripti sunt in libro vitae Agni.

---

divine presence (*shekinah* in Hebrew), a presence revealed by the descent of the cloud of the glory of God.

In the heavenly Jerusalem there is no longer any need for God to have a dwelling-place, because God the Father himself and the Lamb are always present. The Godhead does not need to be brought to mind by the temple (the symbol of his invisible presence), because the blessed will always see God face to face. This sight of God is what causes the righteous to be forever happy. "There are no words to explain the blessedness which the soul enjoys, the gain which he obtains once his true nature has been restored to him and he is able henceforth to contemplate his Lord" (Chrysostom, *Ad Theodorum lapsum*, 1, 13).

In the Old Testament theophanies of Yahweh, a splendid brightness revealed the divine glory. And so, the presence of God will fill the heavenly Jerusalem with such a brightness of light that there is no need of sun or moon. Beside God the Father, with equal rank and dignity, is the Lamb, whose glory will also shine out, revealing his divinity.

This light will illuminate all those who worship the Lord, thereby fulfilling the messianic prophecies of Isaiah (cf. Is 60:3, 5, 11; 65-66).

The gates of the Holy City will stay open by day, that is, always, because there will be no more night, nor anything unclean: the saints will be the only ones to enter.

[1]Then he showed me the river of the water of life, bright as crystal, flowing from the throne of God and of the Lamb [2]through the middle of the street of the city; also, on either side of the river, the tree of life[r] with its twelve kinds of fruit, yielding its fruit each month; and the leaves of the tree were for the healing of the nations. [3]There shall no more be anything accursed, but the throne of God and of the Lamb shall be in it, and his servants shall worship him; [4]they shall see his face, and his name shall be on their foreheads. [5]And night shall be no more; they need no light of lamp or sun, for the Lord God will be their light, and they shall reign for ever and ever.

Ezek 47:1, 7
Zech 14:8

Ezek 47:12
Gen 2:9

Zech 14:11
Rev 7:15

1 Jn 3:2
1 Cor 13:12
Ps 17:15; 42:3

Rev 21:25; 5:10
Is 60:19
Dan 7:18, 27

---

[1]Et ostendit mihi fluvium aquae vitae splendidum tamquam crystallum, procedentem de throno Dei et Agni. [2]*In medio* plateae eius et *fluminis ex utraque parte lignum vitae* afferens fructus duodecim, *per menses* singulos reddens *fructum suum*, et *folia* ligni *ad sanitatem* gentium. [3]Et omne maledictum non erit amplius. Et thronus Dei et Agni in illa erit; et servi eius servient illi [4]et videbunt faciem eius, et nomen eius in frontibus eorum. [5]Et nox ultra non erit, et non egent lumine lucernae neque lumine solis, quoniam Dominus Deus illuminabit super illos, et regnabunt in saecula saeculorum. [6]Et dixit mihi: "Haec verba fidelissima et vera sunt, et Dominus, Deus spirituum prophetarum, misit angelum suum ostendere servis suis, quae oportet fieri cito. [7]Et ecce venio

---

1-5. Because the water of life is a symbol of the Holy Spirit (cf. 21:6), some Fathers and modern commentators have, justifiably, read a trinitarian meaning into this passage—interpreting the river which flows from the throne of God and of the Lamb representing the Holy Spirit who proceeds from the Father and the Son.

The trees whose leaves never fade (cf. Ps 1:3), with their fruit and medicinal foliage, symbolize the joy of eternal life (cf. Ezek 47:1-12; Ps 46:5).

The passage also takes up the prophecy in Zechariah 14:11 that nothing will be accursed—a reference to the terrible practice of anathema (Hebrew *herem*) which marked the Israelite conquest of Canaan: to avoid being tainted by idolatrous pagans, the Israelites laid cities and fields waste, putting them to torch and killing inhabitants and livestock. Peace and security will now reign supreme. And the dream of every man will come true—to see God (something impossible to attain on earth). Now all the blessed will see God (cf. 1 Cor 13:12); and because they see him they shall be like him (cf. 1 Jn 3:2). The name of God on their foreheads shows that they belong to God (cf. Rev 13:16-17).

[r]Or the Lamb. In the midst of the street of the city, and on either side of the river, was the tree of life, etc.

The visions come to an end

Dan 2:28
Rev 1:1

⁶And he said to me, "These words are trustworthy and true. And the Lord, the God of the spirits of the prophets, has sent his angel to show his servants what must soon take place. ⁷And behold, I am coming soon."

Rev 3:11; 1:3

Blessed is he who keeps the words of the prophecy of this book.

Rev 19:10

⁸I John am he who heard and saw these things. And when I heard and saw them, I fell down to worship at the feet of the angel who showed them to me; ⁹but he said to me, "You must not do that! I am a fellow servant with you and your brethren the prophets, and with those who keep the words of this book. Worship God."

---

velociter. Beatus, qui servat verba prophetiae libri huius." ⁸Et ego Ioannes, qui audivi et vidi haec. Et postquam audissem et vidissem, cecidi, ut adorarem ante pedes angeli, qui mihi haec ostendebat. ⁹Et dicit mihi: "Vide, ne feceris. Conservus tuus sum et fratrum tuorum prophetarum et eorum, qui servant verba

6-9. The author concludes his account of his visions by reaffirming that everything he has written is true (vv. 5-9) and by issuing a solemn warning: it will all come to pass and people will either be blessed or rejected (vv. 10-15).

The truth of what the book says is grounded on God, who is truth itself. This is St John's usual way of referring to the authority and reliability of his teaching (cf. Rev 1:1, 9; Jn 19:35; 1 Jn 1:1ff). He is acutely conscious of having written in the same manner as the prophets spoke—inspired by "the God of the spirits of the prophets". That is why he presents his book as "prophecy".

He also insists on the fact that the Lord's coming is imminent: he says this no less than three times in this chapter (vv. 7, 12 and 20): this is designed to make it quite clear that the Lord will come, and to create a climate of vigilance and hope (cf. note on Rev 1:1, on the imminence of the second coming).

Because this is a genuine book of prophecy those who read it and tell others its message are described as "blessed". This is the attitude which Jesus required people to have towards the word of God and towards his own words: when a woman proclaims his Mother "blessed", our Lord replies, "Blessed rather are those who hear the word of God and keep it" (Lk 11:28), and he promises that a person who listens to his word and keeps it is like someone who builds on solid foundations (cf. Mt 7:24). St James gives a similar warning: "be doers of the word, and not hearers only, deceiving yourselves" (Jas 1:22).

10-15. Unlike other revelations (cf. Rev 10:4; Dan 8:26), God makes it plain that he wants everyone to know the things St John has just written; Christians needed to be consoled and strengthened in the trials that lay ahead. They must keep pressing on, for the end is near (v. 11); these words are somewhat ironic,

[10]And he said to me, "Do not seal up the words of the prophecy of this book, for the time is near. [11]Let the evildoer still do evil, and the filthy still be filthy, and the righteous still do right, and the holy still be holy."

[12]"Behold, I am coming soon, bringing my recompense, to repay every one for what he has done. [13]I am the Alpha and the Omega, the first and the last, the beginning and the end."

[14]Blessed are those who wash their robes,[s] that they may have the right to the tree of life and that they may enter the city by the gates. [15]Outside are the dogs and sorcerers and fornicators and murderers and idolaters, and every one who loves and practises falsehood.

Dan 8:26; 12:4
Rev 10:4; 1:3

Dan 12:10

Ps 28:4; 62:13
Jer 17:10
Is 40:10
Is 44:6; 48:12
Heb 13:8
Rev 1:17, 8

Gen 2:9; 3:22
Rev 7:14

Rev 21:8, 27

---

libri huius; Deum adora!" [10]Et dicit mihi: "Ne signaveris verba prophetiae libri huius; tempus enim prope est! [11]Qui nocet, noceat adhuc, et, qui sordidus est, sordescat adhuc, et iustus iustitiam faciat adhuc, et sanctus sanctificetur adhuc. [12]Ecce venio cito, et merces mea mecum est, reddere unicuique sicut opus eius est. [13]Ego Alpha et Omega, primus et novissimus, principium et finis. [14]Beati, qui lavant stolas suas, ut sit potestas eorum super lignum vitae, et per portas intrent in civitatem. [15]Foris canes et venefici et impudici et homicidae et idolis

---

ridiculing as they do those who are bent on continuing to live a depraved life, unwilling to admit their sin and unwilling to mend their ways in time. The passage makes it quite clear that there will be a judgment made by Christ when he comes again; when he exercises this judicial authority which belongs to God alone, he appears with divine attributes (cf. note on Rev 1:8). The message contained in these verses should be reassuring for the Christian. As St Teresa of Avila says, "May His Majesty be pleased to grant us to experience this before he takes us from this life, for it will be a great thing at the hour of death to realize that we shall be judged by One whom we have loved above all things. Once our debts have been paid we shall be able to walk in safety. We shall not be going into a foreign land, but into our own country, for it belongs to him whom we have loved so truly and who himself loves us" (*Way of Perfection*, 40).

The robes washed in the blood of the Lamb (cf. note on Rev 7:14) are a reference to the fact that the righteous have been cleansed by having applied to them the merits of the passion, death and resurrection of Christ.

16. In a formal, solemn manner Jesus Christ addresses believers and confirms the genuineness of the prophetic content of the book. This marks the start of the epilogue, which records the testimony of the Church (v. 17) and the writer (vv. 18-19) and once again, before the words of farewell, Christ's own confirmation (v. 20).

EPILOGUE

¹⁶"I Jesus have sent my angel to you with this testimony for the churches. I am the root and the offspring of David, the bright morning star."

Prayer of the Spirit and the Bride. Words of warning and farewell

Zech 14:8
Jn 7:37
Is 55:1
Rev 21:6

¹⁷The Spirit and the Bride say, "Come." And let him who hears say, "Come." And let him who is thirsty come, let him who desires take the water of life without price.

Deut 4:2; 13:1

¹⁸I warn every one who hears the words of the prophecy of this book: if any one adds to them, God will add to him the plagues described in this book, ¹⁹and if any one takes

---

servientes et omnis, qui amat et facit mendacium! ¹⁶Ego Iesus misi angelum meum testificari vobis haec super ecclesiis. Ego sum radix et genus David, stella splendida matutina." ¹⁷Et Spiritus et sponsa dicunt: "Veni!" Et, qui audit, dicat: "Veni!" Et, qui sitit, veniat; qui vult, accipiat aquam vitae gratis. ¹⁸Contestor ego omni audienti verba prophetiae libri huius: Si quis apposuerit ad haec, apponet Deus super illum plagas scriptas in libro isto; ¹⁹et si quis abstulerit de

---

The titles applied to Jesus focus on his Hebrew and Davidic ancestry, without which he could not be the Messiah. Instead of the word "root", other passages speak of his being a young, vigorous shoot which grows out of the ancient trunk of Jesse (cf. Is 11:1). The morning star is another metaphor designating the Messiah (cf. Num 24:17).

17. The Bride is the Church who, in reply to Christ's promise (cf. 22:12), ardently desires and prays for his coming. The prayer of the Church is inspired by the Holy Spirit, the voices of both Church and Spirit fusing in a single cry. Every Christian is invited to join in this prayer and discover in the Church the gift of the Spirit, symbolized by the water of life (cf. 21:6); this gift allows the Christian to taste in anticipation the good things of the Kingdom. The language of this verse reminds us of the liturgical dimension of the Church with its prayer and celebration of the sacraments.

18-19. Using language similar to Deuteronomy 4:2 (cf. also Dt 13:1; Prov 30:6), the author warns that nothing in this book may be altered, for the very good reason that it is a revelation from God. No one may tamper with it, no one may add or subtract anything, or if he does God will call him to account. What St John says here is applicable to all divine Revelation. That is why St Paul told the Galatians that anyone—even an angel—would be accursed, excommunicated, who dared to change the Gospel, the message of received faith (cf. Gal 1:8).

away from the words of the book of this prophecy, God will ~~Rev 21:10 - 22:2~~
take away his share in the tree of life and in the holy city,
which are described in this book.
²⁰He who testifies to these things says, "Surely I am ~~1 Cor 16:22~~
coming soon." Amen. Come, Lord Jesus!
²¹The grace of the Lord Jesus be with all the saints.ᵗ ~~1 Cor 16:23~~
Amen.

---

verbis libri prophetiae huius, auferet Deus partem eius de ligno vitae et de
civitate sancta, de his, quae scripta sunt in libro isto. ²⁰Dicit, qui testimonium
perhibet istorum: "Etiam, venio cito." "Amen. Veni, Domine Iesu!" ²¹Gratia
Domini Iesu cum omnibus.

The Revelation made by Christ has been entrusted to the Church, who guards
it faithfully with the aid of the Holy Spirit. As St Vincent of Lerins teaches, "in
the catholic Church the greatest care must be taken to keep what has been
believed everywhere, always and by all [. . .]. The very nature of religion
demands that everything be passed on to children as faithfully as it has been
received by parents" (*Commonitorium*, 2 and 6). The deposit of faith is so
inviolable that "true ecumenical activity means openness, drawing closer,
availability for dialogue, and a shared investigation of the truth in the full
evangelical and Christian sense; but in no way does it or can it mean giving up
or in any way diminishing the treasures of divine truth that the Church has
constantly confessed and taught" (John Paul II, *Redemptor hominis*, 6).

20. Christ himself replies to the supplication of the Church and the Spirit:
"I am coming soon." This idea occurs seven times in the course of the book (cf.
2:16; 3:11; 16:15; 22:7, 12, 17, 20), showing that this is a promise which will
certainly be kept. On the basis of this passage, John Paul II makes this
exhortation: "Therefore, let Christ be your sure point of reference, let him be
the basis of a confidence which knows no vacillation. Let the passionate
invocation of the Church, "Come, Lord Jesus!" become the spontaneous sigh
of your heart, a heart never content with the present because it always tends
towards the 'not yet' of promised fulfilment" (*Homily*, 18 May 1980).
This invocation—"Come, Lord Jesus"—was so often on the lips and in the
hearts of the first Christians that it was even expressed in Aramaic, the language
which Jesus and the Apostles spoke: *Marana-tha* (cf. 1 Cor 16:22; *Didache*,
10, 6). Today, translated into the vernacular, it is used as an acclamation at
Mass, after the elevation. And so "the earthly liturgy harmonizes with that of
heaven. And now, as in every Mass, there reaches our heart, which is so much
in need of consolation, that reassuring reply: "He who testifies to these things
says, 'Surely I am coming soon [. . .].'

ᵗOther ancient authorities omit *all*; others omit *the saints*

"Strengthened by this certainty, let us set out again along the ways of the earth, feeling greater unity and solidarity with one another, and at the same time bearing in our heart the desire that has become more eager to make known to our brothers and sisters, still enveloped by the clouds of doubt and depression, the 'joyful proclamation' that there has risen over the horizon of their lives 'the bright morning star' (Rev 22:16), the Redeemer of man, Christ the Lord" (John Paul II, *Homily*, 18 May 1980).

Headings added to the scriptural text for this edition

The Navarre Bible (New Testament)

St Matthew's Gospel
St Mark's Gospel
St Luke's Gospel
St John's Gospel
Acts of the Apostles
Romans and Galatians
Corinthians
Captivity Epistles
Thessalonians and Pastoral Epistles
Hebrews
Catholic Epistles
Revelation

ESSAYS ON BIBLICAL SUBJECTS

In addition to special introduction(s) in each volume, the following essays etc. are
published in the series:

St Mark	General Introduction to the Bible; Introduction to the Books of the New Testament; Introduction to the Holy Gospels; and The Dates in the Life of our Lord Jesus Christ
St Luke	Index to the Four Gospels
Acts	The History of the New Testament Text
Romans & Galatians	Introduction to the Epistles of St Paul
Corinthians	Divine Inspiration of the Bible
Captivity Epistles	The Canon of the Bible
Thessalonians	The Truth of Sacred Scripture
Hebrews	Interpretation of Sacred Scripture and the Senses of the Bible; Divine Worship in the Old Testament
Catholic Epistles	Rules for Biblical Interpretation
Revelation	Index to the New Testament

New Testament Subject Index

This is an index both to passages in the New Testament and to explanations in the Notes and Introductions. Parallel passages are not usually indexed; these can be found in the shoulder notes to the RSV text.

References to the Introductions are indicated by 'Intro', followed by the *volume* short title (as given below) and the *page* number; whereas reference to NT text or Notes are in the standard form, e.g. 'Jn 4:28-32'.

The index has been compiled by members of the Department of Sacred Scripture at Navarre University.

Volume No.	Short title	Content of Volume
1	Mt	St Matthew's Gospel
2	Mk	St Mark's Gospel
3	Lk	St Luke's Gospel
4	Jn	St John's Gospel
5	Acts	Acts of the Apostles
6	Rom	Romans and Galatians
7	Cor	Corinthians (1 & 2)
8	Capt	Captivity Epistles (Ephesians, Philippians, Colossians, Philemon)
9	Thess	Thessalonians (1 & 2) and Pastoral Epistles (1 & 2 Timothy, Titus)
10	Heb	Hebrews
11	Cath	Catholic Epistles (James, 1 & 2 Peter, 1-3 John, Jude)
12	Rev	Revelation

Abandonment *in God's hands*
Mt 1:19; 6:25-32; Lk 22:42;
1 Pet 5:5-11. *See* Filiation, divine; Providence.

Abraham
(a) **Patriarch:** Mt 1:2, 17; 8:11; 23:32; Lk 13:28
(b) **father of the chosen people:** Mt 3:9; Lk 1:55, 73; 13:16; 19:9; Jn 8:31-59; Acts 7:1-8; Heb 7:1-10
(c) **his exemplary faith:** Rom 4:1-25; Gal 3:6-9; Heb 6:13-15; 11:8-12,

17-19; Jas 2:20-26
(d) **bosom of A.:** Lk 16:19-31.

Adoration Mt 2:11; 4:8-10; 14:33; 28:16-20; Lk 2:15-20; Jn 4:20-26; Heb 1:6; Rev 4:8-11; 22:9.
See Worship; Liturgy.

Adultery Mt 5:27-32; 19:9-12; Jn 8:3-11; Jas 4:4.

Almsgiving
(a) **recommended by Christ:** Mt 5:42; 19:21; 25:35-46; Lk 12:33

(b) upright intention needed:
Mt 6:2-4; Lk 14:12-14
(c) generosity: Mk 12:41-44;
Lk 11:40-41; Acts 11:27-30;
Gal 2:10; Tit 3:12-14
(d) reward for: Lk 14:12-14;
Acts 9:36-43; 10:1-8; 2 Cor 8:10-12;
9:6-15
(e) duty of: Acts 10:4; Jas 2:15-16.
See Mercy.

Altar
(a) in Old Law: Mt 5:23-24;
23:18-20; Rom 11:3
(b) of the Eucharist: 1 Cor 10:14-22;
Heb 13:10
(c) eschatological: Rev 6:9-11; 8:3-5.

Andrew, St Mt 4:18-20; 10:2;
Mk 1:29; 13:3; Jn 1:35-44; 6:8; 12:22;
Acts 1:13.

Angels
(a) inferior to Christ: Eph 1:20-21;
3:10-12; Col 1:16; 2:10, 15;
Heb 1:4 - 2:18; 1 Pet 3:22
(b) in life of Christ: Mt 1:20, 25;
2:13-23; 4:11; 26:53; 28:2-7;
Lk 1:11-20, 26-38; 2:9-15, 21; 22:43;
Jn 20:12-13
(c) their mission to men: Mt 18:10;
Acts 5:19-21; 8:26; 10:1-8; 12:6-11,
15; 27:23-24; Heb 1:14;
Intr. Rev pp. 25-26;
Rev 1:20; 5:11-14; 12:7-9
(d) in heaven: Mt 22:30; Lk 15:10;
Jn 1:51; 1 Pet 1:12; Rev 5:11-14
(e) at Last Judgment: Mt 13:39-42;
16:27; 24:31; 25:31; Lk 12:8-9; 16:22;
Jude 14:16
(f) hierarchies of: Rom 8:38;
Eph 1:32; 3:10-12; 6:12; Col 1:16;
2:10, 15; 1 Pet 3:22.

Angelus, the Lk 1:26-38; Jn 1:14.

Anna Lk 2:36-38.

Annas Lk 3:2; Jn 18:13-24; Acts 4:6.

Anointing of the Sick Mk 6:13;
Intr. Jas, p. 30; Jas 5:14-15.

Antichrist 2 Thess 2:3-12; 1 Jn 2:18,
22; 4:3; 2 Jn 7; Rev 13.

Apollos Acts 18:24-28; 19:1;
1 Cor 1:12; 3:4, 6, 22; 4:6; 16:12.

Apostles
(a) calling: Mt 4:18-22; 9:9; 17:1;
26:37; Mk 5:27; 13:3; Jn 1:35-51;
15:16; Acts 9:1-19; 26:16-18;
Rom 1:1; Gal 1:1, 15-16
(b) training: Mt 10:5-42; 13:10, 52;
15:12-20; 16:5-12; 18:1-35;
Mk 6:30-31; 7:17-20; Jn 4:31-38;
13-17
(c) Christ-given mission: Mt
28:16-20; Mk 3:14; Lk 6:12-16
(d) Apostolic College: Mk 3:14;
Acts 1:12-26; Eph 2:20; Rev 21:10-14
(e) witnesses to Christ: Acts 1:1-8,
21-26; 2:32; 4:33; 5:17-42; 10:40-42;
1 Cor 15:1-11; 1 Jn 4:15-15
(f) their authority in Church:
Acts 1:26; 4:35; 6:2; 8:14-17;
9:26-28; 11:1-18; 15:2; 1 Cor 3:4-17;
Rev 1:9, 11.
See Church.

Apostolate
(a) task of every Christian:
Mt 5:13-16; Lk 5:4; 8:1-3; 19:24-26;
Jn 4:32-38; Acts 9:6; 11:19-21; 16:10;
18:10, 24; 26:27; 1 Cor 9:16;
12:14-27; Eph 4:29; Col 4:5-6;
1 Thess 2:1-2; 2:10-12; Jas 5:19-20
(b) some features: Mt 13:31-33;
15:33-38; Mk 6:30-31; Lk 10:3-4;
Jn 4:32-28; Phil 1:15-18;
1 Thess 2:1-6; *see* Daring (b).
**(c) union with God as main means
of:** Mt 9:37-38; 10:1-4, 9-10;
Mk 3:14; Jn 1:45-51; 15:1-8;
Acts 13:2-3; 1 Cor 1:27;
2 Cor 5:14-15
(d) urgency: Lk 5:19-20; 12:49-50;
Acts 17:16-17; 26:27; 1 Cor 9:16
(e) purpose: Lk 10:5-6; Jn 1:40-41;
15:26-27; Jas 3:18.

Aquila Acts 18:2, 18, 26; 1 Cor 16:19;
2 Tim 4:19.

Asceticism
(a) need, importance: Mt 10:34-39;
11:12; Mk 10:46-52; Acts 20:21, 24;
Gen. Intr. St Paul in Rom, p. 42;
Rom 7:14-25; 13:11-14;
2 Cor 12:5-10; 1 Tim 4:7-11;
Heb 3:14; 6:9-12; 1 Pet 4:1-6;
Rev 5:8-10

(b) metaphor used:
1. narrow gate: Mt 7:13-14
2. competitive running:
1 Cor 9:24-27; Gal 5:7; Phil 3:12-14;
2 Tim 4:6-8
3. warfare, combat: 2 Cor 10:2-6;
Eph 6:10-20; 1 Thess 5:7-8;
1 Tim 1:18-19; 6:12; 2 Tim 2:3-7;
4:6-8. *See* Lukewarmness.

Authority
(a) of Jesus: Mt 9:6; 21:23; Mk 1:22;
Jn 13:13
(b) of the Apostles: Lk 10:16-19;
1 Cor 5:3-5; 1 Thess 2:6-10
(c) in Church: Mt 18:18; 20:24-28;
Jas 3:1-2. *See* Magisterium.
(d) in society: Mt 23:11;
Lk 22:24-27; Jn 13:12-18;
Rom 13:1-7; Col 3:22; Eph 6:5;
1 Pet 2:13-17; Rev 17:1 - 19:10

Azymes. *See* Festivals.

Babylon 1 Pet 5:13; Rev 14:8; 16:19;
17:5; 18:1-24.

Banquet
(a) Kingdom of God as: Mt 8:11-12;
22:1-14; 26:29
(b) Eucharist as: Mt 26:26-29;
1 Cor 10:14-22; 11:17-22, 33-34;
see Eucharist.

Baptism
(a) John's: Mt 3:6-12; 21:23-27;
Acts 19:1-7
(b) of Jesus: Mt 3:13-17
(c) of Christian:
1. prefigured in OT: 1 Cor 10:1-4;
1 Pet 3:20-22
2. nature: Mt 3:11; Jn 3:3-8;
Acts 8:36-39; 19:5; Rom 6:1-11;
Col 2:11-12; Intr. 1 Pet in Cath,
pp. 81-82; 1 Jn 5:6
3. necessary: Mt 19:13-14; Mk 1:9;
16:16; Intr. Jn, p. 34; Jn 3:5-8
4. removes sins: Mt 3:11; Mk 1:8;
Rom 6:1-11; 1 Cor 6:11
5. makes us children of God:
Jn 4:21-24; 5:3-4; Acts 2:37-38;
Gal 3:2-5: 2 Cor 5:16-17; Rev 7:1-8
6. makes us members of Christ:
1 Cor 1:2, 13-16
7. prints a "character":
2 Cor 1:21-22; 2 Pet 3:21-22

(d) of children: Mt 16:16; Acts 8:36;
16:15-33; 1 Cor 1:16
(e) of blood: Mt 2:16-17.

Barnabas Acts 4:36-37; 9:26-30;
11:22-30; 12:25; 13:1 - 15:39;
1 Cor 9:6; Gal 2:1, 9, 13; Col 4:10.

Bartholomew Mt 10:3; Jn 1:45-51;
21:2; Acts 1:13.

Beatitudes
(a) Sermon on the Mount: Mt 5:3-12
(b) the disciples are blessed:
Mt 13:16-17; Lk 11:27-28; Jn 13:17;
20:29.
See Joy.

Bethany Mt 21:17; 26:6-13;
Mk 11:1, 11; Lk 10:38-42; 24:50;
Jn 1:28; 11:1-45; 12:1-11.

Bethlehem Mt 2:1-18; Lk 2:4-20;
Jn 7:42.

Bethsaida Mt 11:21; Mk 6:45; 8:22;
Lk 9:10; Jn 1:44; 12:21.

Bible. *See* Scripture, Sacred.

Bishops
(a) successors of Apostles: Mt 18:18;
28:20; Acts 1:26; 20:28; 1 Cor 4:21;
2 Cor 2:5; 13:10; Phil 1:1
(b) hierarchical mission:
1. teaching: 1 Tim 5:17; 6:20-21;
Tit 1:5
2. ruling: 1 Tim 3:5; 5:1-16; Tit 2:1-10
3. hallowing: 1 Tim 4:12; Tit 2:7-8
(c) collegiality: Mt 18:18; 28:16-20;
Mk 3:13-14.
See Church (f).

Blasphemy
(a) against God: Rom 2:24;
2 Tim 3:2; Rev 13:1-6; 16:9, 11, 21;
17:3
(b) against Christ: Mt 27:39-44;
Jas 2:7
(c) against the Holy Spirit:
Mt 12:31-32
(d) against angels: 2 Pet 2:10-12;
Jude 8-10
**(e) Christ and Christians accused
of:** Mt 9:3; 26:65; Jn 10:33-38;
Acts 6:8-14
(f) grave sin; its punishment: Jn
18:29-32; Eph 4:31; Col 3:8;
1 Tim 1:20.

Blessing

(a) **God blesses men:** Mt 25:34-36; Acts 3:25; Gal 3:6-9,14

(b) **Christ b.:** Mt 14:19; 26:26; Mk 10:16; Lk 24:30

(c) **Christian b.:**1 Cor 10:16; 1 Pet 3:8-10

(d) **formal:** Mt 21:9; Lk 1:42; 2:34; Eph 1:3.

Body. *See* Flesh; Man.

Brethren

(a) **Christ's relatives:** Mt 12:46-50; Mk 6:1-3; Jn 2:12; 7:1-5; Acts 1:14

(b) **Chrisitian fraternity:** *see* Charity; Fraternity.

Brothers. *See* Brethren.

Caesar Mt 22:15-22; Lk 2:1; 3:1; Jn 19:12, 15; Acts 25-26.

Caiaphas Mt 26:3, 57-66; Lk 3:2; Jn 11:49-53; 18:13, 14, 24, 28; Acts 4:6.

Calling

(a) **of Apostles:** *see* Apostles.

(b) **of some disciples:** *see* Disciples.

(c) **of the Christian**

1. a divine choice: Mt 2:2; 9:9; 19:20-22; Mk 5:18-19; Lk 19:5-6; Jn 6:44, 65; 15:16; 1 Cor 1:26-31; Gal 1:15-16; 1 Thess 5:24; 2 Tim 1:9-10; Jude 1-2

2. demands implied by: Mt 4:18-22; 8:19-22; 10:34-37; Mk 6:8-9; 10:21-22, 28-30, 46-52; Lk 5:11; 14:26; Jn 1:43; 1 Cor 7:17-24; Eph 4:1; 2 Pet 1:10-11

3. how to discern: Mk 10:21-22

4. joy at discovering: Mt 2:10; Lk 5:27-29; 19:5-6

5. excuses: Mt 9:9; Lk 14:16-24; 18:18-27

6. reward: Mt 19:27-30; Lk 10:20; Jn 1:40-41.

(d) **Mary's:** Lk 1:26-38

See Holiness.

Calumny

(a) **against the Lord:** Mt 10:25-27; 11:16-19; 12:24-37

(b) **against his disciples:** Mt 5:11; 10:25-31; 2 Pet 2:12; 3:16; 4:12-19.

See Persecution.

Cana Jn 2:1-11; 4:46; 21:2.

Canticles. *See* Hymns.

Capernaum Mt 4:13; 8:5; 11:23-24; 17:24; Mk 1:21; 2:1; 9:33; Lk 4:23; Jn 2:12; 4:46, 48; 6:17, 24, 59.

Captivity Epistles Gen Intr. St Paul in Rom, pp. 23-26; Intr. Eph, Col. Phil, Philem in Capt.

Catechesis. *See* Preaching d) 3.

Celibacy. *See* Purity; Virginity.

Cenacle Mk 14:12-16; Acts 1:12-14; 12:12.

Centurion Mt 8:5-13; 27:54; Mk 15:29.

Charisms. *See* Gifts, spiritual.

Charity

(a) **the mark of Christians:** Jn 13:34-35; 15:12, 17; 1 Cor 14:1; 1 Pet 1:22-25; 1 Jn 2:9-11

(b) **fulness of the Law:** Mt 22:37-40; Rom 13:8-10; Jas 2:8-12

(c) **practice of:** Mt 5:38-42; 7:12; 9:2; 18:15-17; 25:40-45; 26:50; Lk 6:36; 7:41-50; 10:29-37; Acts 2:44-45; 4:32-37; 28:14-15; Rom 12:9-21; 15:1-3; 1 Cor 8:1-13; 9:19-23; Gal 6:2; Eph 4:2-3; Col 3:12-14; 1 Thess 4:9-10; Heb 12:15; 13:1; Jas 1:26-27; *see* Almsgiving

(d) **features of:** Mt 7:1-2; Lk 6:45; 1 Cor 13:2; 2 Cor 6:11-13; 1 Thess 3:12-13; 1 Tim 1:5; Tit 3:15; Philem 17-21; 1 Pet 3:8-12; 1 Jn 3:16-18; Rev 2:4

(e) **order in:** Mt 5:23-24; 22:34-40; Lk 10:25-37

(f) **some faults against:** Mt 5:22; 7:1; 25:41-46; Lk 9:54-56; 14:1-6; 1 Cor 6:1-10; Jas 2:1-4, 8-11; 3:2-12; 4:11-12; 1 Jn 3:14-15. Cf. Intr. Jn, pp. 31-33; Intr. 1 Jn, pp. 157-158.

Chastity. *See* Purity.

Childhood, spiritual Mt 11:25; 18:1-6; 19:13-14; 1 Pet 2:1-3. *See* Filiation, divine; Humility.

Choice

(a) **Christ chosen by the Father:** Mt 12:18; Lk 9:35; 1 Pet 2:4-6

(b) divine initiative in: Mt 22:14:
24:22-31; Jn 6:70; 13:18; 15:16, 19;
Rom 8:28-34; 1 Cor 1:26-31; Eph 1:4;
1 Thess 1:4; 2 Thess 2:13-14;
1 Pet 1:1-2.
See Vocation.

Christ, Jesus

(a) announced in OT: Intr. Mt, p. 22;
Mt 12:17-21; 21:4-5, 42; Lk
24:25-27; Jn 1:45; 5:39; 19:36; 20:9;
Heb 1:5-14; 2:6-8, 12-13; 5:5-6;
7:1-28

(b) name of:
1. meaning: Mt 1:21:25; Lk 1:31; 2:21
2. works done in: Acts 5:26-42; 10:43;
19:17; 1 Cor 5:3-5; 6:11;
2 Thess 1:11-12
3. miracles worked in: Acts 3:1-26;
4:5-22; 9:32-35

(c) dates in life of: Gen. Intr. Gosp. in
Mk, pp. 45-50; Mt 2:1; Lk 2:1-2;
3:1-2, 23

(d) his Blessed Humanity:
1. during his life on earth: Mt 1:1-17;
4:2; 8:24; 9:36; 26:36-46; 27:45-50;
Mk 11:12; Lk 2:52; 7:13; 24:39-43;
Jn 1:14; 4:6; 11:33; 17:1-5; 19:28;
20:27
2. testified to in Epistles: Rom 1:3-4;
Gal 4:4; Phil 2:5-8; Col 1:22;
Heb 2:9, 16-17; 5:7-8; 10:19-20;
1 Jn 1:1-4

(e) his divinity:
1. and his life on earth: Intr. Mt, p.
23; Mt 1:23; 8:29; 9:1-8; 11:27;
14:33; 16:16; 26:63-66; Mk 1:1, 24;
16:19; Lk 1:35; 20:41-44;
Intr. Jn, pp. 28-30; Jn 1:1-18; 5:31-40;
6:46-69; 8:58; 10:34-39; 12:45;
14:8-13; 20:17
2. in faith of Church: Intr. Rom, pp.
33-34; Rom 1:3-4; 1 Cor 10:1-4; 2
Cor 4:1-6; Gal 4:4; Phil 2:5-11;
Col 1:15-20; 2:9; Tit 2:13; Heb 1:1-4;
13:8; 1 Jn 1:1-4; Rev 2:8, 18; 3:7, 14;
5:11-14; 19:11-16; 22:10-15

(f) his hidden life:
1. Incarnation: Mt 1:18-25; Lk
1:26-38; Jn 1:14; 2 Tim 1:9-10;
1 Jn 4:2-3
2. birth: Mt 2:1-12; Lk 2:1-20
3. infancy: Mt 2:13-23; Lk 2:21-52

(g) his public life:
1. J. announced by Baptist:
Mt 3:1-12; Lk 1:76; Jn 1:6-8, 15-19
2. his baptism and temptations:
Mt 3:13-17; 4:1-11
3. J. and the Apostles: Mt 4:18-22;
10:1-42; 15:12; 16:5; 18:1-35; Mk
3:13-19; 6:30-31; Jn 1:39, 42, 45-51;
13-17
4. J. and Kingdom of God: Mt 4:23;
5-7; 13:1-52; 18:1-34; Jn 6:26-59
5. Transfiguration: Mt 17:1-13; 2 Pet
1:16-18
6. J. and forgiveness of sins:
Mt 9:1-7; Lk 7:36-50; 19:1-10;
Jn 8:1-10; 20:22-23
7. sign of contradiction: Intr. Mt, pp.
22-23; Mt 2:16-18; 10:34-39;
21:33-45; Lk 2:34; 7:23; 7:31-32;
11:14-23; 11:45-54; 19:7;
2 Cor 2:14-16
8. revealed by the Father: Mt 11:27;
Jn 1:18: 5:24, 36; 6:45, 57; 8:19, 26;
14:4-11; 17:2-6; Heb 10:19-21

(h) his redemptive sacrifice:
1. Passion and Death: Mt 16:21-23;
17:22-23; 20:17-19; 26-27;
Acts 2:22-23; 3:11-16; 4:10; 5:30;
10:39; 13:27-29
2. redemptive value: Intr. Rom, p. 35;
Rom 3:21-26; Heb 2:9; 9:11-28;
10:5-18; 1 Pet 2:21-25; 3:18

(i) glorification:
1. foretold by himself: Mt 12:40;
16:21-23; 17:22-23; 20:17-19; 24:30;
Jn 2:19-22; 12:32; 16:14; 17:1-5
2. Resurrection: Mt 28:1-20;
Mk 16:1-20; Lk 24:1-49; Jn 20:21;
Acts 1:1-6, 17-19; 2:8; 2:22-36;
3:11:26; 4:1-22; 10:40-42; 13:30-37;
17:30-34; Gen. Intr. St Paul in Rom,
pp. 35-36; Intr. Cor, pp. 32-34;
1 Cor 15;1 Thess 1:20; 2 Tim 2:8;
1 Pet 1:21
3. Ascension: Mk 16:19; Intr. Lk, pp.
22-23; Lk 9:51; 24:50-53; Acts
1:6-11; 2:32-36; 5:31; 7:55-56
4. descent into hell: 1 Pet 3:19-20; 4:6
5. Lord of All: Mt 25:34; Lk 1:33;
Jn 12:13; 18:33-37; 19:13-22;
1 Cor 15:23-28; 16:21-24; Eph
1:20-23; Phil 2:9-11; Heb 1:5-14; 2:8;
1 Pet 3:21-22; Rev 1:5-6, 17-19;

2:24-28; 3:20-21; 17:9-15; 19:11-16
6. Judge: Mt 13:36-43; 16:27;
25:31-46; Jn 5:22-30; Rom 2:1-16;
Acts 1:9-11; 10:40-42; 17:30-31; 2
Tim 4:6-8; 1 Thess 1:10; Heb 1:8; 1
Jn 2:28-29; Rev 2:12-13; 6:12-17;
22:10-15
(j) titles of Christ:
1. The Word: Intr. Jn, pp. 28-29;
Jn 1:1-18; 1 Jn 1:1-2; Rev 19:13
2. Christ or Messiah: Mt 1:16; 2:4;
16:16; 22:41-46; 26:63; Intr. Mk, p.
62; Mk 1:1; Lk 2:11-26; 24:26, 46;
Jn 1:41; 4:25-29; 10:24-25; 11:27;
20:31; Acts 2:14-26; 3:11-26; 17:2-3;
Heb 1:9; 2:13; 1 Jn 2:22; Rev 1:5-6;
22:16
3. Lamb of God: Jn 1:29, 36;
19:14-36; 1 Cor 5:7-8; Intr. Rev, p.
24; Rev 5:6-14; 14:1-5; 19:9-15;
19:5-9; 21:1 - 22:5
4. Servant of Yahweh: Mt 3:17; 8:17;
12:17-21; 20:28; 26:28; Jn 1:32-34;
Acts 3:13; 8:26-35; Heb 2:12;
1 Pet 2:21-25
5. rabbi or master: Mt 9:11; 17:24;
19:16; 23:7; Mk 10:51; Lk 20:39;
Jn 1:38, 49; 3:2; 13:13-14; 20:16
6. King of Israel: Mt 2:2; 21:5; 27:11,
37; Lk 1:33; 23:2; Jn 18:28-39;
19:19-22
7. Son of David: Mt 1:17; 9:27; 20:30;
21:9, 15; 22:41-46; Lk 1:32;
Rom 1:3-4
8. Son of man: Mt 8:20; 9:6; 10:23;
12:8; 13:37; 16:27-28; 17:22;20:28;
24:37-39; 26:64; Lk 6:22; Jn 1:51;
3:13-15; 5:27; 6:27, 53; 8:28; 9:35;
Rev 1:12-16; 5:1-5; 14:14-20
9. Son of God: Mt 3:17; 8:29; 11:27;
14:33; 16:16; 17:5; 26:63; 27:54;
Mk 1:1; Lk 1:35; 4:41; Jn 1:18, 34,
49; 3:16-17; 10:36; 11:27;
Acts 9:19-20; Rom 1:3-4; Heb 1:5;
Rev 2:18
10. Lord: Mt 3:3; 7:21; 8:2, 25; 9:28;
14:28-30; 15:22-27; 17:4; 22:41-46;
Mk 16:19-20; Lk 1:43; 2:11; 5:8; 7:6;
17:5; 18:41; 24:3, 34; Jn 1:23; 4:49;
6:34, 68; 9:36, 38; 11:27, 32;
13:13-14; 20:18, 28; 21:15-17;
Acts 10:36; 11:20; 22:10; 1 Cor 2:8;
5:4; 8:6; 2 Cor 4:5; 1 Pet 3:15

11. first-born of all creation:
Intr. Eph in Capt, pp. 26-27;
Intr. Col in Capt, pp. 155-157;
Col 1:15-20
12. The Righteous One: Acts 3:15;
7:52; 22:14; Heb 2:11; 4:15; Rev 3:7,
14
13. Mediator: Heb 2:17; 7:20-22;
12:24; 2 Tim 2:5
14. eternal high priest: Heb 3:1;
9:11-28; 10:5-18
(k) Son of Mary: Mt 1:16, 25; Lk
1:26-38; 2:1-52; 11:27-28; Jn 2:1-12;
19:26-27
(l) Christological hymns: Phil
2:6-11; Col 1:15-20; 1 Tim 3:16;
6:15; 2 Tim 2:11
See Trinity, Blessed.

Christian, the
(a) dignity of: Jn 14:22-23;
Acts 16:37-39; 1 Cor 3:21-23;
6:11-19, 20;
Intr. Phil in Capt, pp. 101-106
(b) union with Christ: Mt 10:40;
Lk 10:16; Jn 6:56-57; 15:1-8;
17:20-26; Rom 8:29; 14:7-9;
1 Cor 6:15-18; 1 Cor 8:11-13;
15:20-28; 2 Cor 1:5-11; 3:28; 4:7-12;
Gal 2:19-20; Eph 4:13; Col 3:5-17;
1 Jn 3:1-3; 4:17
(c) the name: Acts 11:26; 1 Pet 4:16.

Christianity
(a) its newness compared with OT:
Mt 5:21-46; 9:14-17; 19:1-12;
see New Testament (b) & (c).
(b) proven by miracles: Mt 10:7-8;
Mk 16:17-20; Jn 10:37-38;
see Miracles.
(c) is man's salvation: Mk 16:15-16;
Lk 4:16-21; Jn 6:14-15; *see*
Conversion.

Christians, first
(a) some features of their lifestyle:
Acts 2:42-47; 4:32-37; 5:12-16;
Rom 16:1-16
(b) charity: Acts 2:44-47; 11:27-30;
30:36-38; 28:14-15
(c) almsgiving: Acts 4:32-37;
1 Cor 16:1-4; 2 Cor 8:9
(d) Eucharist: Acts 2:42-47; 13:2;
20:7-12; 1 Cor 10:14-22; 11:17-34
(e) apostolic zeal: Acts 8:29-30;

18:24-28
(f) prayer: *see* Prayer (h)

Church

(a) divine origin: Mt 10:1-4; 16:18;
Jn 7:39; 14:26; 19:34; Acts 2:1-13;
Eph 1:4; 2:18
(b) and salvation: Mt 28:16-20;
Lk 4:18-19; Jn 20:21;
Intr. Rom, pp. 46-47; Col 1:24-27;
Intr. Past. Epis. in Thess pp. 82-83.
(c) nature of:
1. visible society: Mt 13:36-43; 18:17;
Lk 20:20-26
2. spiritual dimension: Mt 4:8-10;
Lk 19:11; Jn 7:17-18; 17:24;
18:36-37; Intr. Eph in Capt,
pp. 27-28; Eph 4:16; 1 Thess 1:1;
1 Tim 3:15
3. cannot stray: Mt 16:18; 28:20;
Rev 11:1-2, 13-17
(d) compared to:
1. sheepfold: Jn 10:1-18; 1 Pet 2:25
2. field: Mt 20:1-16; 21:33-44;
Jn 15:1-8; 1 Cor 3:9
3. house and temple: Eph 2:19-22;
2 Tim 2:20-21; Heb 3:2; 1 Pet 2:4-10
4. new Jerusalem: Lk 21:20-24;
Rev 21:1 - 22:5
5. Bride of Christ: Eph 5:22-33;
Rev 21 - 22
6. body: Acts 9:4-5; Gen. Intr. St Paul
in Rom, pp. 44-46; Rom 12:4-5;
Intr. 1 Cor, pp. 29-30;
1 Cor 12:12-31; 15:20-28;
2 Cor 1:5-11; 5:14-15; Eph 1:22-23;
4:15-16; Col 1:18; Rev 1:9-11
7. people of God: Gen. Intr. St Paul in
Rom, p. 44; Eph 1:13-14;
1 Pet 1:13-16; 2:9-10
(e) properties of:
1. unity: Jn 10:16; 15:1-8; 17:20-23;
19:23-24; Acts 4:32-37;
Gen. Intr. St Paul in Rom, pp. 43-44;
Intr. 1 Cor, p. 29; 1 Cor 1:10-17
2. holiness: Eph 5:27
3. catholicity: Mt 10:5-6; 13:31-32;
21:43; 28:16-20; Lk 21:24;
Jn 11:49-53; 17:21
4. apostolicity: Mt 19:28;
Mk 3:13-19; Jn 17:20;
Acts 1:21-22, 26; Tit 1:5

(f) hierarchically structured:
1. primacy: Mt 16:18; Lk 22:31-34;
Jn 21:15-19
2. collegiality: Mt 18:18; Mk 3:14;
1 Cor 12:28-30; 1 Thess 5:12-13;
Intr. Past. Epis. in Thess, pp. 83-84;
Heb 13:7-19
(g) eschatological dimension:
1. on earth: Acts 3:20-21; Eph 1:10;
Col 1:20; 2 Pet 3:11-16
2. in heaven: Heb 12:23;
Rev 21:1 - 22:5
3. communion of saints: Eph 4:16;
Col 1:24
(h) Mary and C.: Jn 19:25-27;
1 Tim 2:5
(i) particular churches:
Acts 4:32-37; 1 Cor 1:2; 4:17;
14:26-40; 16:19.

Circumcision

(a) among Jews: Lk 1:59; 2:21; Jn
7:22-23; Acts 7:8
(b) and Christianity: Acts 11:1-2;
15:1-35; 16:1-3; Rom 4:9-12; Gal
2:3-16; 5:1-12; Tit 1:10
(c) true c.: Rom 2:25-29; 1 Cor
7:18-19; Gal 5:6; 6:12-16; Phil 3:1-6;
Col 2:11-14; 3:10-11.

Colossians, Epistle to *See* Gen. Intr.

St Paul in Rom, pp. 24-25;
Intr. Col in Capt, pp. 149-157.

Coming, Second. *See* Parousia.

Commandments

(a) must be kept: Mt 5:17-19; 15:3-
9; 19:16-19; 1 Cor 7:19; Jas 2:10-11
(b) obedience shows love of God:
Jn 14:15-21; 15:10; 1 Jn 2:3-6
(c) first c.: Mt 22:34-40
(d) new c.: Jn 13:34-35; 15:12;
1 Jn 2:7-11; 3:11, 23-24; *see* Charity.
See Law.

Communion. *See* Eucharist; Unity.

Communion of Saints 1 Cor

12:12-31; 2 Cor 1:5-11; Col 1:12.
See Body, mystical, *in* Church (d), 6.

Compassion. *See* Mercy.

Concupiscence

(a) Inclines one to sin: Mt 15:19;
Mk 4:19; Lk 4:28-29; Rom 7:7-13;
Jas 1:13-15; 4:1-6; 1 Jn 2:15-17

(b) to be resisted: Rom 6:12-14; Gal
6:16-26l Eph 4:17-24;
Col 3:5-11; 1 Pet 2:11-12.

Confession
(a) **of faith:** Mt 8:5-13; 10:32;
14:28-33; 16:16; Mk 15:39; Jn 1:20;
12:42-43; 20:28; 1 Jn 2:23; 4:1-3
(b) **of sins:** Mt 3:6; 9:2-7; Mk 1:5;
Lk 7:50; 15:17-21; Jn 20:22-23;
Heb 5:2-3; Jas 5:16; *see* Penance (e).

Confirmation
Lk 9:20; Acts 8:14-17;
91:6; 1 Cor 11:12-13; 2 Cor 1:21-22;
1 Jn 2:20.

Conscience
(a) **what it is:** Acts 5:29; Rom 2:15;
13:5; 14:22-23; 1 Jn 3:19-21
(b) **upright c.:** Acts 23:1;
1 Cor 4:3-5; 2 Cor 1:12-14;
1 Tim 3:9; 5:19; 2 Tim 1:3
(c) **examination of:** 1 Cor 4:3-5;
2 Cor 13:5-10; Gal 6:35.
See Heart.

Consolation. *See* Sorrow; Mercy.

Contemplation
(a) **by angels in heaven:** Mt 18:10;
1 Pet 1:12
(b) **by Blessed Virgin:** Lk 2:19-33, 51
(c) **of believers:** Mt 17:1-9; Lk
2:15-17, 26; 10:38-42
(d) **in ordinary life:** Lk 2:51;
10:38-42; Jn 12:31-33

Contradictions
Mt 1:19-20; 11:28-30;
Jn 12:42-43; 15:18-21; 1 Pet 2:11-12;
3:13-17; *see* Persecution.

Conversion
(a) **because of the nearness of the
Kingdom:**
1. Baptist's preaching: Mt 3:2-12
2. Jesus' preaching and works:
Mt 4:17; 11:20-24; 12:41; 21:32;
Lk 5:32; 7:36-50; 13:1-5; 19:1-10;
23:48; Jn 4:1-42
(b) **need for:** Mt 22:1-14; Lk 8:13;
13:1-9; 16:30-31; 24:46-47; Acts
20:21; Gen. Intr. St Paul in Rom, pp.
36-39; Rom 13:13-14; Col 3:5-17;
Heb 3:7-8; Jas 4:7-10; Rev 2:5,14-16,
20-23; 3:2-3; 9:20-21; 11:3-6; 16:1-6
(c) **and Apostles' preaching:**
Mk 6:12-13; Acts 2:37-41; 3:17-26;
26:17-18

(d) **joy over:** Lk 15:7, 11-32;
Acts 8:5-8, 39.
See Penance.

Corinthians, Epistle
Gen. Intr. St
Paul in Rom, pp. 21-22; Intr. 1 Cor,
pp. 24-34; Intr. 2 Cor, pp. 161-164.

Correction, fraternal
Mt 18:15-17;
Acts 20:26-27; 1 Cor 5:1-2;
2 Cor 7:5-16; Gal 2:11-14; 6:1;
Eph 6:18; 1 Thess 5:14;
2 Thess 3:14-15.

Courage. *See* Fortitude.

Covenant
(a) **Old C. and Law:** Gen. Intro.
Gosp. in Mk, pp. 17-18; Rom 9:4-6;
Gal 3:15-18; 4:24-26
(b) **New C.:** Heb 7:22; 8:1-13;
9:1-10; 9:23-28; 2 Cor 3:4-11
(c) **New C. & Eucharist:** Mt 26:28;
Mk 2:18-22; Jn 4:21-24; 6:44-45;
1 Cor 11:24.

Cowardice. *See* Fortitude (d).

Creation
(a) **God the Creator:** Mt 19:4;
Mk 13:19; Jn 1:3; 4:10;
Acts 17:22-28; Rom 1:19; 4:17;
2 Cor 4:6; Heb 1:2-3, 12; 2:10; 11:3;
Rev 3:14; 10:6
(b) **Christ and c.:** Jn 1:1-3;
1 Cor 8:6; 15:23-28; Col 1:15;
Heb 1:2-3, 10-12; 3:3-6; Rev 3:14
(c) **redeemed:** Rom 8:19-21; Eph
1:10; Gal 3:26
(d) **new:** 2 Cor 5:17; Gal 6:15; Eph
4:22-24; Rev 21:1-8.

Cross
(a) **sign of God's love:** Jn 3:16;
19:37; Acts 13:28; Heb 2:9, 14;
1 Pet 2:21-25
(b) **symbol of glory:** Mt 24:30;
Jn 3:14-15; 8:28; 12:31-33; 13:31-32;
Gal 6:14
(c) **a need for Christian:** Mt 10:38;
16:23-24; 27:32; Acts 14:20-22;
2 Cor 7:14-16; 11:22-23; Heb 12:4-13
(d) **wisdom of** 1 Cor 1:18 - 3:3;
Gal 3:1.
See Christ (h); Mortification;
Suffering.

Crucifixion. *See* Christ (h).

Cures. *See* Miracles.

Daring

(a) **in Christian life:** Mt 10:9-10; 20:22; Mk 15:43; Acts 21:39-40; Rom 1:16

(b) **in apostolate:** Acts 4:13-22; 5:40-42; 18:1-11, 24; 24:24-27; 26:24-29; 28:30-31.

Dates. *See* Christ (c); Testament, New (a).

David Mt 1:1-6, 16-17; 22:41-46; Lk 2:4-11; Acts 1:16; 2:25-36; 7:45-46; 13:22-34, 36; Rom 1:3; 4:6; 2 Tim 2:8; Rev 3:7; 5:5; 22:16. *See* Christ, (j), 7.

Day

(a) **Passion of Christ:** Mt 9:15; Lk 9:51; Jn 12:7

(b) **end of world, and General Judgment:** Mt 7:22; 10:15; 11:22-24; 12:36; 24:21-51; 25:13; Lk 17:24; Jn 12:48; Rom 2:16; 1 Cor 1:7-9; 3:12-13; 2 Cor 1:12-14; Phil 1:6, 10; 2:16; 1 Thess 5:1-3; 2 Thess 2:2; 2 Pet 3:12

(c) **d. of glorification:** Mt 26:29; Jn 8:56; 14;20; 16:23-26. *See* Parousia.

Deacons Acts 6:1-6; Phil 1:1; 1 Tim 3:8-13.

Death

(a) **inescapable:** Lk 12:20; 1 Cor 7:29-31; 2 Cor 5:1-10; Heb 9:27-28; 13:14; Jas 1:9-11; 4:13-17; 5:1-6

(b) **result of sin:** Rom 5:12-21; 6:23; 1 Cor 15:54-58

(c) **Christ's power over:** Mt 9:24-25; Lk 7:14; Jn 10:17-18; 11:25, 43-44; 1 Cor 15:54-48

(d) **d. of Christ:** *see* Christ, Jesus (h). *1. Christ has overcome d.:* 2 Cor 4:7-12; Heb 2:14; *see* Christ, Jesus (i), 2. *2. redemptive value:* Mt 26:28; Jn 11:50-53; Gen. Intr. St Paul in Rom, p. 35; 1 Cor 8:11-13; 2 Cor 5:11-21; Heb 2:14-15

(e) **spiritual d.:** Lk 15:24, 32; Jn 5:24; 8:21-24, 51-53

(f) **as eternal punishment:** Mt 10:28; Lk 13:5; Jn 6:49-51; Rev 2:11; 20:6, 14; 21:8

(g) **Christian attitude to:** Mt 10:28; Mk 15:39; Jn 11:24-26; Phil 1:21-26; 1 Thess 4:13; 5:9-10; Rev 3:2-3; 14:13.

Demon. *See* Devil.

Detachment Mt 6:24-34; 13:44-46; 19:20-22; Lk 6:24; 12:33; 14:33; 19:8; Jn 12:2-3; Act 2:44-45; 4:32-37; 1 Cor 7:29-31; Eph 5:5-7; Heb 13:5-6, 14; Jas 1:9-11. *See* Poverty.

Devil(s)

(a) **Satan, prince of devils and father of lies:** Mt 9:34; 12:24; Jn 8:44; 2 Cor 11:13-15

(b) **condemned forever:** Mt 25:41; 2 Pet 2:4; Jude 6; Rev 20:7-10

(c) **opposed to Christ:** Mt 4:1-11; 8:28-34; Lk 4:34; Jn 14:30; 16:11; Rev 12:1-17; 16:12-16; 20:1:10

(d) **calls Baptist and Christ "possessed":** Mt 10:25; 11:18; 12:24; Jn 7:20; 8:48-49; 10:20

(e) **is expelled by Jesus:** Mt 4:24; 8:16; 9:32-34;12:22-30; 15:22-28; 17:18; Mk 1:32-34; Lk 4:35; 13:16, 32

(f) **Apostles given power to expel:** Mt 10:1, 8; Mk 6:7, 13; 16:17; Lk 10:17-20; Acts 16:16-18; 19:11-12

(g) **their expulsion a sign of divine power:** Mt 12:22-30; Act 19:13-16

(h) **recognise Jesus as son of God:** Mk 1:24; 5:7; Lk 4:41

(i) **actions against man:** Mt 12:43-45; 13:19-39; Lk 9:39; 13-16; 22:3-31; Jn 13:27; Acts 16:16-18; Eph 2:1-2; 1 Thess 2:18; 1 Jn 2:13; Rev 9:1-12; 12:1-17; 13:1-18

(j) **how to defeat them:** Rom 16:20; 2 Cor 2:11; Eph 4:27; 6:16; 1 Thess 3:5; 2 Thess 3:3; Jas 4:7; 1 Pet 5:5-11; 1 Jn 3:6-9.

Disciples

(a) **of John Baptist:** Mt 9:14; 11:2; Lk 11:1; Jn 1:35-39; 3:25-26; Acts 19:1-7

(b) **of Jesus:** *1. calling:* Mt 8:19-22; 21:1; 22:57; Lk 10:1-24; Jn 2:11-12 *2. training:* Mt 5-7; 11:1; 13:10-22;

15:12-20; 16:13-28; 17:19-20;
18:1-35; 19:10-15; 20:17-19;
21:20-22; 28:16-20; Mk 4:34; 9:31;
Lk 10:17-24; 12:22-53; 17:1-10;
Jn 9:2-5; 13-17
3. mission: Lk 10:1-20; 22:19;
Jn 20:22-23
4. weaknesses: Mt 14:26; 26:8, 35,
56; Mk 7:18; 8:15-21; 9:33, 37;
Lk 22:24; Jn 6:60
(c) all the baptized: Acts 6:1-6;
9:10-26
(d) dignity: Mt 10:40; Lk 10:16
(e) demands:*1. self-denial*: Mt 8:21;
16:24; 19:21; Mk 10:28-30;
Lk 14:26-27
2. humility: Mt 10:24-42; 19:13-15
3. charity: Jn 13:34-35; 15:12-17;
1 Jn 2:8; 3:7-12
(f) Mary, Mother of the disciples:
Intr. Jn, pp. 36-37; Jn 19:25-27.
See Apostles; Christian, the.

Divorce. *See* Marriage.

Docility
    (a) Christ's: Mt 26:36-46; Lk 2:51;
Jn 4:34
    (b) in doing God's will:
Mt 21:28-32; Lk 11:28; Jn 2:7;
Acts 8:26-31; 26:19
    **(c) in seconding inspirations of the
Spirit:** Jn 7:37-39; Acts 8:29-30
    (d) of Mary and St Joseph:
Mt 1:18-25; 2:13-14, 19-23; Lk 1:38.
See Obedience; Will of God.

Doctrine. *See* Teaching.

Doxology. *See* Blessing (d); Hymns (d).

Ecumenism Jn 10:16; 17:21;
Acts 4:32; Eph 4:1-6; Col 3:17.
See Church.

Elders. *See* Bishops; Priests.

Election. *See* Choice.

Elijah
    (a) prophet: Lk 4:25-26;
Rom 11:2-4; Jas 5:17-18
    (b) and John Baptist: Mt 11:14;
Lk 1:17; Jn 1:21, 25
    (c) and Christ: Mt 16:14; 17:3-13;
27:47, 49; Lk 9:8.

Elizabeth, St Lk 1:5-63.

Emmanuel. God with us: Mt 1:23;

Jn 1:14.

Emmaus Lk 24:13-35.

Enemy, love of one's Mt 5:43-48;
Lk 6:27-38; Rom 12:14, 17-21.

Envy, a sin Mt 20:9-15; 27:18;
Mk 7:22; Lk 15:25-32; Jn 11:48;
12:19; Phil 1:15-18; 1 Tim 6:3-5;
Jas 4:1-3.

Ephesians, Epistle to; Ephesus
Gen. Intr. St Paul in Rom, pp. 25-26;
Intr. Eph in Capt, pp. 21-28; Intr. 1
Tim in Thess, pp. 87-88; Rev 2:1-7.

Epistles. *See under* title of Navarre
Bible volumes.

Eschatology
    **(a) the fulness of time begins with
Christ:** 1 Cor 10:11; Gal 4:4;
Eph 1:1; Intr. Thess, pp. 25-26; 2 Tim
3:1-5; 1 Jn 2:18
    (b) last things:
1. for individual: 2 Cor 5:8-10;
Phil 1:5; *see* Death; Judgment;
Heaven; Hell.
2. end of the world: Acts 3:21;
Rom 8:19-22; Eph 1:10; Col 1:20;
2 Pet 3:10-13; Rev 21:1
    (c) vigilance: Mt 25:13: Eph 6:11-13;
Heb 9:27; 1 Thess 1:1-2.
See Parousia.

Eucharist
    **(a) prefigured in OT and
proclaimed by Christ:** Jn 6:26-59;
1 Cor 10:1-4
    (b) institution of: Mt 26:26-29;
Intr. 1 Cor, pp. 30-31; 1 Cor 11:23-26
    (c) mystery of faith: Jn 6:28-34, 48,
60-71
    **(d) Mass is renewal of sacrifice of
Cross:** Mt 26:26-29; Intr. 1 Cor,
p. 31; 1 Cor 10:14-22; 11:23-26;
Heb 9:18-22, 25-26; 10:2-4;
Rev 4:8-11
    (e) real presence: Mt 2:11; 26:26-29;
Jn 6:48, 53-58; Intr. 1 Cor, pp. 31-32;
1 Cor 10:14-22; 11:27-32
    (f) food for the soul: Mt 6:11;
14:22-23; 26:26-29; Jn 6:27, 35,
48-58; Acts 2:42; 1 Cor 10:16-17;
1 Pet 2:1-3; Rev 2:17
    (g) dispositions for receiving:
Mt 5:23-24; 7:6; 8:5-13; Jn 1:29;

6:57; 11:55: 13:7-14; 1 Cor 11:27-32
(h) relationship with Christ:
Intr. 1 Cor, pp. 31-32;
1 Cor 10:16-17; 11:17-22; 12:12-13.

Evangelisation. *See* Preaching.

Examination. *See* Conscience (c).

Example
(a) of Christ: Mt 11:29; Jn 13:1-20;
14:4-7; Acts 1:1; 1 Thess 1:6;
Heb 12:1-3; 1 Pet 2:21-25
(b) giving good: Mt 5:13-16;
Phil 3:17; 1 Thess 1:7-8; 1 Tim
4:12-16; Tit 2:6-8; Heb 12:12-13;
1 Pet 2:11-17; 3:1-7; 4:1-6; Jn 11.
See Christ.

Exodus. Symbolizes divine salvation
Acts 7:17-45; 1 Cor 10:1-13;
Heb 11:23-29; Intr. 1 Pet in Cath,
pp. 81-82; 1 Pet 1:13; Rev 15:2-4.

Expiation
(a) Mass is expiatory sacrifice: Mt
26:26-29; Rom 3:25; *see* Eucharist.
(b) Christ's death atones for sin:
Mt 27:45-50; Heb 9:11-28; 10:5-18
(c) need for: Lk 2:22-24;
2 Cor 12:20-21
See Forgiveness; Redemption;
Sacrifice.

Faith. *See* Gen. Intr. St Paul in Rom,
pp. 37-39.
(a) content and object:
1. belief in God: Jn 14:1, 8-12; 17:8;
Heb 6:1-3; 11:1, 6
2. belief in Christ: Mk 10:46-52;
Jn 4:39-42; 6:29, 69; 7:31; 9:35-38;
11:25-27, 45; 13:19; 14:9-12;
16:27-31; Acts 13:38-41; 16:30-34;
20:21; 1 Cor 1:2; Eph 3:16-17;
1 Pet 3:18-22; Intr. 1 Jn, pp. 155-156;
1 Jn 5:1-5
3. belief in Gospel: Mk 1:15; Jn 20:31
(b) necessary for salvation:
Mk 16:16; Jn 3:16-21; Acts 14:8-10;
16:30-34; Rom 1:7; 3:21-31; 4:5;
Gal 5:6; Heb 2:1-4; 3:17-19; 11:6
(c) gift of God: Mk 9:19-24; Lk 17:5;
22:32; Jn 3:14-15; 6:44-45, 65;
10:26-29; 12:37-40; 2 Cor 3:5; 4:6;
Eph 2:8; 2 Tim 1:12; Heb 11:1
(d) reasons for believing:
Mt 28:1-15; Mk 16:17-20; Jn 2:11,

23-25; 4:48; 9:14-16, 25-34; 10:25,
37-38; Acts 5:12-16; 8:5-8; 9:32-43;
13:6-12; 14:4; 1 Cor 1:20-25; 2:1-5;
14:23-25; 1 Thess 1:5
(e) some features:
1. supernatural: Acts 16:4; 17:30-34;
2 Cor 10:5; 2 Thess 3:2
2. firm: Mt 15:21-28; Lk 5:12;
Jn 5:24; 16:31-32; 1 Cor 9:19-23;
2 Thess 2:13-17; 1 Tim 1:18-19;
Heb 11:4-40; Rev 2:2-3
3. must be active: Jn 1:35-39; 9:6-7;
15:2; Rom 10:10; 2 Cor 4:13-14;
1 Thess 1:3; Tit 2:1-10; Intr. Jas in
Cath, pp. 30-31; Jas 2:14-26
4. calls for fortitude: Mt 10:32-33;
Acts 4:5-22; 2 Thess 1:3-4
5. docile: Jn 10:26-29; Rom 1:5
(f) examples of:
1. the Apostles: Lk 5:5; Jn 1:45-51;
2:11; 6:67-71
2. others: Mt 8:5-13; 9:1-8, 20-22;
15:21-28; Mk 10:46-52; Lk 23:42-43;
Jn 9:6-7; 11:25-27; Rom 4:1-25;
Heb 11:1-40; Jas 2:20-26
(g) lack of:
1. among disciples: Mt 8:26;
14:28-31; 16:8; 17:20; 26:70-75;
Mk 16:9-14; Jn 6:66; 20:24-29
2. among others: Mt 13:53-58;
Lk 1:18-20; Jn 7:5; 8:21-24
(h) punishment for unbelief:
Mk 6:5-6; Jn 3:18-21, 36; 8:24; 16:9;
Heb 3:7-19
(i) some effects of:
1. salvation: Mk 5:34; 10:52; 16:16;
Lk 7:50; 17:19; Jn 3:15; 5:24; 6:35;
11:25-26, 40; 12:46; Eph 2:8-10;
Heb 11:6; 1 Jn 5:13
2. divine filiation: Mt 6:25-32; Jn 1:12
3. miracles: Mt 9:27-31; 17:14-20;
Mk 5:35-43; 8:22-25; 9:23; 16:17-18;
Jn 14:12; Acts 3:1-26
(j) passing it on: 1 Cor 1:10; 2:13; 2
Cor 4:1-6; Gal 1:6-9; Phil 1:28;
2 Tim 1:12-14; 2:1-2
(k) our Lady's: Lk 1:34-38, 45; 2:48,
50; 11:27-28; Jn 2:3-5.

Faithful, the. *See* Christian, the;
Faithfulness.

Faithfulness
(a) of God and Christ: Mt 27:50;

Rom 3:1-8; 11:29; 1 Cor 1:9; 10:13;
2 Cor 1:17-20; Phil 1:6; 1 Thess 5:24;
2 Thess 3:3; 2 Tim 2:11-13;
Heb 3:1-6; 1 Jn 1:9; Rev 1:5; 19:11
(b) importance of: Mt 25:21-23;
Lk 9:57-62; 16:9-12; 2 Tim 1:15-19;
2:11-13; 3:14-15; 4:10; Heb 13:7-14;
12:4-13; 1 Jn 2:18-27; Rev 2:10-13
(c) reward for: Lk 12:41-44;
22:24-30; Rev 2:10; 3:4-5
(d) sin of infidelity and its
punishment: Mt 21:33-46; Lk
12:45-48; Heb 3:17-19; 6:4-8;
10:26-31
(e) Our Lady's: Mt 1:19-25; 2:14; Lk
11:27-28.

Family
(a) Holy F.: Mt 2:13-23; Mk 6:1-3;
Lk 2:1-52; Jn 6:42
(b) Christian f.: Acts 18:2-3;
2 Tim 1:4-5; Tit 2:4-5; Philem 22:25
(c) duties of spouses: 1 Cor 7:1-16;
Eph 5:22-33; Col 3:18-19; 2 Pet 3:1-7
(d) parents and children: Eph 6:1-4;
Col 3:20-21
See Marriage.

Fasting Mt 4:2; 6:16-18; 9:14-17;
Mk 9:28-29; Acts 13:2-3; 2 Cor 6:5;
11:27; Col 2:16-18.

Father. See Filiation, divine; Trinity,
Blessed.

Fear
(a) of God: Lk 1:50; 23:39-43;
Acts 10:2; 19:17-19; 2 Cor 5:11-13;
Heb 10:31; 1 Jn 4:17-18
(b) of the supernatural:
Mt 14:25-27; 28:1-10; Lk 1:30;
2:9-10; 7:16; 24:36-43; Acts 2:43;
5:1-11; Heb 12:18-21
(c) of those who can harm the soul:
Mt 10:28.
See Trust.

Festivals See Gen. Intr. Heb, pp. 32-35
(a) Passover: Mt 26:2, 17-19; 27:15;
Mk 14:1; Lk 2:41-42; 22:1, 7-20;
Jn 2:13-23; 6:4; 11:55; 12:1, 12; 13:1;
19:14
(b) unleavened bread: Mt 26:17;
Mk 14:1
(c) Tabernacles: Jn 7:2, 10, 37-39
(d) Dedication of Temple: Jn 10:22

(e) Lord's day, Sunday: Acts 20:7;
1 Cor 16:1-4; Heb 10:22-25;
Rev 1:9-11.

Filiation, divine
(a) Jesus':
1. revealed by the Father: Mt 3:17;
17:5
2. revealed by Christ: Mt 11:27;
Lk 2:49; Jn 3:35-36; 5:18-26; 10:36;
15:15; 17:1; 20:17
3. other testimonies to it in Gospel:
Mt 4:3-6; 8:29; 14:33; 16:16;
26:63-64; 27:43, 54; Intr. Mk, p. 62;
Mk 1:1; Lk 1:32, 35; Jn 1:18-34, 49;
11:27; 19:7; 20:31
(b) man's:
1. children of God: Mt 5:9; 6:9; 23:9;
Mk 10:13-16; Jn 1:12-13;
Gen. Intr. St Paul Rom, p. 40;
Rom 8:14-30; Gal 4:6-7; 2 Cor
6:17-18; Eph 1:5; 5:1; Intr. 1 Jn in
Cath, p. 158; 1 Jn 3:1-2; Rev 21:5-8
2. trust in the Father: Mt 6:7-9, 26,
32; 7:11; 10:29; Lk 15:11-32;
1 Pet 1:17
3. and fraternity: Mt 5:43-48;
6:14-15; Gal 3:26-29; 1 Jn 5:1.
See Christ; Trinity, Blessed.

Flesh
(a) man as created being: Mt 16:17;
Lk 3:6; Jn 1:13-14; 17:2; 2 Cor 10:3;
11:18; Gal 2:20
(b) Humanity of Christ: Jn 1:14;
6:51-56; Col 1:22
(c) as opposed to spirit and to
goodness: Mt 26:41; Jn 3:6; 6:62;
Gen. Intr. St Paul in Rom, p. 30;
Rom 8:1-4; 2 Cor 10:2-6; Gal 3:17-21.

Forgiveness
(a) of sins:
1. announced by John Baptist:
Mk 1:4; Lk 1:77
*2. promised and given by Christ: see
sin (c).*
3. fruit of death of Christ: Mt 26:28;
Acts 13:38-39; 2 Cor 5:11-21;
Col 2:13-14
(b) towards neighbour: Mt 6:12-15;
18:21-35; Mk 11:25; Lk 17:3-4;
1 Cor 6:1-11; Eph 4:26, 31-32;
1 Thess 5:15

170

(c) towards enemies: Mt 5:38-48;
Acts 7:60; Rom 12:14-21; 1 Tim 2:2;
1 Pet 3:8-9.
See Sin; Penance.

Fortitude
(a) based on God: Mt 7:24-27;
10:20; 14:28-35; Jn 12:27; Rev 3:8-12
(b) need for: Mt 27:32; 1 Cor 4:21;
16:13-14; 2 Cor 2:1-4; Rev 2:2-3
**(c) example of Mary and holy
women:** Mt 27:55-56; Jn 19:25
(d) faults against: Mt 27:24;
Mk 10:22; 2 Tim 4:10.

Fraternity
(a) among Christians: Mt 23:8;
Lk 22:32; Jn 20:17; 21:23;
Acts 2:44-47; 11:27-30; 28:14-15;
Phil 2:25-30; 1 Jn 5:1
(b) duties it implies: Mt 5:22-24;
18:15-17, 21-35; Col 3:12-17;
Heb 3:13; 1 Pet 4:7-11.
See Love; Charity.

Freedom
(a) of Christ: Mt 26:51-54;
Jn 10:17-18; 18:4-11
(b) of man:
1. won by Christ: Lk 1:72-75;
Jn 8:31-36; Gal 5:1; 1 Cor 7:21-23;
Jas 1:25
2. true f.: Rom 8:9-21; 1 Cor 6:12-14;
2 Cor 3:17; Philem 13-14;
2 Pet 2:18-19; Jude 4; Rev 13:5-8
3. and self-surrender: Mt 6:18-22;
19:16-22; Jn 10:17-18; Rom 14:2-12
4. and liberation: Lk 4:18-21;
Jn 6:14-15; 8:30-32; Rom 7:6;
Intr Philem in Capt, p. 196.

Friendship Lk 10:38-42; Jn 1:35-39;
3:27-30; 11:1-45; 12:1; 15:12-15.

Gabriel Archangel, St Lk 1:11-20,
26-38.

Galatians, Epistle to
Gen. Intr. St Paul in Rom, p. 21;
Intr. Gal in Rom, pp. 48-59.

Generosity
(a) God's: Mt 7:11; 19:27-30;
Lk 12:32; Jn 6:38; 14:16; 15:16;
16:23; Jas 1:16-18
(b) Christ's: Mt 20:28; 26:26-29;
Mk 6:42-43; Jn 1:12; 10:28; 14:27;
19:30

(c) men's towards God: Mt 2:11;
26:6-16; 27:57-61; Lk 8:1-3; 21:1-4;
Jn 12:1-8
(d) towards one another: Mt 5:42;
10:8, 41-42; 19:21; Lk 3:11;
10:30-37; 11:41; 12:33; 19:8;
2 Cor 8:9
(e) reward for: Mk 10:29-30;
Lk 6:38; 2 Cor 9:6-15; Phil 4:17-19
(f) faults against: Mt 20:20-28;
Mk 9:33-40; Jn 6:26; 12:4-6.
See Alms; Magnaminity.

Gifts, spiritual
(a) come from Holy Spirit:
Acts 2:5-11; 1 Cor 12:14
(b) types of: Rom 12:6-9;
1 Cor 2:7-11, 28-30
(c) and unity in Christ:
1 Cor 12:4-11; 14:2-25; Eph 4:7
(d) discernment of: 1 Thess 5:19-22.

Glory
(a) God's: Lk 2:8-14; Jn 12:28; Rev
4:11; 21:21-27
(b) Christ's: Mt 17:1-13; 25:31;
Jn 1:14, 51; 2:11; 8:49-59; 11:4;
12:28; 13:31-32; 17:1-26; 1 Cor 2:8;
Heb 2:9; Jas 2:1; 2 Pet 3:18; Rev 1:6;
5:12-13
(c) glorification of God:
1. by Christ: Jn 13:31-32; 14:13;
17:1-26; Rom 16:27; Eph 3:20-21;
1 Pet 4:11
2. by men: Mt 5:16; 9:8; Lk 13:13;
17:15-18; 23:47; Acts 12:20-23;
1 Cor 1:30-31; 6:20; 10:31;
2 Cor 10:17-18; 1 Pet 4:7-11;
Rev 19:6-7.
See Rectitude of Intention.

God
(a) nature and attributes:
1. one and only: 1 Cor 8:4-6; Jas 2:19
2. transcends creation: Mt 5:34;
22:31-32; 23:22; Jn 1:18; 4:24;
Acts 17:24-29; 1 Tim 6:15-16;
1 Jn 1:5; Intr. Rev, p. 23; Rev 4:1-11
3. almighty: Mt 3:9; 19:26; Lk 1:37;
9:43; Jn 1:12-13; 9:3; Intr. Rev, p. 23;
Rev 1:4, 8; 4:6-11
4. creator: Mt 19:4; Mk 13:19;
Acts 14:15-17; 17:24-28; Rev 14:6-7
5. all-knowing: Mt 6:4, 6, 18;
Lk 16:15; 1 Cor 1:21

6. *provides for us*: Mt 6:8, 30;
Lk 12:6-7; Acts 17:24-28
7. *merciful*: Lk 6:38; 15:1-32;
Jn 3:16-21; 1 Cor 7:25; 2 Cor 1:3;
1 Tim 1:13
8. *just*: Lk 18:7; 19:24-26; Rom 2:11;
3:1-8
9. *full of love*: Jn 3:16; 1 Jn 4:8, 16, 19
10. *faithful*: Rom 3:1-8; 1 Cor 1:8-9;
10:13; 1 Thess 11:23
(b) Revelation of God:
1. *in theophanies*: Mt 3:16-17; 17:5;
Lk 3:2; Jn 12:23-30
2. *in Christ*: Mt 22:16; Mk 1:14;
Jn 1:18; 3:2, 31-36; 7:16-18;
Rom 3:21-22; Heb 1:1-4
3. *through angels*: Mt 1:20-23;
2:13-19; Lk 1:11-20; 1:26-38; 2:8-14
4. *through other created things*:
Rom 1:20; 1 Cor 1:18-21
5. *divine Revelation and its
transmission*: Gen. Intr. in Cor,
pp. 13-16
(c) as Father: Mt 6:25-32; Lk 11:2;
Jn 1:12; 5:30-47; 6:46-47;
Rom 8:14-17; Gal 4:6; Eph 3:14-15;
1 Jn 4:7-17; *see* Filiation, divine
(d) union with: Mt 4:10; 6:24; 22:37;
Lk 2:20, 28, 38; 7:16; 23:47; Jn 3:16;
Rom 5:8; 8:38-39; 1 Cor 8:3;
1 Thess 5:9-11; 1 Tim 1:17;
1 Jn 4:11-13, 16, 19
**(e) man finds fulfilment and
happiness in:** Mt 5:8; 6:24; Lk 11:28;
Jn 7:37-38.
See Trinity, Blessed.

Gospel

(a) general questions: Gen. Intro.
Gosp. in Mk, pp. 29-49; *see* Intro. to
each Gospel
**(b) joyful proclamation of Christ &
and Kingdom:** Mk 1:1; Lk 1:1-4;
Jn 21:25; Acts 5:42; 8:4; 1 Thess 1:9
(c) preached by Jesus: Mt 4:23;
9:35; Mk 1:14;
**(d) to be proclaimed to whole
world:** Mk 13:10; 16:15-16;
Acts 10:1-48; Rom 1:1;
1 Cor 9:14-18
(e) need to believe in: Mk 1:15;
16:15-16; Rom 1:16; 1 Tim 1:11
(f) demands it makes: Mk 8:35;

10:29; 13:9-13.
See Testament, New; Scripture,
Sacred.

Grace

(a) in Christ: Lk 2:52; Jn 1:14;
Heb 5:9
(b) given by Christ: Jn 1:16-17;
4:10-15; 7:37-39; 17:22-23;
Rom 3:24; 1 Cor 1:4-9; Gal 2:8
(c) action of: Acts 18:1-11, 22:10;
Rom 2:12-14; 8:1-13; 1 Cor 1:49;
2 Cor 3:6; 1 Pet 1:4; 4:10-11;
1 Jn 5:18
(d) response to: Mt 10:11-15; 13:12;
Jn 1:12-17; 3:16-21; Acts 26:19;
2 Cor 6:1-2; Heb 3:8; 13:20-21;
Jas 2:22-24
(e) Christian greeting: Rom 1:7; 1
Cor 1:1-3; 2 Cor 1:1-2; 1 Thess 1:1; 2
Thess 1:1-2; 3:18; 2 Jn 1-3; Rev 1:4
(f) in Mary: Lk 1:28, 30, 46-49.

Greed

(a) to be avoided: Mt 6:19-34;
Mk 8:36; Lk 12:15-21; 1 Cor 5:11-13;
Heb 13:5-6; Jas 5:2-3
(b) cause of perdition: Mt 26:14-16;
Jn 12:4-6; 1 Tim 6:10.
See Detachment; Riches.

Happiness. *See* Joy; Beatitudes.

Heart

**(a) centre of thoughts, desires and
passions:** Mt 6:21; 12:34; 13:19;
22:37; Mk 7:20-23; Lk 1:17-51; 2:35;
Jn 14:1, 27; 16:6, 22; Eph 3:7
(b) conscience: Mt 5:28; 1 Cor 4:3-5;
Gal 4:6; Heb 10:19-22
(c) man's interiority: Mt 9:4; 18:35;
Lk 8:15; 9:47; 16:15; Jn 2:25;
Rom 19:9; Heb 4:12
(d) H. of Jesus: Mt 11:29
(e) H. of our Lady: Lk 2:19, 35, 51.

Heaven

(a) where God dwells: Mt 3:16-17;
5:16, 45, 48; Mk 16:19; Lk 11:13;
15:7; Jn 3:13; 6:38; Col 1:20;
Heb 4:14; 9:24
(b) where angels dwell: Mt 18:10;
22:30; Lk 2:13
(c) reward for the just: Mt 5:12;
19:21; 25:46; Lk 6:23; 10:20; 12:33;
16:22-26; 1 Cor 2:9; 13:11-12;

2 Cor 4:13; 2 Thess 1:6, 10; Heb 4:1;
1 Pet 1:3-5; 4:6; 1 Jn 3:2; Rev 7:9-17;
14:13; 21:21
(d) **new heavens:** Rev 21:1 - 22:5.
See Glory; Kingdom of God.

Hebrews, Epistle to
Gen. Intr. St Paul in Rom, pp. 28-29;
Intr. Heb, pp. 37-48.

Hell
(a) **where devils dwell:** Mt 25:41;
Lk 8:31
(b) **punishment after death:**
Mt 5:22, 29-30; 10:28; 13:39-42,
49-50; 19:8-9; 22:13; 24:51;
25:41-46; Lk 16:19-31; Jn 15:6;
Rom 2:2-11
(c) **pains of:** Mt 5:22; 7:23; 8:12;
24:51; 25:10-12, 30, 41; Lk 3:17;
16:23-24; Rev 19:17-21; 21:8
(d) **eternity of:** Mt 18:8; 25:41, 46;
Mk 9:43, 45, 48; Lk 16:26; Jude 7;
Rev 14:9-11; 20:7-10.
See Punishment.

Heresy. *See* Teaching (e).

Herod
(a) **the Great:** Gen. Intro. Gosp. in
Mk, pp. 45-46; Mt 2:3-22; Lk 1:5
(b) **Antipas:** Mt 14:1-12; Mk 3:6;
Lk 3:1; 13:31-33; 26:6-12
(c) **Agrippa I:** Acts 12:1-23; 24:24
(d) **Agrippa II:** Acts 25:13-26:32.

Hierarchy. *See* Church.

History of Salvation Mt 1:1;
Mk 12:1-12; Jn 2:9-10; Intr. Lk, pp.
18-19; Acts 7:1-53; 13:16-41;
Rom 3:21-31; Rev 5:1-5.

Holiness
(a) **of God:** Mt 5:48; 6:9; 19:17
(b) **of Christ:** Mk 1:24; 7:37;
Lk 1:35; 2:52: 23:41, 47; Jn 8:46;
16:8-12; Rev 3:7
(c) **in Gospel h. is often termed
"righteousness":** *see* Righteousness.
(d) **of the Christian**
1. all are called to h.: Mt 5:48;
Lk 2:51; 3:23; 6:20-49; 12:33-34;
Jn 15:16; Rom 1:6-7; 1 Cor 1:2;
Eph 1:1; 1 Thess 4:3; Heb 3:2;
1 Pet 1:13-16
2. seeking and imitating Christ:
Mt 11:28-30; Mk 10:46-52; Lk 2:16;

19:4; Jn 14:4-7; 15:9-11; 1 Cor 11:1;
Heb 3:14
3. in work and ordinary life: Mt 2:2;
9:9; 25:14-30; Mk 6:1-3; Lk 2:51;
3:14, 23; 10:38-42; Jn 12:31-33;
Acts 19:3; Intr. Phil in Capt, pp.
105-106; Phil 1:27; Col 3:1-4, 17
4. zeal for h: see Asceticism
5. it is God who makes one holy:
Mt 5:20; 17:14-21; Jn 17:17-19;
Acts 20:32; Phil 3:10-12; 1 Thess 5:23
(e) **linked to apostolate:** Mt 5:13-16;
Lk 17:3-4; Jn 12:31-33; Rom 11:2-5
(f) **Mary's h.:** Lk 1:28, 38
(g) **St Joseph's h.:** Mt 1:19; 2:14.
See Apostolate; Asceticism; Will of
God.

Hope
(a) **Christ the hope of Israel:**
Lk 2:25-38; 24:21
(b) **Christ the hope of the
Christian:** Lk 24:50-53; Rom 5:1-11;
2 Cor 4:13 - 5:10; Col 1:27;
2 Thess 2:16-17; Tit 2:11-14;
Heb 10:19-25; 1 Jn 3:3
(c) **virtue:** Mt 10:16-33; 11:28-30;
24:13; Mk 13:33-37; 1 Cor 15:12-28,
58; Eph 1:18-19; 1 Thess 4:13;
1 Tim 4:10; Tit 1:2; Heb 3:6; 6:9-20;
11:1; 1 Pet 3:15; 2 Pet 3:11-16.
See Trust.

Humility
(a) **of Christ:** Mt 11:29; 20:25-28;
21:1-5; 27:14; Jn 6:37-40; 13:1-20;
Phil 2:3-11; Heb 2:9
(b) **need for:**
1. to recognise and follow Christ:
Mt 11:25-26; 18:1-5; 19:13-15;
21:15-17; Lk 4:22-29; Jn 9:39-41;
2 Cor 10:5; Jas 4:7-10
2. to pray: see Prayer (d), 2.
3. to show others: Mt 20:25-28;
23:11-12; Lk 1:38-39; Jn 13:1-20;
1 Cor 12:22-23; Eph 3:8; Phil 2:3-4
4. to understand and forgive:
Mt 7:1-5; Lk 7:39-50
(c) **danger of pride:** Mt 23:12;
26:30-35; Lk 1:51-53; 14:7-11; 18:14;
22:66-71; Acts 18:1-11; 1 Cor 5:1-2;
2 Cor 3:5; 10:17-18
(d) **reward for:** Mt 23:12; Lk
1:48-49, 52; 14:7-11; 18:14; Jas 4:6;

1 Pet 5:5
(e) **examples of:** Mt 3:11; 8:8-9;
15:21-28; Lk 5:8; Jn 1:19-27;
3:25-30; 1 Cor 4:8-16; 15:9-10;
2 Cor 12:7-11
(f) **Mary's:** Lk 1:26-38, 48.
See Rectitude of intention.

Hymns
(a) **in infancy narrative:** Lk 1:46-55,
68-79; 2:14, 29-32
(b) **of thanksgiving:** Mt 11:25;
Rom 1:8-15; 1 Cor 1:4-9;
2 Cor 1:3-11; Eph 1:3-14;
Phil 1:3-11; Col 1:3-8;
1 Thess 1:2-10; Philem 4-8; 1
Pet 1:3-12
(c) **christological:** Phil 2:5-11;
Col 1:15-20; 1 Tim 3:16; 6:15;
2 Tim 2:11
(d) **doxologies:** Rom 1:25: 9:15;
16:25-27; 2 Cor 11:31; Eph 1:3-14;
Phil 4:20; 1 Tim 1:17; 2 Pet 3:18;
Jude 24-25; Rev 7:12.

Hypocrisy. *See* Sincerity.

Idleness. *See* Work.

Idolatry Acts 14:11-18; 15:20, 29;
19:23-40; Rom 1:18-32;
1 Cor 5:11-13; 8-10; Rev 19:23-40.

Immortality
(a) **the Living God is the author of
life:** Mt 16:16; 26:63; Jn 1:4; 5:21;
Rom 9:26; 1 Tim 6:16
(b) **of Christ:** Acts 3:15; Rom 6:8-11;
see Life (b), 2
(c) **of soul:** Lk 16:19-31; 20:27-40;
2 Cor 5:8-10; Heb 9:27-28
(d) **of man when risen:** 1 Cor
15:35-55; 2 Cor 4:14; Phil 3:21.
See Resurrection.

Incarnation. *See* Christ (d) and (f), 1.

Indwelling. *See* Trinity, Blessed (h).

Instruments of God: Acts 10:25-26;
18:27; 21:19; 1 Cor 3:4-17;
2 Cor 3:1-4; 5:20-21; 1 Thess 3:2.
See Apostolate; Apostles.

Israel
(a) **people of God:** Mt 2:6, 15;
Lk 1:16, 54, 68; 2:25: 24:21;
Jn 19:15; Acts 13:16-25; 7:1-53;
Rom 3:1-8; 9:4-6; 1 Cor 10:1-13;

Eph 1:11-12
(b) **Messiah will come again:** Mt
2:6; Lk 2:32; Acts 13:23
(c) **first to hear Christ's message:**
Mt 10:6; 15:24; Lk 2:34; Jn 1:31
(d) **its leaders reject Christ:** Mt
21:33-45; 27:9; Jn 11:53; 19:15
(e) **and early Church:** Acts 4:5-22;
5:17-42; 8:1-4; 22:27 - 25:12;
1 Thess 2:14-16; Rev 2:9;
see Judaizers.
(f) **Jesus, King of** Mt 27:37, 42;
Jn 1:49; 12:13
(g) **Church is new I.:** Mt 19:28;
Act 28:25-28; Gen. Intr. St Paul in
Rom, p. 44; Rev 4:4; 7:1-8
(h) **conversion of:** Rom 11:25-32.

James the Greater, St Mt 4:21-22;
10:2; 17:1-13; 20:20-28; 26:37;
Mk 5:37; 13:3-4; Lk 5:10-11;
9:54-56; Jn 21:2-14; Acts 1:13; 12:2.

James the Less, St Mt 10:3; 13:55;
27:55; Mk 6:3; Acts 1:13; 12:17;
15:13-21; 21:18; 1 Cor 15:7;
Gal 1:19; 2:9-12; Intr. Jas in Cath, pp.
25-26; Jas 1:1; Jude 1:1.

Jerusalem *See* Intr. Lk, p. 22.
(a) **child Jesus in:** Lk 2:22-50
(b) **and activity of Jesus:**
1. journeys to: Mt 20:17;
Lk 9:51 - 14:35; Jn 2:13; 5:1; 7:10;
12:12
2. entry in triumph: Mt 21:1-17;
3. ministry: Mt 21:23; Jn 2:13 - 3:21;
5:1-47; 7-10
*4. Death, Resurrection and
Ascension:* Lk 9:31; 19:28;
see Christ, Jesus.
(c) **Jesus foretells its destruction:**
Mt 23:37-39; 24:1-35
(d) **Council of:** Acts 15:1-35; 16:4
(e) **the heavenly J.:** Gal 4:26;
Heb 12:22-24; Rev 21:1 - 22:5;
see Church (d), 4.

Jesus Christ. *See* Christ, Jesus

Jews. *See* Israel.

John Baptist, St
(a) **birth:** Lk 1:5-25, 39-45, 57-80
(b) **mission and message:** Mt 3:1-12;
Jn 1:6-8, 15, 19-36; Acts 13:23-25
(c) **his disciples:** Mt 9:14; 11:2-6;

14:12; Jn 3:25-30
(d) **his greatness:** Mt 11:7-15;
Mk 6:16-29
(e) **imprisonment and death:**
Mt 4:12; 11:2; 14:3-12.
See Baptism (a).

John the Evangelist, St
(a) **Apostle:** Mt 4:21; 10:2; 17:1;
Mk 5:37; 9:38; 10:35-41; 13:3; 14:33;
Lk 5:10; 9:54; 22:8; Intr. Jn, pp.
18-22; Jn 1:35-39; Acts 4:1-22;
8:14-25
(b) **beloved disciple:** Jn 13:23;
19:26-27; 20:2; 21:7, 20
(c) **his writings:** Intr. Jn, pp. 13-18,
22-39; Intr. 1, 2 & 3 Jn in Cath, pp.
151-158, 203-206.

Joseph, St
(a) **husband of Mary:** Mt 1 :16-25;
Lk 1:27; 2:4-52
(b) **foster father of Jesus:** Mt 1:16,
25; 13:53-58; Mk 6:1-3; Lk 2:4-52;
3:23; 4:22; Jn 1:45; 6:42
(c) **model of virtues:** Mt 1:19-25;
2:13-14, 19-23
(d) **patron of whole Church:**
Mt 1:16.

Joseph of Arimathea Mt 27:57-60;
Jn 19:38-42.

Joy
(a) **Christ's:** Mt 18:13; Lk 10:21;
15:1-32; Jn 11:15; 15:11; 17:13
(b) **at the coming of the Kingdom:**
Mt 2:10; 13:44; Lk 1:14-17, 39-58;
2:10; 9:49-50; 10:17-20; 13:17; 19:6,
37; Jn 3:29; 4:36; 8:56; 15:11; 17:13;
Acts 8:5-8, 39; 13:52; 16:34
(c) **in tribulation:** Mt 5:12; Acts
5:40-42; 2 Cor 6:10; 7:4-16; 8:1-6;
1 Thess 1:6; Jas 1:2-4; 1 Pet 1:6-9
(d) **a typical Christian virtue:**
Lk 1:46-50; Acts 2:46; 2 Cor 9:7;
13:11; Phil 1:4; 3:1; 4:4; 1 Thess 5:16
(e) **sadness, a danger:** 2 Cor 2:5-11;
Jas 5:13.
See Conversion.

Judaizers Acts 15:1-35; 2 Cor 10-13;
Intr. Gal, pp. 48-50; Gal 2:11-21; 3-4;
Phil 3:1-6; Col 2:11-12.

Judas Iscariot Mt 10:4; 26:14-16,
21-25, 47-50; 27:3-8; Jn 6:71; 12:4-6;
13:2, 26-30; 17:12; 18:2-3; 19:11;
Acts 1:15-26.

Jude, St
(a) **Apostle:** Lk 6:12-16; Jn 14:22
(b) **author of the epistle:** Intr. Jude
in Cath, pp. 221-224; Jude 1-2.

Judgment
(a) **Day of:** Mt 3:12; 10:15; 11:22-24;
12:36, 42; 25:31-46; 1 Cor 1:8-9;
3:12-13; Rev 6:12-17
(b) **Last:** Mt 7:22-23; 13:40-43, 47,
50; 16:27; 24:27-31; 25:31-46;
Mk 8:38; Acts 1:11; 10:42;
1 Cor 15:23-28; 1 Thess 1:10;
2 Thess 1:6-10; Heb 9:27-28;
1 Pet 4:1-6, 17-19; Rev 11:16-18;
14:6-20; 20:11-15; 22:10-15
(c) **immediately after death:**
Mt 3:12; Lk 16:19-31; 23:43;
Rom 2:2-11; 1 Cor 3:14-15;
2 Cor 5:10; Phil 1:21-26; Heb 9:27-28
(d) **human judgment:** Mt 7:1-5;
Lk 7:41-50; 1 Cor 4:3-5
(e) **trial of Jesus:** Mt 26:57 - 27:26.

Justice. *See* Righteousness.

Justification
(a) **unmerited gift:** Rom 3:24;
11:16-24
(b) **praised by Christ:** Mt 3:14-15;
Jn 17:1-4; Acts 3:14; Rom 4:25;
5:16-19
(c) **and faith:** Acts 13:28-41;
Gen. Intr. St Paul in Rom, pp. 36-37;
Rom 3:21-31; 4:1-25; Gal 2:16-18;
3:6-9; 5:6; Phil 3:9; Tit 2:11-14
(d) **and works:** Intr. Jas in Cath, pp.
30-31; Jas 2:14-26.

Kerygma, apostolic. *See* Preaching.

Kingdom of God
(a) **announced by John Baptist:**
Mt 3:2
(b) **proclaimed by Christ:**
Mt 4:17, 23; 9:35; 11:11; 12:28;
13:11; 16:3; Lk 8:1; 9:11; 16:16;
17:20-21; 21:31-32
(c) **preached by Apostles:** Mt 10:7;
24:14; Acts 19:8; 20:25; 28:23-31
(d) **nature:**
1. universal: Mt 8:11; 20:1-16;
22:1-14; Lk 13:29-30; Acts 1:6-8;
Heb 12:28-29; 1 Thess 2:12

2. *new and in future*: Gen. Intr. Gosp.
Mk, pp. 27-28; Mt 13:1-52;
Mk 4:26-32; Lk 19:11-27; 21:31;
1 Cor 15:23-28. Rev 21:1-4
3. *mysteries of K.*: Mt 4:11-12;
Acts 1:3;
Gen. Intr. St Paul in Rom, pp. 32-33
(e) **and Church:** Mt 3:2; 16:18-19;
Mk 9:1; Lk 21:31
(f) **demands it makes:** Mt 3:2; 4:17;
5:19-20; 6:33; 7:21; 11:2; 13:44-46;
18:1-9, 23-35; 19:12; 21:28-32;
22:1-4; 25:1-46; Mk 9:47; 10:13-15;
Lk 9:62; 16:16; Jn 3:3-5; Acts 14:22.

Knowledge
(a) **God's:**
1. *of the Son*: Mt 11:27; Jn 10:15
2. *of man*: Mt 6:8-32; Lk 16:15; 1 Cor
8:3; Gal 4:8-10
(b) **Christ's:**
1. *of the Father*: Mt 11:27; Jn 7:29;
8:55; 10:15
2. *of his divinity*: Mt 5:30; Jn 8:14;
11:42; 13:3; 19:28
3. *of future events*: Mt 16:21-23;
17:22-23; 20:17-19; 24:1-41;
Jn 6:70-71; 21:18-23
4. *of man*: Mt 9:4; 12:25; Lk 7:39-50;
Jn 1:48; 2:24-25; 6:61-71; 21:17
(c) **man's:**
1. *of God*: Mt 11:27; 13:11; Jn 1:10;
7:27-30; 14:7-17; 17:3-26;
Rom 1:18-33; 1 Jn 2:3-6
2. *through Revelation*: 1 Cor 2:10;
Gal 2:1-10; Heb 1:1-3
3. *of the natural law*: Rom 2:12-14
4. *of truth*: Jn 8:30-32; 14:17; 16:13

Lamb of God. *See* Christ (j), 3.

Law
(a) **Natural:** Rom 1:29:31; 2:12-15
(b) **Old:**
1. *witnesses to Christ*: Mt 11:13;
Lk 24:44; Jn 12:34; 15:25
2. *finds fulfilment in Christ*: Mt 5:18;
8:4; 17:24-27; 22:36-40; Lk 2:21-24,
39
3. *Christ, its interpreter*: Mt 15:3-6;
19:1-9; 23:23; Jn 8:5
4. *Christ perfects it*: Mt 5:17-48;
12:1-13; Lk 13:10-17; Jn 1:17; 7:23
(c) **New:**
1. *Christ, lawgiver*: Mt 5:21-48

2. *new commandment*: Jn 13:34-35;
15:12; 1 Jn 2:7-11; 3:11, 23-24
3. *supersedes Old*: Acts 9:43;
10:9-16; 15:1-35; 21:20-26; Gen. Intr.
St Paul in Rom, p. 3; Rom 3:27-31;
7:7-13; 1 Cor 16:56-57; 2 Cor 3:4-18;
Gal 3:10-12; 4:24-26; 5:1-5, 14-15
(d) **Christ and man-made laws:**
Mt 17:24-27; 22:15⸲22.
See Commandments.

Lay people. *See* Christian, the; Holiness (d); Work (d).

Lazarus Lk 10:38-42; Jn 11:1-45; 12:1-11.

Laziness Mt 25:24-30; Lk 19:24-26; Heb 6:12. *See* Work.

Levi. *See* Matthew, St.

Liberation. *See* Freedom; Redemption; Salvation.

Life
(a) **natural:**
1. *its value*: Mt 6:25
2. *Christ, Lord of life*: Mt 9:23-26;
Lk 7:11-17; Jn 10:18; 11:1-45;
Acts 3:15
(b) **supernatural:**
1. *given by Christ*: Jn 10:10, 28; 17:2
2. *Christ is L.:* Jn 1:4; 11:25; 14:6;
Gal 2:20; Phil 1:21; Col 3:4; 1 Jn 1:2;
5:11-12
(c) **living in Christ:** Rom 6:8-11;
14:7-9; 2 Cor 5:14-15; Gal 2:19-20;
Col 3:3-4; Phil 1:21.
See Life, eternal; Life, ordinary.

Life, eternal
(a) **same features:** Mt 22:30;
Lk 23:43; Jn 14:2-3; 17:3, 24-26
(b) **Christ compares it to:**
1. *a banquet*: Mt 26:29; Lk 13:25-28;
14:15-24
2. *the Kingdom*: Mt 5:3, 20; 7:21;
18:3; 25:31-46; *see* Kingdom of God.
(c) **other similes:** Rev 2:7, 10; 7:17;
20:15; 22:1, 2, 17, 19
(d) **how to attain it:**
1. *by faith*: Jn 3:14-16, 36; 5:24; 6:40,
47; 8:51; 10:25-29; 11:25-26; 20:31;
1 Tim 1:16
2. *by doing what God says*:
Jn 5:39-40; 6:63, 68-69
3. *by receiving Eucharist, pledge of*

eternal life: Jn 6:27, 50, 58
4. other requirements: Mt 7:13-14,
21-23; 16:24-27; 18:3-5; 25:31-46; Lk
13:1-5, 25-28; Jn 12:25;
1 Tim 6:12.
See Heaven; Kingdom of God;
Salvation.

Life, ordinary. *See* Naturalness;
Holiness (d), 3; Work.

Light
(a) **opposed to darkness:** Mt 6:2-23;
Jn 1:4-5; 11:9-10; Col 1:12-14;
1 Thess 5:4-8;1 Jn 1:5-7
(b) **sign of God's glory:** Mt 17:2-5;
Lk 2:9
(c) **Christ, l. of world:** Mt 4:16;
Lk 1:78-79; 2:32; Jn 1:4-9; 3:19-21;
8:12; 9:5; 12:35-36, 46; 2 Cor 4:3-6
(d) **Christian, l. of world:**
Mt 5:14-16; Lk 16:8; Eph 5:8-13;
Phil 2:14-15.

Little things: importance of
Mt 5:18-19; 10:42; 25:21-23; Mk
6:42-43; Lk 7:44-47; 16:10; Jn 2:7.
See Holiness (d), 3.

Liturgy Mt 26:6-13; Lk 24:30-31;
1 Cor 11; 14:26-40; Eph 5:19;
Heb 10:22-25; Rev 1:3; 4:4-11;
19:5-8. *See* Worship.

Love
(a) **of the Father for the Son:** Mt
3:17; 12:18; 17:5; Mk 12:6; Jn 3:35;
5:20; 10:17; 17:23-26; Rom 5:5;
Eph 1:6; Col 1:13
(b) **of God for man:** Lk 1:54-55;
12:49-50; Intr. Jn, pp. 31-33; Jn 1:14;
3:16-21; 14:21-23; 16:27; 17:20-26;
Gen. Intr. St Paul in Rom, pp. 42-43;
Jas 4:5, 1 Jn 4:7-10; Jude 1-2
(c) **of Son for the Father:**
Mt 27:26-50; Jn 14:31; 15:9-11
(d) **of Christ for man:** Mt 27:26-50;
Mk 10:21; Intr. Jn, p. 32; Jn 11:3-5,
33-45; 13:1, 23, 34; 14:21; 15:9-17;
Eph 3:19; 5:12; Rev 1:5-6
(e) **of man for God and Christ**
Mt 10:34-39; 19:27-29; 22:37-40;
Mk 3:20-21; Lk 7:47; Intr. Jn, pp.
31-33; Jn 3:16-21, 14:15-31;
15:12-15; 21:15-17; Gen. Intr. St Paul
in Rom, pp. 42-43; 1 Jn 4:16

(f) **of one's neighbour:** Mt 5:43-47;
10:34-37; 22:34-40; Lk 10:25-37;
Intr. Jn, pp. 32-33; Jn 13:34-35;
15:12-17; Rom 9:3; Phil 1:8;
1 Pet 4:8; Intr. 1 Jn in Cath, pp.
157-158; 1 Jn 4:20-21;
2 Jn 4-6; Jude 22:23.
See Charity; Mercy; Providence.

Loyalty. *See* Fidelity.

Luke, St
(a) **disciple:** Intr. Lk, pp. 15-17;
Acts 16:10-17; 20:5-21, 17; 27:1-28,
16; 2 Cor 8:16-24; Col 4:41;
2 Tim 4:11; Philem 24
(b) **his writings:** Intr. Lk, pp. 17-26;
Lk 1:1-5; Intr. Acts, pp. 21-22;
Acts 1:1-5.

Lukewarmness Mt 24:12; 25:18,
24-30; Rev 3:14-22.

Man
(a) **created by God:** Mt 19:4; Jn 1:3;
Acts 17:26-28
(b) **his dignity:**
1. receives divine Revelation: Mt 4:4;
Jn 1:4-18; Acts 17:26-28
2. is loved by God: Mt 18:12-14; Lk
2:14; Jn 3:16-21; Acts 17:25-29
3. is called to enjoy God forever:
Mt 16:26; 25:34; Lk 12:29-34;
Heb 11:13-16
4. reborn to life of grace: Jn 1:12-13;
3:3-8; 1 Cor 2:14-16; Gal 6:15;
Eph 4:22-24; *see* Grace.
(c) **all equal in God's eyes:** Gal 3:28;
Col 3:9-11.
See Soul; Flesh; Christ.

Magi Mt 2:1-12.

Magisterium
(a) **of Christ:** Mt 7:28-29; 28:18;
Lk 19:48; Jn 7:16-18; 8:28, 38
(b) **of Apostles:** Mt 28:18-20;
Mk 6:30
(c) **of Church:** Mt 16:13-20;
Jn 10:1-5; Acts 11:27; 15:22-29;
Eph 4:14; 2 Tim 2:19.
See Church; Teaching.

Magnaminity
(a) **God's:** Lk 1:49; 6:38; 11:13
(b) **Christ's:** Mt 15:32-38; 19:27-30;
Mk 6:42-44; Jn 2:9-10; 3:34; 6:12-13
(c) **man's:** Mt 5:38-42; 10:9-10;

26:6-13; Jn 12:2-8; 2 Cor 8:1-6.
See Generosity.

Mark, St Intr. Mk, pp. 55-57;
Acts 12:12-17, 25; 13:4-13; Col 4:10;
2 Tim 4:11; Philem 24; 1 Pet 5:13.

Marriage
(a) **raised by Christ to level of
sacrament:** Jn 2:1-2; Eph 5:28-32;
1 Tim 4:3-5
(b) **ends and properties:** Mt 5:31-32;
19:1-12; 1 Cor 7:1-11, 39-40;
(c) **a divine calling:** 1 Cor 7:7;
Heb 13:4
(d) **renouncing m. for sake of
Kingdom:** Mt 19:10-12, 29; *see*
Virginity
(e) **Pauline privilege:** 1 Cor 7:12-16.
See Family; Wedding.

Mary. *See* Virgin, Blessed.

Mary Magdalene Mt 27:56, 61; 28:1;
Lk 8:2; Jn 20:1-18.

Mary, sister of Martha Lk 10:38-42;
Jn 11:1-45; 12:1-8.

Martha, St Lk 10:38-42; Jn 11:1-45;
12:2.

Martyrdom Acts 7:54-60; 22:20;
Rev 2:12-13; 6:9-11; 7:9-17; 11:7-10;
13:9-10; 17:1-6; 18:20-24.

Mass. *See* Eucharist.

Matthew, St Intr. Mt, pp. 15-24;
Mt 9:9-13; 10:3; Acts 1:13.

Matthias, St Acts 1:15-26.

Meekness. *See* Patience.

Mercy
(a) **God's:** Mt 9:13; 12:7; Lk 1:54,
58, 78; 2:14; 6:36; 10:29-37; 15:1-32;
Rom 3:23-26; 2 Cor 1:3-4; Eph 2:4;
Heb 4:16; Jas 5:11; 1 Pet 1:2;
1 Jn 3:19-22
(b) **Christ's:** Mt 9:36; 14:14; 15:32;
20:34; Mk 1:41; Lk 7:11-17; 23:34,
43; Jn 8:3-11
(c) **the Christian's:** Mt 5:7;
18:21-35; 23:23; Lk 6:29, 36;
10:29-37; Heb 13:3; Jas 2:13.
See Charity; Almsgiving; Forgiveness.

Messiah. *See* Christ.

Michael Archangel, St: Jude 9;
Rev 12:7.

Miracles
(a) **worked by Christ:**
1. some cures of specific individuals:
the blind: Mt 9:27-31; 20:29-34;
Mk 8:22-26; 10:46-52; Jn 9:1-38
paralytics: Mk 2:1-12; Jn 5:1-14
lepers: Mt 8:1-4; Lk 17:11-19
man with withered hand: Mk 3:1-6
woman with flow of blood:
Mk 5:25-34
centurion's son: Mk 8:5-13;
Jn 4:46-54
Peter's mother-in-law: Lk 4:38-39
Canaanite woman: Mt 15:21-28
Malchus: Lk 22:50-51
others: Mk 7:31-37; Lk 13:11-13;
14:1-6
2. various cures: Mt 4:23-24;
8:16-17; 12:15; 15:30-31;
Mk 3:10-12; Lk 6:17-19; 9:11
3. cures of possessed people:
Mt 8:28-34; 9:32-33; 12:22; 17:14-20
4. raising people to life: Mk 5:22-43;
Lk 7:11-17; Jn 11:1-45
5. m. over nature:
wine at Cana: Jn 2:11
storm at sea: Mt 8:23-27
walking on water: Mt 14:22-33
money in fish: Mt 17:24-27
loaves and fish: Mt 14:13-21;
15:32-39
Transfiguration: Mt 17:1-9
miraculous draught of fish: Lk 5:1-11;
Jn 21:1-4
(b) **Jesus bestows his power to work
m.:** Mt 10:1; Mk 3:15; 16:17-20
(c) **m. a credential of Christ:**
Mt 9:3-7; 12:22-30; Jn 2:11; 5:31-40;
10:37-38; 11:41-42; Heb 2:4
(d) **m. worked by Apostles:**
Acts 2:43; 3:1-10; 4:5-22; 9:32-43;
13:6-12; 14:3, 8-12; 16:16-18;
19:11-12; 20:8-12; 28:1-9
(e) **symbolism:**
1. Baptism: Jn 5:3-4; 9:8-34
2. Eucharist: Mk 6:41; Jn 6:11
3. Penance: Mt 9:3-7; Lk 5:24
4. Church: Mt 8:23-27
5. divine gifts: Mt 15:33-38; Acts
3:3-8.

Mission

(a) **of divine Persons:**

1. given by Father to Son: Mk 9:37;
Lk 10:16; Jn 3:17-34; 5:30-37; 6:44;
7:28; 8:16, 29, 42; 11:42; 12:44-50;
14:24; 16:5; 17:3-8, 18-25; 20:21;
Rom 8:3; Gal 4:4; 1 Jn 4:9

*2. given by Father and Son to Holy
Spirit*: Jn 14:16, 26; 15:26; 16:7-15;
Gal 4:6

(b) **given by Jesus to Apostles.** *See*
Apostles.

See Disciples; Church.

Morality

(a) **moral demands of faith:**
Gen. Intr. St Paul in Rom, pp. 38-39;
1 Cor 5:9-11; 6:9-11

(b) **Law of Christ:** Mt 5-7;
Mk 10:17-22; Jn 13:34-35.

See Law.

Mortification

(a) **need and importance:** Mt 3:4;
7:13-14; Lk 9:23; 1 Cor 9:26-27; 2
Cor 4:10-11; Phil 2:17; Heb 13:15-16

(b) **reward for:** Mt 6:16-18;
19:38-39; Jn 12:24-26.

See Fasting; Cross; Repentance.

Moses

(a) **his importance in OT:** Mt 17:3;
Jn 3:14-15; 5:45-46; 9:28-29;
Acts 7:17-45; Heb 12:21

(b) **Israel's lawgiver:** Mt 19:3-9;
22:24; 23:2-3; Lk 5:14; 16:29-31;
Jn 1:17; *see* Law

(c) **Christ superior to:** 2 Cor 3:4-18;
Heb 3:2-6

(d) **model of faith:** Heb 11:23-29.

Mystery

(a) **of God:** Rom 11:25, 33-36; 5:25;
1 Cor 2:1, 7-9; 4:1; Col 2:2;
2 Thess 2:7

(b) **of Christ:** Eph 1:3-14; 3:1-7, 18;
Col 1:26-27

(c) **of Kingdom (Church):**
Mk 4:11-12; Gen Intr. St Paul in
Rom, pp. 32-33

(d) **of our religion:** 1 Tim 3:16.

Nathaniel. *See* Bartholomew.

Nicodemus Jn 3:1-21; 7:50-52;
19:39-42.

Oath-taking: Mt 5:33-37; 14:6-12;
23:16-22; 2 Cor 1:17-24;
Heb 6:13-20; Jas 5:12. *See* Sincerity.

Obedience

(a) **of Christ:**

1. to Father: Mt 3:15; 26:36-46;
Lk 2:49; Jn 4:32-34; 5:30; 6:38;
10:17-18; 18:11; 19:30; Phil 2:8;
Heb 5:7-9; 10:5-10

2. to Mary and Joseph: Lk 2:51

3. to those in authority: Mt 17:24-27

(b) **of Christian:**

1. to God's plans: Mt 2:12; 4:18-22;
6:10; 9:9; 21:1-6, 28-32; Jn 2:5-7;
Rom 1:5

2. in apostolate: Lk 5:1-11; Jn 21:4-8;
Acts 5:29; Phil 2:19-24

3. to civil authority: Rom 13:1-7;
Tit 3:1-2; 1 Pet 2:13-17

4. some examples: Mt 2:12; 21:1-6;
Mk 14:12-16; Lk 17:14; Jn 2:7-9;
9:6-7; 2 Cor 8:16-17; Heb 11:17-19;
see (c) & (d).

(c) **of Mary:** Mt 12:48-50; Lk 1:38;
2:22-24; 11:27-28

(d) **of Joseph:** Mt 1:19-25; 2:13-14,
19-23.

See Docility; Will of God.

Order, sacrament of priestly. *See*
Priesthood.

Pain. *See* Suffering.

Parables

(a) **purpose and dispositions to
understand them:** Mt 13:10-15,
34-35

(b) **p. of the Kingdom:**

1. sower: Mt 13:1-23

2. weeds: Mt 13:24-30, 36-43

3. mustard seed and leaven:
Mt 13:31-33

4. hidden treasure, pearl and net:
Mt 13:44-50

5. workers in vineyard: Mt 20:1-16

6. two sons: Mt 21:28-32

7. murderous vineyard tenants:
Mt 21:33-46

8. wedding guests: Mt 22:1-14

9. wise and foolish virgins: Mt 25:1-13

10. talents: Mt 25:14-30

(c) **p. of mercy:**

1. lost sheep: Lk 15:1-7

2. *lost coin*: Lk 15:8-10
3. *prodigal son*: Lk 15:11-32
(d) other p.:
1. *wicked servant*: Mt 18:21-35
2. *good Samaritan*: Lk 10:25-37
3. *foolish rich man*: Lk 12:13-21
4. *barren fig tree*: Lk 13:6-9
5. *unjust steward*: Lk 16:1-12
6. *rich man and Lazarus*: Lk 16:19-31
7. *unjust judge*: Lk 18:1-8
8. *Pharisee and publican*: Lk 18:9-14
9. *good shepherd*: Jn 10:1-21
10. *vine and branches*: Jn 15:1-8
(e) various similes: Mt 5:13-16;
7:2-5, 13-20; 15:13-14; 16:6-12;
Mk 3:23-27; Lk 12:35-48.

Parousia
(a) second coming of Christ:
Mt 16:27; 26:64; Acts 3:21;
1 Cor 15:26-27; Phil 3:20-21;
1 Thess 2:19-20; 4:13 - 5:1;
2 Thess 2:1-12; Heb 9:27-28;
Jas 5:7-9; 1 Pet 1:7; Intr. 2 Pet, pp.
123-124; 2 Pet 3:1-16; Rev 1:7;
14:14-20
(b) we do not know time:
Mt 24:36-41; 1 Thess 5:1-2;
2 Thess 2:1-2; Heb 9:27; 2 Pet 3:8-10
(c) hope in: Rom 8:19-25; Phil 1:23;
Eph 6:13; 2 Tim 2:11-13; Rev 2:7.

Passion. *See* Christ (h).

Passover. *See* Festivals.

Pastoral Epistles
Gen. Intr. St Paul in Rom, pp. 26-27;
Gen. Intr. Tim & Tit in Thess.

Patience
(a) God's: Gen. Intr. Gosp. in Mk,
pp. 16-17; Mt 18:21-27; Lk 13:6-9;
Rom 3:23-26; 2 Pet 3:9
(b) Christ's: Mt 11:29; 16:8-11;
17:17; 20:25-28; Lk 9:51-56;
22:24-30; 24:13-35; Jn 8:50;
20:26-29; 21:15-18; 2 Thess 3:5
(c) the Christian's: Mt 5:5, 38-42;
Lk 8:15; 21:19; 2 Cor 6:4-5; 12:12;
Heb 10:35-39; Jas 1:2-4; 5:7-11;
Rev 2:2-3; 14:12
(d) faults against: Mt 5:21-26;
Gal 45:20; Eph 4:31-32; Col 3:8;
Jas 1:19-20.
See Peace; Serenity.

Paul, St
(a) life:
1. *dates*: Gen. Intr. St Paul in Rom,
pp. 13-19
2. *before conversion*: Acts 7:58; 8:1-3
3. *conversion*: Act 9:1-19; 22:1-16;
26:9-18; Gal 1:11-12; 1 Tim 1:12-13
4. *miracles*: Acts 13:6-12; 16:16-18;
19:11-12; 28:1-9
5. *visions*: Acts 18:9-10; 22:17-21;
23:11; 27:21-26; 2 Cor 12:1-10
6. *apostolic journeys*: Acts 13:1-14,
28; 15:36 - 18, 22; 18:23 - 21:16: 27:1
- 28:16; Gen. Intr. St Paul in Rom,
pp. 15-16.
7. *addresses*: Acts 13:16-41;
17:22-31; 20:18-35; 22:1-21;
24:10-21; 26:1-29
8. *persecution*: Acts 9:23-30;
13:50-51; 14:19-20; 16:19-40;
17:13-14; 18:12-17; 19:23-40;
20:18-27; 2 Cor 4:7 - 5:10; 6:1-10;
11:21-23; 2 Tim 2:9-10; 3:10-13;
4:6-18
9. *imprisonment*: Acts 21:27-40;
22:22-29; Gen. Intr. St Paul in Rom,
pp. 17-18
(b) Apostle:
1. *title*: Rom 1:1; 1 Cor 1:1; 9:1-23;
15:9-11; Intr. 2 Cor, pp. 163-164; 2
Cor 1:1-2, 3-6; Tit 1:1; 2 Tim 1:1-3
2. *Apostle of Gentiles*: Act 9:15;
13:46-49; 18:5-8; 22:21; 28:28;
Rom 1:5-7
(c) ministry:
1. *qualities*: Acts 20:34;
1 Cor 4:14-21; 9:1-27; 2 Cor 1:12-14;
3:1-3; 5:13; 6:11-13; 7:2-16;
10:15-16; 11:7-15, 28, 29; 12:11-18;
Gal 4:19; 1 Thess 2:17-19; 3:6-10;
2. *in Jerusalem*: Acts 9:26-30; 15:1-35
3. *in Damascus*: Acts 9:19-25
4. *in Antioch*: Acts 11:25-30
5. *in Athens*: Acts 17:16-34
6. *in Ephesus*: Acts 18:18-22;
19:1-40; 20:17-38
7. *in Corinth*: Acts 18:1-17;
Intr. 1 Cor, pp. 25-26; 1 Cor 2:1-5
8. *in Thessalonica*: 1 Thess 2:1-12
(d) Epistles: Gen. Intr. St Paul in
Rom, pp. 17-29; Intr Rom, pp. 54-55;
2 Pet 3:15-16

(e) teaching: Gen. Intr. St Paul in Rom, pp. 29-45.

Peace
(a) gift brought by Christ: Mt 11:28-30; Lk 1:7-9; 2:14; 8:48; 24:36; Jn 14:27; 16:33; 20:19, 21, 26; Eph 1:2; 2:14-18; Col 3:15; 2 Thess 1:1-2; 3:16; Heb 13:20
(b) the Christian's: Mt 6:25-34; 10:11-15, 34-36;11:28-30; Lk 7:50; Acts 21:12-14; 1 Cor 1:3; 2 Cor 1:1-2; Heb 4:9-10; *see* (d).
(c) Christians, sowers of: Mt 5:9; 10:11-15; Lk 10:5-6; Heb 12:14; Jas 3:18
(d) Christian greeting: Rom 1:7; Eph 1:2; 1 Thess 1:1; 1 Tim 1:1-2; 2 Tim 1:1-2; Tit 1:4; 1 Pet 1:2; 3 Jn 15; Jude 2; Rev 1:4
See Joy.

Penance
(a) sign of conversion: Mt 3:1-12; 4:17; 11:20-24; Mk 6:12; Lk 5:32; 13:1-5; Heb 3:7-8
(b) examples of: Mk 1:6; Lk 7:36-50; 19:1-10; 22:62
(c) sacrament of:
1. instituted by Christ: Jn 20:22-23
2. need for: Mt 5:23-24; Lk 7:47; Jn 11:44; 1 Cor 11:28; 2 Cor 4:7; 5:18-21; Heb 5:3
3. sign of God's mercy: Lk 7:50; Jn 20:20-23; Heb 5:2-3; 6:4-8.
See Confession; Conversion; Forgiveness.

Pentecost. *See* Spirit, Holy (c).

Persecution
(a) of Jesus: Mt 12:14; Lk 13:31; Jn 5:16-18; 7:1; 8:59; 15:20
(b) Jesus foretells his disciples will suffer p.: Mt 10:16-39; 24:9; Mk 10:28-30; Lk 21:10-19; Jn 15:20; 16:2-4
(c) suffered by Christians: Acts 4:5-22; 5:17-42; 8:1-4; 12:1-19; 1 Thess 2:14; 3:3-4; 2 Tim 3:10-13; Heb 10:32-34; Intr. 1 Pet in Cath, pp. 80-81; 1 Pet 4:12-19; Rev 11:1-13; 12:13-17; 13:9-10
(d) duty to pray for persecutors: Mt 5:44; Acts 7:60; Rom 12:14

(e) reward for: Mt 5:5, 10-12; 24:13; Lk 21:19; Acts 14:20-22; Rev 11:11-13; 19:1-4.

Perseverance
(a) gift of God: 1 Cor 9:27; 10:11-13; Phil 1:6; 2:12-13; 2 Thess 1:11-12
(b) need and reward: Mt 10:22; Mk 13:13; Lk 8:15; 21:19; Gal 6:7-10; 2 Thess 3:13; Heb 6:9-12; 10:19 - 11:40; 12:3, 25
(c) in prayer: *see* Asceticism.

Peter, St
(a) life: Intr. 1 Pet in Cath, pp. 75-77.
1. calling: Mt 4:18-22; 10:2; Jn 1:40-42
2. a favourite Apostle: Mt 17:1-13; 26:37; Mk 5:37; 13:3; Lk 22:8
3. acts in name of disciples: Mt 15:15; 19:27-30; Lk 12:41; Jn 6:68-69
4. other actions in Gospel: Mt 14:24-33; 17:24-27; 18:21-22; Mk 1:36; 11:21; 16:7; Lk 8:45; 24:34; Jn 13:6-10; 18:10-11; 21:2-15
5. denies Christ: Mt 26:30-35, 69-75
6. apostolate: Acts 1-6; 8:1-25; 9:32 - 12:19; 15:1-35
7. addresses: Acts 2:14-36; 3:11-26; 4:8-12, 19-20; 10:34-43; 11:4-17; 15:7-11
8. miracles: Acts 3:1-10; 5:1-11; 9:32-42; 12:1-19
(b) first among Apostles:
1. primacy promised and bestowed: Mt 16:13-20; Lk 22:31-34; Jn 12:15-33
2. he acts as Primate: Acts 1:15-26; 2:14-41; 15:6-11
(c) writings: Intr. 1 & 2 Pet in Cath, pp. 77-83, 121-125.
See Pope.

Pharisees
(a) their sect and its teaching: Mt 3:7; 9:14-17; Mk 7:1-13; 9:11-13; Acts 15:5; 23:6-11
(b) their opposition to Christ: Mt 9:34; 12:1-14, 22-42; 16:1-12; 19:1-9; 22:15-22; 26-27; Lk 15:1-2; Jn 4:1-3; 8:3-11; 9:8-34; 11:46-57
(c) Jesus' criticism of: Mt 15:1-4; 21:33-46; 23:1-36; Lk 18:9-14; Jn 9:40-41.

Philemon, Epistle to
Gen Intro. St Paul in Rom, p. 24;
Intr. Philem in Capt, pp. 195-196.

Philip, St Mt 10:3; Jn 1:43-48; 6:5-7;
12:21-22; 14:8-9; Acts 2:13.

Philippians, Epistle to
Gen. Intr. St Paul in Rom, p. 24;
Intr. Phil in Capt, pp. 110-107.

Piety. *See* Religion.

Pilate Mt 27; Lk 3:1; 13:1;
Jn 18:28 - 19:38; Acts 3:13; 4:27;
13:28; 1 Tim 6:13.

Pope Mt 16:13-20; Lk 10:16; 22:31-34;
Jn 21:15-17; Acts 1:26; Gal 1:17-20.
See Church; Peter.

Poverty
(a) **Christ's:** Mt 8:20; 27:35;
Lk 2:6-7; 2 Cor 8:9
(b) **need for:** Mt 6:19-24, 33; 13:22;
19:16-26; Lk 6:24; 12:13-21; Rev 2:9
(c) **how to practise:** Lk 6:20; Jn
6:12-13; Heb 13:5-6
(d) **and trust in God:** Mt 6:25-34;
10:9-10; Lk 1:53; 2 Cor 8:1-6; Jas 2:5
(e) **and use of material things:**
Mk 10:23-27; Lk 6:20-24; 10:7;
16:19-31; 19:8; 21:1-4; Phil 4:10-20
(f) **as state of need before God:**
Mt 5:3; Lk 4:18-21
(g) **reward for:** Mt 5:3; 11:5;
19:27-30.
See Detachment. Almsgiving.

Praise
(a) **of Christ to the Father:**
Mt 11:25-27
(b) **of angels to God:** Lk 2:13-15;
(c) **of men to the Lord:** Mt 9:8;
15:31; 21:8-19, 15-16; Mk 7:37;
Lk 24:53; Eph 3:20-21; Rev 5:6-14;
19:1-8
(d) **to Mary:** Lk 1:26-33, 41-45;
11:27-28.
See Thanksgiving, Blessing.

Prayer
(a) **of Christ:**
1. in solitude: Mt 14:23; Mk 1:35;
Lk 5:16; 9:18
2. in Gethsemani: Mt 26:36-46;
Heb 5:7-9
3. on Cross: Mt 27:46; Lk 23:34, 46

4. at some key moments: Lk 3:21;
6:12; 9:39; Jn 11:41-42; 12:27-28
5. for disciples: Lk 22:32; Jn 17:1-36
(b) **some teaching of Jesus
concerning:** Mt 6:5-13; 7:7-11; 9:38;
27:41; Lk 18:1-4
(c) **the Our Father:** Mt 6:9-13;
Lk 11:1-4
(d) **qualities of:**
1. concentration: 1 Cor 14:15-17
2. humility: Mt 6:5-8; 8:2-4;
15:21-28; Lk 7:1-10; 18:90-14
3. faith and trust: Mt 15:21-28;
17:14-21; 21:21-22; Lk 1:13;
Jn 11:21-22
4. perseverance: Mt 7:7-11; 15:21-28;
20:29-34; 26:36-46; Mk 10:46-52;
Lk 18:1-8; Acts 2:42-47; 12:5-12;
Col 4:2
5. backed by deeds: Mt 7:21-23
(e) **effectiveness:** Mt 18:19; 21:22;
Lk 4:38-39; 7:1-10; 11:5-12;
Jn 14:13-14; 15:7, 16; 16:23-27;
Acts 10:1-8; 16:25-34; 1 Thess 3:10;
Jas 1:5-8; 4:2-3; 5:13, 17-18;
1 Jn 5:14-15; Rev 8:3-5
(f) **need for:** Lk 5:16; Acts 13:2-3;
Eph 6:18; 1 Thess 5:17;
2 Thess 3:1-2; 1 Tim 2:1; Rev 3:20-21
(g) **of Blessed Virgin:** Lk 1:46-55;
2:19, 33:51; Jn 2:3, 11
(h) **of first Christians:** Acts 1:12-14,
23-26; 2:42-47; 3:1; 4:23-31; 9:40;
10:9-16; 12:5, 12; 16:13-16, 25;
20:36; 21:5-6.

Preaching
(a) **of John Baptist:** Mt 3:1-12;
Jn 1:15
(b) **of Christ:**
1. authoritative: Mt 5:21-48; 2:28-29;
Jn 3:34; 7:46; 8:26-28, 38; 10:37-38;
12:49-50
2. confirmed by miracles:
Gen. Intr. Gosp. in Mk, p. 31; Mt 8-9;
Jn 5:36; 10:37-38
(c) **of Apostles:** Mt 10:7, 27;
28:18-20; Acts 5:17-42; 6:1-6;
Intr. Thess, p. 24; 1 Thess 1:5
(d) **of Church:**
1. need for: Mt 9:37-38; Mk 1:38;
Lk 4:18-19; 1 Cor 1:17; 2:1-5;
Eph 3:7; 4:11-12

2. *in line with Gospel*: Acts 2:36;
1 Cor 2:1-5; 2 Cor 4:1-6;
2 Tim 2:14-18; Tit 1:1, 12-14
3. catechesis: Acts 2:42; 19:2;
Rom 10:14-17; 1 Cor 3:10-11;
Heb 6:1-3.
See Teaching.

Presence of God Mt 6:4, 6, 18;
Lk 16:15; Acts 17:26-28; Eph 1:4;
1 Thess 3:9; Heb 4:12-13.

Pride
(a) **God resists the proud:**
Lk 1:51-52; 18:9-14; Jas 4:6; 1 Pet 5:5
(b) **grave sin:** Lk 1:51; 20:9-19;
Jn 9:39-41; 1 Cor 4:7; Jas 4:13-17.
See Humility.

Priesthood
(a) **levitical:** Mt 2:4; Lk 1:8-10;
Intr. Heb, pp. 29-30
(b) **chief priests:** Mt 2:4; 26:3-4,
47-68; 27; Lk 3:2; Jn 7:32; 11:47-53;
18:13-14; Acts 4:5-22; 5:17-42; 7:1;
23-24
(c) **Christ's p.:** Mt 20:28; Jn 17:1-26;
Heb 2:17; 3:1; 5:1-10; 7:4-19
(d) **ministerial:**
1. institution: Mt 26:26-29; Lk 22:19;
1 Tim 4:14-16; 5:22; 2 Tim 1:6
2. mission: Acts 10:25-26; 1 Cor
16:10-12; 2 Tim 1:6; 2:4-7; 4:22;
Heb 5:1-10; 7:3
3. qualities: Acts 14:23; 1 Cor 4:1-2;
2 Cor 12:15; 2 Tim 2:22-26; 3:17;
Tit 1:5-9
(e) **common p. of faithful:** Rom 12:1;
1 Pet 2:4-10; Heb 13:15-16; Rev
1:5-6; 20:6.
See Bishop; Priests.

Priests
(a) **ordained by sacrament:**
Acts 14:23; 1 Tim 4:14; 5:22;
2 Tim 1:6
(b) **co-workers of bishops:**
Acts 11:30; 20:17-38; 1 Tim 5:17-19;
Tit 1:5
(c) **hierarchical mission:**
1. preaching: 1 Tim 4:13; 2 Tim 2:15;
4:1-5
2. ruling: Acts 15:2-35; 21:18-26;
1 Pet 5:1-4; 1 Tim 5:19; Tit 2:1-10;
3:1-2

3. hallowing: Tit 1:5-9
(d) **qualities:** 1 Cor 4:21; Tit 1:5-9.
See Priesthood.

Priscilla. *See* Aquila.

Prophecies
(a) **of OT fulfilled in NT:**
1. in Jesus: Mt 1:22-23; 2:5-7, 15, 23;
3:17; 8:17; 12:17-21; 13:35; 21:4-5,
42; 26:24, 31, 56; Lk 4:17-21; 18:31;
22:37; 24:25-27; Jn 6:45; 7:42;
12:14-16, 38; 15:25; 19:24, 28, 36,
37; 20:9; Acts 2:14-36; 3:11-26; 4:11;
13:32-41; 2 Pet 1:19-21
2. in Mary: Mt 1:22-23; Lk 1:27
3. in the people and events: Mt
2:17-18; 3:3; 4:14-16; 11:10;
13:14-15; 15:7-9; 24:15; Mk 7:6-7;
Lk 7:27; Jn 12:14-15, 37-41
(b) **John Baptist as prophet:**
Mt 3:11; 11:9; 14:5; 21:26; Lk 1:76;
Jn 1:6-8, 15
(c) **other NT p.:**
1. concerning Jesus: Lk 2:25-38;
Jn 11:51-52
2. concerning Mary: Lk 1:45, 48; 2:35
(d) **Jesus is the Prophet:** Mt 21:22;
Mk 6:15; Lk 7:16; 13:33; 24:19;
Jn 4:19; 6:14; 7:40; 9:17
(e) **some p. made by Jesus:**
1. on his Passion: Mt 12:39-40;
16:21; 17:22-23; 20:17-19; Jn 2:19-22
2. on Peter's denials: Mt 26:34
3. on Judas' betrayal: Mt 26:21-25;
Jn 6:70-71
*4. on Last Judgment and destruction
of Jerusalem*: Mt 24:1-41
(f) **p. in the Church:**
1. among early Christians: Acts
11:27-30; 13:1-3; 21:9-14; 1 Cor 14;
1 Thess 5:19-22. *See* Gifts.
2. rejection of false prophets:
Mt 7:15, 21-24; 24:24; 1 Tim 1:6-7;
6:3-10; Jude 17-19.

Providence
(a) **universal:** Mt 4:4; 6:11, 25-34;
10:9-10, 28-31; 12:32-34;
Acts 17:26-28; Rom 8:28; Col 1:27;
Heb 1:3; 1 Pet 5:6-7
(b) **towards Church:** Mt 8:23-27;
16:18; 28:20; Mk 16:20; Jn 10:1-18.
See Filiation, divine; Suffering.

Prudence Mt 7:24-27; 10:16-23; 11:25-26; 24:45-51; 25:1-13; Lk 16:1-12; Jn 4:1-3; Acts 9:30; 2 Cor 8:20-21.

Publicans Mt 5:46; 9:9-13; 11:19; 21:31-32; Lk 3:12-13; 7:29; 18:10-14; 19:1-10.

Punishment
(a) **reasons for:** Mt 3:7; 18:34; 22:1-14; Lk 21:20-24; Jn 3:36; 9:2-3; 2 Thess 2:8-12; Rev 2:20-23; 8-9; 16:1-21; 17:16-18; 18:4-24
(b) **eternal p.:** Mt 25:46; 2 Thess 1:6-10; 2 Pet 2:4-10
See Hell; Suffering.

Purgatory Lk 16:22-26; 1 Cor 3:12-15; Heb 9:23.

Purity
(a) **Christ's example:** Lk 23:8-11; Jn 4:27
(b) **positive virtue:** Mt 5:8, 27-30; Jn 19:26-27; 1 Cor 6:12-14, 20; Eph 5:3-4; 1 Thess 4:4-8; 2 Pet 2:6-14
(c) **ways to practise:** Mt 5:27-30; 18:8-9; 1 Cor 6:15-18; 2 Pet 2:13-14
(d) **of Mary:** Lk 1:34
(e) **grave sin of impurity:** Mt 5:27-28; Acts 15:29; 1 Cor 5:11-13; 6:9, 12-20; Heb 13:4; Rev 17:1-6.
See Virginity.

Reconciliation of man with God through Christ Rom 5:6-11; 2 Cor 5:11-21; Eph 2:11-22; Col 1:2-23; 2:13-15.
See Penance; Forgiveness.

Rectitude of intention
(a) **needed for recognizing and following Christ:** Mt 11:25-26; Lk 11: 33-36, 52-54; Jn 5:41-47; 6:26; 7:17-18, 45-53; 9:13-41; 11:46-53; 12:37-43; Acts 17:11; 23:12-22; 24:24-27
(b) **in one's action:** Mt 6:1-8, 16-18, 22-23; 15:10-20; 21:1-39; Mk 11:13-14; Jn 12:4-6; 18:28; Rom 3:8; Gal 1:10; 1 Thess 2:3-6
(c) **some examples:** Jn 1:19-27; 2:25-30; 2 Cor 11-12; 1 Thess 2:3-6.
See Humility; Simplicity.

Redemption
(a) **Israel's hope in:** Lk 1:68; 2:38; 24:21
(b) **brought about by Christ:** Mt 20:28; 26:28; 27:50; Lk 4:18-19; 21:28; Jn 1:29; 3:16-17; 10:11-15; Acts 20:28; Rom 3:21-31; 1 Cor 1:30-31; 2 :1-5; 6:19-20; 2 Cor 5:11-21; Eph 1:7-8; 3:9; Intr. Phil in Capt, þp. 106-107; 1 Tim 2:6; Tit 2:14; Heb 9:11-14; 1 Pet 1:17-21; 3:18-20; 1 Jn 4:10
(c) **need for:** Gen. Intr. St Paul in Rom, pp. 29-32; Rom 3:23-26; Eph 2:5-6; Heb 5:10
(d) **Mary, co-redeemer:** Lk 2:34-35; Intr. Jn, pp. 35-37; Jn 2:3; 19:25-27.
See Justification; Salvation.

Religion (piety) Gen. Intr. Gosp. in Mk, pp. 22-23; Mk 11:15-18; Eph 3:14; Intr. Past. Epis. in Thess, pp. 84-86; 1 Tim 2:10; 3:16; 4:7-11; 6:3-10; Tit 1:1; 2 Pet 3:11. *See* Worship; Filiation, divine.

Repentance. *See* Conversion.

Respect, human Mt 10:26-27, 32-33; 27:24; Mk 8:38; Lk 19:4; Jn 7:13; 9:22; 12:42-43; 19:6-8; Acts 4:13-22; Rom 1:16.

Resurrection
(a) **of all men at end of time:** Mt 22:23-33; Lk 14:12-14; Jn 5:28-29; 11:24-26; Acts 23:6-9; 24:14-16; Intr. 1 Cor, pp. 32-34; 1 Cor 15:12-58; Rev 20:11-15
(b) **Jesus raises people to life:** Mt 9:18-26; Lk 7:11-17; Jn 11:1-45
(c) **Christ's own:** *see* Christ, Jesus (1), 2
1. foretold in Scripture: Lk 24:46; Jn 20:9
2. announced by him: Mt 12:40; 16:21; 17:9, 23; 20:19; 26:32; 27:63; Lk 24:6-8; Jn 2:19-22
3. empty tomb: Mt 28:1-15; Jn 20:1-10; 1 Cor 15:4
4. appearances of Christ after R.: Mt 28:9-20; Mk 16:9-18; Lk 24:13-53; Jn 20:11 - 21:23; Acts 1:3; 1 Cor 15:1-11

(d) to eternal life through Christ:
Jn 6:39-44, 54; 11:23-26;
Acts 24:14-16; 2 Cor 4:13 - 5:10;
1 Thess 4:14-17
(e) signs of coming of kingdom:
Mt 10:8; 11:5; 27:52-53.

Revelation
(a) natural: Acts 14:15-18; 17:22-31;
Rom 1:18-32
(b) supernatural: Acts 17:30-31;
Rom 2:12-14; Gen Intr. Heb, pp.
45-46; Heb 2:3-4; 1 Tim 1:11;
Rev 1:1; 5:1-7
(c) Christ, fulness of R.: Mt 11:25;
Jn 1:9, 18; 6:46; 14:8-11; Heb 1:1-2;
1 Jn 5:9-12; Rev 1:1-3
(d) its transmission: Gen. Intr. Gosp.
in Mk, pp. 13-15; Rom 1:16; Gen Intr.
Cor, pp. 13-16; 2 Thess 2:15; Jude 3
(e) content: 1 Tim 6:20;
2 Tim 1:12-14
(f) Church, guardians of R.:
Lk 10:16; 1 Cor 1:10; Gal 1:6-9;
1 Tim 6:20-21; 2 Tim 1:12-14.
See Magisterium; Scripture, Sacred;
Tradition.

Revelation, Book of *See* Intr. Rev.

Riches
(a) can be obstacle to salvation:
Mt 6:19-21, 24; 13:22; 19:16-26;
Lk 6:24; 12:15-21; 14:33; 16:19-31;
Acts 5:1 - 11; Jas 2:6-7; 4:2-3; 5:1-6;
Rev 3:17-19; 18:1-3
(b) true: Lk 6:24; 12:33-34; 19:8.
See Poverty.

Righteousness
(a) God's: Mt 3:15; Lk 7:29; 18:7-8;
Rom 1:17 - 3:31; 2 Cor 5:21;
Rev 11:16-19
(b) Christ, the Righteous One:
Mt 27:19; Lk 23:47; Jn 7:18;
see Christ, Jesus (j), 12
(c) means doing God's will: Mt 1:19;
5:6, 10, 20; 6:1, 33; 13:43, 49; 21:32;
25:37, 46; Mk 6:20; Lk 1:6, 75; 2:25;
23:50; 2 Cor 9:9-10
(d) social j.: Mt 17:24-27; 22:15-21;
Lk 16:19-31; Rom 13:1-7; Jas 5:1-6;
1 Pet 2:13-17.
See Holiness.

Rights
(a) of God: Mt 22:15-21; Acts
4:18-20; 5:29
(b) of society: Mt 22:15-21; Jn
19:8-11
(c) human: Lk 16:19-31; Jn 14:27;
Acts 16:37-39; 22:25-30.
See Righteousness.

Romans, Epistle to
Gen. Intr. St Paul in Rom, pp. 22-23;
Intr. Rom, pp. 48-59; Rom 1:8-15.

Sabbath
**(a) dedicated by Jews to divine
worship:** Mt 12:2; Mk 16:1;
Lk 4:16-30
(b) Jesus, Lord of s.: Mt 12:1-13;
Lk 13:10-17; 14:1-6; Jn 5:1-18;
7:19-24; 9:14-16

Sacraments Mt 3:10; Intr. Jn, pp.
33-35; Jn 19:34; Heb 6:1-3.
See Baptism; Confirmation, etc.

Sacrifice
(a) in OT: Rom 3:25; Intr. Heb, pp.
30-32; Heb 10:1-4
(b) Christ's:
on Cross: Mt 20:28; Jn 1:29; 3:14;
11:55; 12:32; Heb 9:11-14; *see* Christ,
Jesus (h).
2. for our sins: Mt 26:26-28; Jn 1:29;
2 Cor 5:18-21; Heb 10:5-18; 1 Pet
1:17-21; Rev 5:6-10
3. renewed in Mass: *see* Eucharist (d).
(c) of the Christian: *see*
Mortification.

Saducees Mt 3:7; 16:1-12; 22:23-33;
Acts 5:17-42; 23:6-11.

Sadness. *See* Joy.

Saints
(a) description of Christians:
Acts 9:13, 41; Rom 1:7; 16:15;
1 Cor 1:2; 6:2; 16:1; 2 Cor 1:1;
Eph 1:1; Phil 1:1; 4:21; Col 1:2
(b) models and intercessors: 3 Jn 11;
Rev 8:3-5.

Salvation
(a) God wants all to be saved:
Mt 1:6; 20:28; 22:1-14;
Intr. Lk, pp. 23-24; Lk 2:8-20, 29-32;
13:23-30; 15:1-32; 19:1-10; 23:39-43;
Jn 6:39-40; 10:16; Rom 3:27-31;

9:14-33; 1 Tim 1:3-4; 2:3-4; Tit 3:1-8
(b) Christ is the Saviour:
Mt 1:20-23; Lk 1:46-55, 68-79; 2:11,
21, 25-38; Jn 3:14-17; 4:42;
Acts 4:12; 3:37-41; 5:29-32; 13:23;
15:11; Gen Intr. St Paul in Rom, pp.
32-36; 1 Thess 5:9-10; 1 Tim 1:15;
2 Tim 1:9-10; Tit 2:13; 1 Jn 4:14;
Rev 5:8-10
(c) Church continues Christ's
mission: *see* Church (b).
(d) Mary's cooperation in: Lk 1:38;
2:34-35; Intr. Jn, pp. 35-37; Jn 2:1-5,
11; 19:25-27.
See History of Salvation;
Redemption; Life, eternal.

Sanhedrin Mt 2:4; 5:22; 26:59-68;
Mk 14:64; Jn 11:46-53; Acts 4:5-22;
5:17-42; 6:8 - 7:60; 23:1.

Scandal
(a) Jesus, an occasion of: Mt 11:6;
13:53-58; 15:12; 26:31-35; Jn 6:60-66
(b) gravity of: Mt 13:41; 14:1-5;
16:23; 17:27; 18:6-9; Mk 9:42-50;
Rom 14:13-21; 1 Cor 5:1-13; 6:1-10;
8:7-13; 10:23-33; 2 Cor 6:3;
Jude 12:13.

Scribes
(a) teachers of the Law: Mt 2:4;
13:52; 23:2; Mk 1:22
(b) some accept Christ: Mt 8:19;
Mk 12:28-34; Lk 20:39
(c) oppose Christ and his disciples:
Mt 12:38; 15:1-14; 16:21; 20:18;
26:57; 27:41; Mk 2:6-7, 16; 3:22;
9:14; 14:1; Lk 11:53-54; Jn 8:3;
Acts 4:5-22; 6:8 - 7:60
(d) upbraided by Christ: Mt 5:20;
23:1-36.

Scripture, Sacred
(a) general questions:
Gen. Intr. Gosp. in Mk, pp. 13-23;
Gen. Intr. Capt, pp. 15-20
(b) inspiration and authority:
Mt 26:54; Lk 24:27, 44; Jn 10:34-36;
Gen. Intr. Cor, pp. 13-23;
2 Pet 1:19-21; 1 Tim 3:16; 2 Pet 1:21;
Rev 2-3; 10:1
(c) announce Christ and are
fulfilled in him: Jn 5:39-47;
Acts 17:2-3, 11

(d) nourishment for soul:
Gen. Intr. Gosp. in Mk, pp. 22-23;
Mt 4:4; Lk 24:27; Jn 14:25;
Acts 8:28; Rom 15:4; Rev 1:3
(e) unity: Lk 24:44- 49; Gen Intr.
Heb, pp. 16-17; 1 Pet 1:10-12
(f) correct interpretation: Lk
24:13-27; Acts 8:31; Gen. Intr. Thess,
pp. 13-21; Gen Intr. Heb, pp. 19-21,
63-67; 2 Pet 1:20; 3:15-16.
See Testament, Old; Testament, New;
Gospel.

Self-denial: *see* Calling; Charity,
Cross; Generosity; Love.

Self-surrender: *see* Love; Charity,
Generosity; Calling.

Selfishness: *see* Generosity.

Serenity
(a) of Christ: Lk 4:28-30; Jn 18:4-11,
22-23
(b) of the Christian: Mt 6:25-34;
10:19-20; 24:6; Jn 14:1, 27; 16:33;
Acts 21:12-14.
See Peace; Persecution.

Servants
(a) duties of: Eph 6:5-8; Col 3:22-25;
1 Tim 6:1-2; Tit 2:9-10; 1 Pet 2:18-25
(b) masters' duties towards:
Eph 6:9; Col 4:1; Philem 15-21.

Service
(a) Christ, Servant: Mt 20:28;
Jn 13:1-20
(b) Church and its rulers, servants:
Mt 18:1-35; 20:26; 23:11; Lk
22:24-27
(c) Christian, as servants:
1. of God: Mt 4:10; 6:24; 25:35-46;
Lk 1:74-75; Jn 2:5-7; 12:26; 18:37;
Rom 1:1, 9; Jas 1:1
2. of others: Mt 10:42; 20:24-28;
23:11-12; 25:35-46; Lk 3:12-13;
22:24-27; 1 Cor 7:21-23; 9:19-23
(d) Mary, servant: Lk 1:39-40, 56;
Jn 2:3.
See Charity; Mercy.

Sickness: *see* Suffering.

Silvanus (Silas) Acts 15:22, 27, 32;
15:36 - 18:22; 2 Cor 1:19;
1 Thess 1:1; 2 Thess 1:1;
cf. Intr. 1 Pet, p. 78; 1 Pet 5:12.

Simeon Lk 2:25-35.

Sin

(a) **offence aginst God:** Lk 11:4;
15:1-32; 18:9-14; Heb 6:6; 10:26-31;
1 Jn 3:4-5; 5:16-17; Rev 3:1; 18:4-8

(b) **cause of Christ's death:**
Mt 20:28; 26:28; Jn 1:29;
Rom 3:23-26; 1 Cor 6:19-20;
2 Cor 5:11-21; Rev 1:5-6

(c) **Jesus and sinners:**
1. he receives them: Mt 9:10-13;
Lk 7:34; 15:1; 19:1-10
2. he pardons s.: Mt 9:1-8;
Lk 7:36-50; Jn 8:3-11; Acts 10:43;
13:38-39
3. he bestows power to forgive s.:
Mt 18:18; Jn 20:23; *see* Penance.

(d) **comes from man's heart:** Mt 5:8,
28; 15:18-19

(e) **original s.**: Rom 5:12-21; 1 Cor
15:20-22; Eph 2:3

(f) **some grave s.**
1. against Holy Spirit: Mt 12:21-32
2. apostasy: Heb 6:4-6; 10:26-31; 2
Pet 2:20-22
3. mortal s.: 1 Jn 5:16-17
4. of angels: 2 Pet 2:4; Jude 6
5. lists of: Rom 1:29-31; 1 Cor 5:11;
6:9-10; Gal 5:17-21; 1 Tim 1:9-10; 2
Tim 3:2-5; Tit 3:3-7; Rev 21:8

(g) **affects all**
1. all men sin: Rom 3:9-18; Jas 3:1-2;
1 Jn 1:8-10; 5:19
2. loss of sense of s.: Mt 13:36-43;
22:12-13; 25:41-46; Lk 3:1-5;
16:19-31; 1 Cor 6:9-10; 1 Jn 1:8

(h) **some consequences of**
1. slavery: Jn 8:34; 2 Pet 1:20-22;
1 Jn 3:6-9
2. eternal punishment
Mt 13:36-43; 22:12-13; 25:41-46;
Lk 13:1-5; 16:19-31; 1 Cor 6:10-11;
15:54-58; Rev 21:8
3. other: Rev 3:1; 6:4-6; 16:1-21;
see Death (b).

(i) **avoiding occasions of:**
Mk 9:43-48; Acts 19:17-19;
1 Cor 5:9-13; Heb 12:1; 1 Jn 2:1-2; 2
Jn 10-11.
See Conversion; Pardon.

Sincerity

(a) **Christ is Truth:** Mt 23:8-10;
Jn 1:14, 17; 14:6; 17:7; 18:37

(b) **virtue beloved by Christ:**
Mt 5:33-37; Jn 1:47; 18:37

(c) **towards God:** Mt 10:26-27;
12:30; Lk 5:13; 16:15; Jn 3:19-21;
Acts 5:1-11

(d) **and oath-taking:** *see* Oath-taking.

(e) **s. of life:** Mt 6:1-8, 16-18; 7:1-5;
15:1-9; 23:1-36; 27:6; Lk 12:1-3;
Jn 12:4-6; Acts 5:1-11; Rom 2:17-24;
Eph 4:15-25; 2 Thess 2:8-12;
Jas 1:7-8.
See Rectitude of intention; Simplicity.

Simon of Cyrene Mk 15:21;
Rom 16:13.

Simplicity

(a) **God prefers simple souls:**
Mt 11:25-26; 18:1-6; 19:13-15;
Lk 1:51-53; 2:8-20, 36-38; 24:9-12;
1 Cor 1:26-31

(b) **recommended by Christ:**
Mt 6:7-8, 22-23; 10:16; Jn 1:47.
See Filiation, divine; Sincerity.

Slavery, Slaves 1 Cor 7:21-23;
Gal 3:28; Eph 6:5-9; Col 3:22 - 4:1;
1 Tim 56:1-2; Tit 2:9-10;
Philem 8:21; 1 Pet 2:18-25.

Sobriety Mt 3:4; 16:26-27;
Lk 12:15-21; 16:19-31; 1 Thess 5:6-8;
Eph 5:18; 1 Pet 1:13; 4:7; 5:8.
See Fasting; Poverty.

Society

(a) **Church as:** Rom 12:4-5;
1 Cor 12:12-27; Eph 1:22-23;
4:12-16; Col 1:18

(b) **the Christian and civil s.:**
1. public authority: Mt 22:17-21;
Acts 16:37-39; 24:10-21;
Rom 13:1-7; 1 Tim 2:2; Tit 3:1-7;
1 Pet 2:13-14
2. human progress: 1 Cor 15:23-28;
2 Cor 5:6; Jas 5:5
3. God is first to be obeyed:
Acts 4:18-21; 5:29.

Son of man: *see* Christ.

Sorrow: *see* Joy.

Soul Mt 10:28; 11:28-30; 16:26;
22:22-33; Lk 16:19-31; 21:29;
Heb 9:27-28.

Spirit, Holy
(a) **in Christ's life:** Mt 1:18-20; 3:16;
4:1; 12:18, 28; Lk 1:35; 4:14, 18;
10:21; Acts 10:38; Heb 9:14
(b) **his coming promised:**Lk 11:13;
24:49; Jn 7:39; 14:16-17, 26; 15:26;
16:7, 13; Acts 1:4-8
(c) **Pentecost:** Acts 2:1-41
(d) **influence on men:**
1. on the prophets and sacred writers:
Mt 22:43; Lk 1:67; 2:25-35;
Acts 4:25-26; 21:10-11;
Gen. Intr. Cor, pp. 13-23;
2 Pet 1:19-21
2. on the Baptist: Lk 1:15, 44;
3. on the Apostles: Mt 10:20;
Jn 14:16, 25-26; 16:13; 20:22;
Acts 4:8; 10:19-20; 15:27-29; 16:6-7;
20:22-23
4. on Church: Intr. Acts, pp. 24-25;
Acts 1:5; 9:31; 10:44-48; 11:4-17;
13:2; 1 Cor 12:12-13; 14:12-20;
Rev 1:4; 2-3
5. on believers: Lk 12:12; Jn 3:5-8;
Acts 2:38; 4:31; 5:32; 7:55; 8:26-40;
13:52; 19:1-7; Gen. Intr. St Paul in
Rom, p. 41; Rom 8:9-11;
1 Cor 2:10-16; 12:3-11;
2 Cor 1:21-22; 3:6, 18; 5:5; 7:6;
Eph 2:18; 4:30; 1 Thess 1:5;
1 Jn 2:27; 4:13
6. on Blessed Virgin: Mt 1:18-25;
Lk 1:35
(e) **sin against:** Mt 12:31-32;
Heb 10:26-31
(f) **his gifts and fruits:** Gal 5:22-23;
1 Thess 1:6; *see* Gift.
See Trinity, Blessed.

Spouse, Christ depicted as Mt 9:15;
22:1-14; 25:1-13; Jn 3:27-29;
2 Cor 11:2-3.

Suffering
(a) **Christ's:** Mt 9:36; 26:36-46;
37:46; Lk 12:50; 19:41-44;
Jn 11:33-38; Heb 2:18; 5:8;
1 Pet 2:21-25; *see* Christ, Jesus (h).
(b) **Christian meaning:** Mt 5:1-12;
10:38-39; 16:24-25; 27:32, 34;
Lk 24:46; Jn 9:2-3; 12:24-25;
Gen Intr. St Paul in Rom, p. 41;
Rom 5:3; 8:18; 1 Cor 4:8-13;
2 Cor 1:3-11; 4:7-12, 17-18; 6:4-10;

7:4-16; 11:21-33; Eph 3:13; Phil
1:12-14, 29-30; 2:25-30; 2 Tim
3:10-13; Heb 2:10, 18; 5:8; 11:23-29,
35-38; 12:5-11; Jas 1:2-12; 1 Pet 1:7
(c) **Mary's:** Lk 2:34-35, 43-50;
Jn 19:25-27. *See* Cross; Persecution.

Supper
(a) **and Kingdom:** *see* Banquet (a).
(b) **Last:** Gen. Intro. Gosp. in Mk, pp.
48-50; Mt 26:17-35; Jn 13-17;
see Eucharist.

Synagogue
(a) **Christ preaches in:** Mt 4:23;
Mk 1:21; Lk 4:16; 6:6; 13:10-17;
Jn 6:59; 18:20
(b) **St Paul preaches in:** Acts 9:20;
13:5, 14-43; 14:1; 17:1; 18:19; 19:8.

Synoptics: *see* Gospel.

Tabernacles: *see* Festivals.

Teaching
(a) **of Jesus:**
1. divine origin: Jn 3:34; 6:63;
7:16-18; 8:28; 12:44; 1 Jn 1:1-3
2. authority: Mt 7:28-29; 22:16;
Mk 1:27
3. binding: Mk 16:16; Jn 3:36;
9:39-41; 1 Jn 5:12
(b) **of the Apostles:**
1. received from Jesus: Mt 28:19-20;
Jn 14:26
2. authority: Lk 10:16; Acts 15:6-21
of the Church:
1. passed on by Tradition:
1 Cor 11:23-26; 15:1-6; 1 Tim 6:20;
2 Tim 13:14
2. binding: Mt 16:13-20; Acts 6:21
(d) **sound doctrine:** 2 Tim 2:14-18;
Tit 1:1, 12-14
(e) **false doctrine:**
1. fact of: Acts 20:29-31; 2 Tim 3:6-9;
3:10-11; 2 Pet 3:3-4; 1 Jn 4:1-3;
2 Jn 7:11; Rev 2:14-16
*2. attitude to take towards its
promoters*: 2 Tim 2:14-18; 3:6-9;
4:3-5; Tit 1:10-11; 3:10-11;
Intr. 2 Pet in Cath, pp. 124-125;
2 Pet 2:1-3; 1 Jn 2:19; Jude 3:4.
See Authority.

Temple
(a) **of Jerusalem:**
1. description: Mt 21:12-13;

Mk 15:38; Intr. Heb, pp. 26-29
2. *cleansed by Christ*: Mt 21:12-13;
Jn 2:14-22
3. *destruction*: Mt 24:1-35
4. *and first Christians*: Acts 2:46;
3:1-10; 4:12; 5:19-21, 42; 21:26-30
(b) **Christ, New T.**: Mt 12:6; 25:51;
Jn 2:18-22; Rev 21:21-27
(c) **the Christian, t. of God**: *see*
Trinity, Blessed (h).

Temptations
(a) **of Christ**: Mt 4:1-11; 26:36-46
(b) **of the Christian**: Mt 4:1; 6:13; Lk
8:13; Rom 7:11; 1 Thess 3:5;
Heb 4:15; Jas 1:13-15
(c) **how to deal with**: Mt 4;11;
Mk 1:13; 13:32-42; Lk 4:13;
22:39-40; 1 Cor 10:11-13
(d) **tempting God**: Mt 4:7;
Mk 8:11-12; Heb 3:9.

Testament, New
(a) **general questions**: Gen Intr. NT
Mk, pp. 25-28; Gen. Intr. Acts, pp.
17-18; Gen Intr. Capt, pp. 18-19
(b) **fulness of OT**: Mt 5:17-19;
Lk 4:20-22; Rom 3:31; 10:4; Gal 3:4:
(c) **new and definitive Covenant**:
Mt 26:28; Jn 19:31-32; Heb 8:7-12.
See Testament, Old; Gospel;
Scripture, Sacred.

Testament, Old
(a) **general questions**:
Gen Intr., Capt, pp. 17-18
(b) **its perennial value**: Jn 5:31-40;
2 Tim 3:16
(c) **a preparation for the NT**:
Lk 16:16-17; 24:44-49; 1 Pet 1:10
(d) **understood in light of NT**:
Mt 5:17-19; Lk 4:20-22;
2 Cor 3:12-18; Intr. Heb, pp. 42-44
(e) **finds fulfilment in Christ**:
Intro. Mt p. 22; Mt 5:17-19; Jn 1:6-8
See Testament, New; Scripture,
Sacred.

Thanksgiving
(a) **of Jesus to the Father**:
Mt 11:25-27; 15:36; 26:27; Jn 11:41
(b) **of men to God**: Mt 11:21-24:
20:30-34; 27:28-31; Lk 1:46-56,
68-79; 2:29-32; 17:11-19; Rom 1:8;
1 Cor 4:7; 2 Cor 4:15; 2 Cor 9:13-15;

Eph 5:20; 1 Thess 5:18;
2 Thess 1:3-4; 2:13-14. *See* Hymns.

Thessalonians, Epistle to
Gen Intr. St Paul in Rom, pp. 20-21;
Intr. 1 & 2 Thess, pp. 22-26.

Thomas, St Mt 10:1-4; Jn 11:16; 14:5;
20:24-29.

Timothy Acts 16:1-3; Gen. Intr. St Paul
in Rom, pp. 26-27; 1 Cor 4:17;
16:10-12; 2 Cor 1:1-2; Col 1:1;
1 Thess 1:1; Intr. 1 Tim in Thess, pp.
87-88; Intr. 2 Tim in Thess, p. 131;
2 Tim 1:1-2; Heb 13:23.

Titus Gen. Intr. St Paul in Rom, pp.
26-27; 2 Cor 2:13; 7:2-16; 8:16-24;
Gal 2:1-3; Intr. Tit in Thess, p. 159.

Tradition
(a) **Christ and Jewish t.**: Mt 9:14-15;
15:1-9; 23:16-26; Mk 7:1-23; Lk
7:44-50; 11:37-42
(b) **Apostolic**: 1 Cor 11:2, 23-26;
15:1-11
(c) **source of Revelation**: Gen. Intr.
Cor, pp. 15-19; 1 Thess 2:13;
2 Thess 2:15; 2 Pet 3:1-2; 1 Jn 1:3-4;
Jude 3
(d) **in Church**: 1 Tim 6:13-14;
2 Tim 1:13-14; 3:14-15.
See Revelation; Scripture, Sacred.

Training, need for: Mt 10:5-15;
28:20; Eph 5:10; Phil 1:9-11, 28;
Heb 5:11-14. *See* Doctrine.

Transfiguration Mt 17:1-9; Jn 12:28;
2 Pet 1:16-18. *See* Christ, Jesus.

Transubstantiation: *see* Eucharist.

Trinity, Blessed
(a) **a mystery**: Intr. Jn, pp. 28-30;
Jn 5:25-30; 1 Thess 3:11
(b) **manifestation of**: Mt 3:16-17;
17:1-5; Lk 1:26-38; Jn 1:32-34
(c) **revealed by Christ**: Mt 28:19;
Lk 4:18-21; Intr Jn, pp. 28-30;
Jn 3:31-36; 14:16, 26; 15:26; 16:14-15
(d) **other testimonies in NT**:
Rom 15:15-19; 2 Cor 1:21-22; 13:13;
Gal: 4:6; Eph 4:4-6; Tit 3:4-7;
1 Pet 1:1-2; 1 Jn 5:5-9
(e) **God the Father**: Rom 3:21-31;
15:6; 1 Cor 8:6; 2 Cor 1:3; Eph 1:3,
17; *see* (f), (g).

(f) God the Son:
1. one in nature with the Father:
Jn 1:1; 5:17-19; 8:19; 10:30, 38;
14:6-11; 17:11, 20-23; 2 Cor 4:4-6;
Col 1:15; Heb 1:1-15
2. only-begotten Son of the Father:
Mt 3:17; 26:63-64; Jn 1:14, 34; 3:16;
5:16-18, 25-30; 6:46; 12:27-28;
20:17; 1 Jn 4:9
3. proceeds from the Father:
Jn 5:25-30; 6:37-40, 46; 8:44-50;
16:27-28; 17:7-8
(g) God the Holy Spirit: *proceeds
from the Father and the Son:*
Jn 14:16, 26; 15:26; 16:13-15;
Acts 16:7; 1 Cor 2:10-16; Rev 22:1-5
(h) dwells in the soul: Jn 14:16-17,
22-23; 17:26; Acts 2:38; 17:26-28;
1 Cor 3:16-17; 6:19-20; 2 Cor 6:16;
2 Pet 1:3-4. *See* Spirit, Holy;
Filiation, divine; Christ, Jesus.

Trust
(a) **in God:** Mt 1:19; 4:4; 6:25-34;
Rom 7:28-31, 39; 11:33-36; Phil 1:6;
4:13; 2 Tim 1:12; 4:18; Heb 6:9-12; 1
Jn 3:19-22; 4:17-18
(b) in Christ: Mt 24:23-28; Mk 2:14;
Jn 6:5-13; 14:1; 16:33; Eph 3:12;
Heb 4:14-16; 1 Jn 2:28-29
(c) in Blessed Virgin: Jn 19:26-27.
See Abandonment; Filiation, divine.

Truth
(a) t. of God: Rom 1:25; 3:7; 15:8
(b) Christ is the t.: Mt 23:8-10;
Jn 1:14-17; 14:6; 17:17; 18:37;
1 Jn 5:20
(c) Holy Spirit and: Jn 14:17; 15:26;
16:13; 1 Jn 5:6
(d) and Gospel: Eph 1:13; Col 1:5;
1 Tim 2:4; 2 Tim 2:15, 25; 3:7;
Tit 1:1; Heb 10:26
(e) and Christian life: Mt 6:1-8;
Jn 8:30-32; 17:17-19; 18:37;
2 Cor 7:14; Col 1:6; 1 Jn 3:19;
2 Jn 1-3; 3 Jn 3-8.
See Sincerity.

Unity
(a) of Christ and the Father:
Mt 11:27; Jn 5:30; 6:57; 8:28-29;
12:44-50; 14:20; 15:9-10,23-24;
16:15, 28; 17:1-11, 21-26; *see* Trinity,
Blessed (f), 1.

(b) of Christ and the Christian:
Jn 6:55-57; 7:37-39; 10:27-29; 12:26;
14:3, 12-14, 20-24; 15:1-8, 14;
17:21-26; Acts 9:4; 1 Cor 3:10-11;
11:4-7; Intr. 1 Jn in Cath, pp. 155-156
(c) of Church: Mt 16:18;
Lk 11:17-18; Jn 10:16; 15:1;
17:20-23; 19:23-24; Acts 2:42-47;
4:32-37; 5:12-16;
Intr. 1 Cor, pp. 29-30; 1 Cor 1:10-7;
12:12-13, 28-30; Eph 4:4-6
(d) of life: Lk 10:38-42; 16:13-14;
Jas 2:14.

Universality: *see* Church (e), 3;
Salvation (a).

Vigilance: *see* Watchfulness.

Virgin, Blessed
(a) her prerogatives and tites:
1. Mother of God: Mt 12:48-50;
Lk 1:31-33, 38, 43
2. Immaculate Conception: Lk 1:28
3. holiness: Lk 1:26-38; 11:27-28
4. ever a virgin: Mt 1:16, 18-25;
12:46-47; Mk 6:1-3; Lk 1:27, 34; 2:7;
Jn 1:13; 19:41; Acts 1:13-14;
1 Cor 9:5-6
5. Co-redeemer: Lk 2:34-35; Jn 2:3;
19:25-27
6. Mediatrix of all grace: Jn 2:11;
1 Tim 2:5
7. Mother of men: Jn 19:26-27
8. Mother of the Church: Acts 1:12-14
9. type of the Church: Rev 12:1-2.
(b) Annunciation of the Lord: Lk
1:26-38
(c) Visitation: Lk 1:39-56
(d) in Christ's hidden life:
1. birth: Lk 2:1-7
2. adoration of shepherds: Lk 2:8-20
3. Purification: Lk 2:22-38
4. adoration of Magi: Mt 2:1-12
5. flight into Egypt: Mt 2:13-23
6. Jesus, lost and found: Lk 2:41-52
(e) in Christ's public life:
1. Cana: Jn 2:1-12
2. tries to see Jesus: Mt 12:46-50
3. is praised by a woman: Lk 11:27-28
4. at the Cross: Jn 19:25-27
(f) the woman of the Apocalypse:
Intr. Rev, pp. 26-27; Rev 12:1-18
(g) her exemplary virtue:
1. faith: Lk 1:34, 38, 45

2. fidelity to God's will: Mt 12:46-50;
Lk 1:34-38; 11:27-28; Jn 19:25
3. abandonment in God's hands:
Mt 1:19
4. charity: Lk 1:39
5. obedience: Lk 1:38; Jn 2:5
6. humility: Lk 1:29-30, 38-56
7. purity: Lk 1:34
8. discretion and simplicity: Mt 1:19;
Lk 1:38
9. teacher of prayer: Lk 2:19, 35, 51;
Jn 2:3-4, 11
10. joy: Lk 1:46-47
(h) some Marian devotions:
1. Hail Mary: Lk 1:28, 42, 48-49
2. Angels: Lk 1:26-28; Jn 1:14
3. Rosary: Lk 2:6-7, 22-24, 41-49.
See Intr. Lk, pp. 24-25;
Intr. Jn, pp. 35-37.

Virginity
(a) charism given to Church:
Mt 19:12; Acts 21:9; 1 Cor 7:7;
Rev 14:4-5
(b) and marriage: Mt 19:11-12;
Lk 1:34; 1 Cor 7
(c) Mary's: *see* Virgin, Blessed (a), 4.
See Purity.

Virtues
(a) required by the Christian:
Mt 5:16; 25:14-30; Eph 2:10; 5:8-9;
Gal 5:6; Jas 2:14-26
(b) merit reward of heaven:
Mt 25:35-46; 1 Cor 15:58; Rev 14:13
(c) lists of: Rom 5:3-5; Gal 5:22-23; 1
Tim 6:11; 2 Pet 1:5-9; Rev 2:19.

Watchfulness
**(a) re death and the Lord's second
coming:** Mt 24:36-51; 25:1-13;
Lk 12:15-21, 35-48; 21:34-46;
2 Pet 3:11-16; Rev 3:2-3
(b) re attacks by devil: Mt 13:24-30;
Lk 11:24-26; 1 Pet 5:8-9
(c) through prayer: Mt 26:36-46;
Lk 18:8; 21:34-36. *See* Judgment.

Water
(a) in Baptism: Mt 3:11; Jn 3:6
(b) symbol of grace: Jn 2:1-11; 4:7,
18; 7:37-39; 19:34-37; Rev 21:6;
22:1-2; 22:17

Way
(a) Christ, w. to Father: Lk 14:27;

Jn 16:4-7; Heb 10:19-20
**(b) John Baptist prepares w. of
Lord:** Mt 3:11-13; 11:10; Lk 1:76,
79; 7:27; Jn 1:19-28
(c) Church as: Acts 9:2; 19:9, 23;
22:4; 24:14-22; 2 Pet 2:2
(d) "walking" = moral conduct:
Gal 5:16; Eph 5:2; Phil 3:17;
Col 1:9-11; 2 Pet 2:15, 21; 1 Jn 2:3-6;
Jn 3:8.

Wedding
**(a) symbol of Church and
Kingdom:** Mt 9:14-15; 22:1-14;
25:1-3; Jn 3:27-29; 2 Cor 11:2-3;
Rev 19:5-9
(b) at Cana: Jn 2:1-12.
See Banquet; Spouse; Marriage.

Wilderness
(a) place to meet God: Mt 3:1-12;
11:7; Lk 1:80; Jn 1:23; Rev 12:6
**(b) where Christ prays and is
tempted:** Mt 4:1-11; 14:13; Mk 1:35;
Lk 5:16; Jn 11:54
(c) abode of devil: Mt 12:43; Lk 8:29.

Will
(a) Jesus does his Father's will: *see*
Obedience (a), 1.
(b) of God:
1. is discovered in Christ: Jn 14:4-7;
3 Jn 3-8
2. must be done: Mt 6:10; 7:21-27;
12:46-50; 21:28-32; Lk 11:27-28;
Acts 20:22-23; 21:10-14; Rom
9:20-23
3. should be loved: Mt 16:24-25;
27:32-34; Lk 14:27; Jn 18:10-11.
See Obedience; Vocation.

Wisdom
(a) of God: Lk 7:35; 11:49;
1 Cor 1:20-25; 2:6-16; *see* Mystery.
(b) of Christ: Mt 13:54; Lk 2:40, 52;
4:22; 7:35; Col 2:2-3
(c) of the Christian: Mt 7:24-27;
11:25-26; Lk 7:35; Acts 27:16-21;
1 Cor 1:18-3:3; Jas 1:5-8; 3:13-18.

Witness
(a) concerning Christ:
1. by Father: Mt 3:17; 17:1-5;
Jn 5:31-40; 8:12-19; 12:27-28
2. by Holy Spirit: Jn 15:26; 1 Jn 5:6-7
3. by OT: Jn 5:39-47

4. by John Baptist: Mt 3:11-12;
Jn 1:6-8, 15, 19-36; 3:25-30
(b) Christ, faithful witness: Jn 3:11,
32-33; 18:37; 1 Tim 6:13; Rev 1:5; 3:14
(c) witnesses to Christ:
1. Apostles: Mt 14:33; 16:16;
Jn 19:35; 21:24; Acts 1:8; 2:32; 10:39;
22:15; 26:16; 1 Jn 1:2; 4:14
2. Christians: Mt 10:22, 32-33;
Mk 10:18; Lk 9:26; Phil 1:12-14;
2 Tim 1:7-8; 4:6; Rev 12:17
(d) gravity by false w.: Mt 18:16;
Jn 8:17; 2 Cor 13:1; 1 Tim 5:19; 6:12; 1
Thess 2:10.

Women

(a) in ancestry of Christ: Mt 1:6
(b) holy women:
Mt 27:55-56; 28:1-10; Lk 8:1-3;
23:55-56; Jn 19:25; 20:1, 11-18
(c) some women in the Gospel:
1. woman with flow of blood:
Mk 5:25-34
2. Canaanite woman: Mt 15:21-28
3. sinful woman: Lk 7:36-50
4. woman who praises Mary:
Lk 11:27-28
5. w. of Jerusalem: Lk 23:27-31
6. Samaritan woman: Jn 4:7-42
7. adulterous woman: Jn 8:3-11
**(d) "woman" as title given Blessed
Virgin:** Intr. Jn, pp. 36-37; Jn 2:4; 19:26
(e) the woman of the Apocalypse: Intr.
Rev, pp. 26-27; Rev 12:1-18
(f) their mission:
1. in Church: Lk 8:1-3; Jn 19:25;
Acts 16:15; 17:34; 1 Cor 11:1-16;
14:33-35; 1 Tim 2:11-15
2. in family: Acts 16:15; 17:34;
1 Tim 2:15; Tit 2:3-5; 1 Pet 3:1-7;
see Family.
3. widows: Acts 6:1, 1 Cor 7:39-40;
1 Tim 5:3-16; Jas 1:27
4. deportment: 1 Cor 11:13-16;
1 Tim 2:9-10; 1 Pet 3:1-6.

Word

(a) of God: Mt 1:22; 2:15; Lk 2:29; 3:2;
5:1; 8:11; 1 Thess 2:13;
2 Thess 3:1; Heb 4:12-13;
Rev 19:15, 20
(b) of Christ:
1. authoritative: Mt 5:21-48; 7:29;
Jn 6:63, 68; 7:45-46
2. able to work miracles: Mt 8:8, 16; Mk
1:25;2:10-11; 4:39; Lk 7:14;
Jn 11:43

(c) one must keep one's w.:
Mt 7:24-27; Lk 8:21; 11:28; Jn 5:24;
8:47, 51; 14:24; Col 3:16;
Heb 10:22-25; Jas 1:20-25
(d) ministers of: Lk 1:2; Acts 6:1-7; 2
Tim 4:2
See Christ (j); Magisterium.

Work

(a) of Christ:*1. in his hidden life*:
Mt 13:55; Mk 6:1-3; Lk 2:51; 3:23
2. in intense ministry: Mk 6:30-31;
Lk 8:23; Jn 4:6; 5:17
**(b) some parables to do with man at
work:** Mt 13:1-50; 20:1-16; 25:14-30;
Lk 15:1-7; 16:1-8; 19:12-27;
Jn 4:35-38; 10:1-21;
(c) the Apostles': Mt 4:18; 9:9;
Jn 21:1-3;Acts 18:3; 20:34;
1 Cor 9:15-18; 2 Cor 11:7-15;
1 Thess 2:9; 2 Thess 3:8-9
(d) the Christian's:
1. a place to meet God: *see* Holiness (d),
3.
2. a duty: Eph 4:28; 1 Thess 4:11-12; 2
Thess 3:7-15
3. making good use of time:
Mt 21:18-22; Lk 13:6-9; 19:20-26; Eph
5:16; Col 4:5; 1 Thess 2:7-9
(e) rights and duties in: Eph 6:5-9; Col
3:22-4:1; Philem 15-16; Jas 5:4.

World

(a) created good by God: Jn 1:3;
17:14-16; 1 Cor 3:21-23; Phil 4:8-9; Heb
1:3
(b) as enemy of God: Jn 1:10; 7:7; 8:23;
14:30; 15:18-19; 16:8, 20, 33; Rom 3:6,
19; 1 Cor 1:20-25; Gal 1:4; Jas 4:4-6; 1
Jn 2:15-17
(c) does not last: Mt 16:26;
1 Cor 7:29-31; 1 Jn 2:17;
see Death (a).
(d) end of: 2 Pet 3:5-13; *see* Judgment
(b); Parousia.

Worship

(a) OT: Gen. Intr. Heb, pp. 23-36; Heb
8:1-6; 9:1-10
(b) of God: Mt 4:10; Acts 17:24;
Heb 10:22-25
(c) the right form: Jn 4:21-24;
Heb 8:1-13; 1 Tim 2:8
(d) generosity in: Mt 26:6-13.
See Adoration; Liturgy.

Zacchaeus Lk 19:1-10.

Zechariah Lk 1:5-25, 59-79.